THE IRISH GRAND NATIONAL
THE HISTORY OF IRELAND'S PREMIER STEEPLECHASE

THE IRISH GRAND NATIONAL
THE HISTORY OF IRELAND'S PREMIER STEEPLECHASE

STEWART PETERS

ACKNOWLEDGEMENTS

Stewart Peters would like to thank the following for their help: Guy Williams, Patricia Erigero, Pat Healy, Derek Gay and Bernard Parkin.

First published 2007
STADIA is an imprint of
Tempus Publishing Limited
The Mill, Brimscombe Port,
Stroud, Gloucestershire, GL5 2QG
www.tempus-publishing.com

British Library Cataloguing in Publication Data.
A catalogue record for this book is available from the British Library.

ISBN-10 0 7524 3691 0
ISBN-13 978 0 7524 3691 3

Typesetting and origination by Tempus Publishing Limited
Printed in Great Britain

CONTENTS

FOREWORD

As a horse-mad youngster in Tullamore I was reared on the legend of Jack Chaucer, hero of the 1940 Irish Grand National for Tullamore owner Larry Egan. 'Jack' might have been dead for years, but his elderly groom kept the flame alive. Paddy Cassells had worked in 'Atty' Persse's during the reign of The Tetrarch.

When I eventually got to experience the happy havoc that was Fairyhouse on Easter Monday – traditionally the Dubliners' day at the races – it was to see Olympia win the Irish National for nearby trainer Tom Dreaper. Kindly invited to stay with the Moores, just across the road in Old Fairyhouse, I suffered from divided loyalties, being then at school with both Arthur Moore and Jim Dreaper.

For the next six years Dreaper supremacy in Ireland's premier steeplechase continued in unbroken sequence. It did not seem to matter what Tom fielded for the race, the outcome had a certain inevitability about it. Admittedly Arkle and Flyingbolt were always going to be hard to beat, however much I hoped our locally-trained mare, Height O' Fashion, might get her deserved turn.

Marriage into the famous Harty racing family reinforced the Irish National connection. My father-in-law, Captain Cyril Harty, had won the 1944 renewal with Knight's Crest, ridden by his apprentice phenomenon, Martin Molony. His son 'Buster' was to come close with Fort Ord, while another son, Eddie, was to come closer still with Sand Pit.

Meanwhile, I had ridden a point-to-point winner at Fairyhouse, which seemed as close to an Irish National as I was likely to get. Jim Dreaper had added to his father's remarkable tally, while Arthur Moore had ridden King's Sprite to victory, as his father Dan had done on Golden Jack and Revelry.

It was on another's whim that I took out a trainer's licence in 1979, lucky to be entrusted with buying a Gold Cup hopeful – Daletta. He gave me my first training success, at Fairyhouse in February 1980, ridden by brother-in-law John Harty. They went on to win the Embassy Final at Haydock Park. Peter Daly, my assistant, was adamant we try for the Irish National. The outcome is recorded later in these pages.

A stint as stipendiary steward for the Jockey Club in the north of England led to a renewed interest in recording Irish racing history. Francis Hyland and I had written the *History of the Irish Derby* in 1980 and duly followed up with the *History of the Irish Grand National* fifteen years later, kindly sponsored by Irish Distillers, in line with their generous endowment of Ireland's premier steeplechase since 1970. In the interim trainer Pat Hughes, likewise married to one of Captain Harty's delightful daughters, had reinforced the family links with the Irish Grand National, saddling Insure to win in 1986.

Now Stewart Peters has updated the history of what has become the Powers Gold Label Irish Grand National. On all known form he has the right credentials for this role and all of us here wish him every success as the newest keeper of a very special flame.

Guy St John Williams

INTRODUCTION

It has often been said that steeplechasing began in Ireland, and although the first Irish Grand National proper did not take place until 1870, racing had taken place at Fairyhouse in County Meath for many years previously. From humble beginnings, the first stepping stones for the rich future that lay in wait were laid out in 1848, when the Ward Union Hunt transferred their annual meeting from Ashbourne to Fairyhouse. In those days, vast green fields set the scene for racegoers, with the *Turf Steeplechase Calendar* publishing some important rules relevant to racing at the time. They read as follows: 'Any rider travelling upwards of one hundred yards on any highroad, lane or public thoroughfare will, in the event of winning, be disqualified. The opening of any gate or wicket will also lead to disqualification, as will wilful crossing, jostling, riding at or driving another from his point while going at a fence.' Spectators would follow the racing in those early years either on horseback or on foot, but what was certain was that the popularity of a days racing at Fairyhouse was increasing all the time.

In 1870, the first ever running of the Irish Grand National took place at Fairyhouse, with the race won by a grey gelding called Sir Robert Peel, owned by Mr L. Dunne and ridden by John Boylan. That initial race was worth 167 sovereigns, and the race quickly established itself as the most important and prestigious in Ireland, with anyone that owned a decent steeplechaser craving the chance to win the race.

Down the years, people have travelled from all over the country, and many from far further, for the big race, which is steeped in tradition and has evolved into a huge national sporting centrepiece. From the days when local people recall walking to the course across fields without ever coming into contact with a road to the modern day, the Irish Grand National, run each year on Easter Monday, holds a very special place in both the eyes of the Irish nation and the racing world as a whole.

Fairyhouse Racecourse is located at Ratoath, approximately twelve miles north-west of Dublin city centre. Today, the course has been transformed from the green fields that were the setting when it first staged point-to-points back in 1848, into a magnificent modern racecourse that boasts fantastic facilities on a par with any course in the country. Fairyhouse opened The Powers Gold Label Stand and the refurbished Jameson Stand in November 1999, offering spectators spectacular viewing.

Fairyhouse is a relatively flat, round, right handed track of approximately one mile and six furlongs in distance, featuring twelve chase fences and eight hurdles. The Irish Grand National is run over an extended two circuits of the course to make up a total distance of three miles and five furlongs, although this distance has been altered at different times throughout the race's history. In total, twenty-three fences are currently jumped in the Irish Grand National, with the obstacles described as 'stiff but fair', while, in addition, the course is two hundred feet wide with a two-and-a-half furlong finishing straight. The race calls for horses to possess both fine jumping ability and strong reserves of stamina.

Each year, there is a great tale associated with the race, and from the day Sir Robert Peel won the inaugural running, many fine horses, jockeys and trainers

have helped to provide a rich and glorious history to one of National Hunt racing's oldest and most loved events. The first dual winner of the race was another grey horse. Owned by Major Browne, Scots Grey won in both 1872 and 1875, ridden on each occasion by Mr Garrett Moore, a hard-drinking youngster but a gifted horseman, who in 1879 won the Aintree Grand National on The Liberator. Scots Grey was one of just five horses (to date) to win the race twice, the others being The Gift (1883 and 1884), Little Hack II (1909 and 1913), Halston (1920 and 1922) and Brown Lad (1975, 1976 and 1978), the lattermost setting a new record when winning for an unprecedented third time in 1978.

Grand National was the name of the 1876 winner, with the horse partnered to success by one member of the astonishing Beasley family, Tommy, who also won on Thiggin Thue in 1877. The brothers, Tommy, Johnny, Harry, James and Willy Beasley, were remarkable amateur riders of the era, all residing on the Curragh. Johnny rode Juggler to win the race in 1878, while Harry won on Controller in 1880 and Citadel in 1889. Tommy also won the Aintree Grand National three times and the Irish Derby three times, while Harry won the Aintree Grand National once. Tommy Beasley was the most prolific of the quintet and was taught to ride by the great amateur rider and trainer, Allen McDonough. Harry was taught by the famous trainer Henry Linde, while Johnny and Willy began with John Hubert Moore, father of Garrett.

Tipperary Boy, the only horse to win the Galway Plate (a race that was established before the Irish Grand National) three times, won the Irish Grand National in 1901, the race then being worth 166 sovereigns, one less than the first race in 1870.

At the start of the twentieth century, one of the famous Irish Grand National winners of the era was Ascetic's Silver. Owned and bred by Mr P.J. Dunne in County Meath, Ascetic's Silver was purchased on the death of Mr Dunne by the Honourable Aubrey Hastings, a fine judge of a horse, who paid 800 guineas for the horse on behalf of Prince Franz Hatzfeldt. Having already won the Fairyhouse showpiece in 1904, Ascetic's Silver went on to triumph at Aintree in 1906, beating Red Lad, a horse that had won the Irish Grand National in 1905. A half-brother to fellow Aintree victors Drumcree and Cloister, Ascetic's Silver is one of just four horses (Rhyme 'N' Reason, Bobbyjo and Numbersixvalverde) to have won both English and Irish Grand Nationals.

The best amateur rider of his era, Reggie Walker set a record for winning rides in the Irish Grand National by emerging victorious four times (1908, 1909, 1912 and 1915). Walker later trained the good horse Royal Danieli to finish second in the 1938 Aintree Grand National. Royal Danieli was ridden at Aintree by Dan Moore, who later enjoyed much success in the Irish Grand National as both a jockey and a trainer. Walker's record of four winning rides was later broken by the great Pat Taaffe, who rode six.

1916 was the year of the Irish Rebellion and all hell was about to break loose in Dublin. Many of the officers and soldiers took the opportunity to enjoy a day out at Fairyhouse, where the winner was All Sorts, and the fourth home was Civil War, a horse that had won the race two years previously.

In 1920 and 1922, Halston won for trainer Jack Rustle, who in his day had been one of Ireland's leading cross-country riders, while little did anyone know that when Don Sancho triumphed in 1928, it would be the last time a British-trained horse would win for fifty-seven years (Rhyme 'N' Reason, 1985). If that drought was incredible, one of the most remarkable victories the Irish Grand National has ever witnessed occurred in 1929. The fact that the good chaser Alike won was of no surprise, but it was the performance of the winning jockey that was most sensational. Riding Alike was 5ft 4in Frank Wise, a jockey missing three fingers and who rode with a wooden leg!

The 1936 winner, Alice Maythorn, was trained by Joe Osborne, who later bred the triple Irish Grand National winner of the 1970s, Brown Lad, while a year after Alice Maythorn's success, Pontet scored for trainer Cecil Brabazon, father of the excellent jockey Aubrey Brabazon. Pontet was ridden at Fairyhouse by Eric McKeever, who as an amateur in 1931 had won on the Charlie Rogers-trained Impudent Barney. Pontet was perhaps the biggest bargain of all Irish Grand National winners, costing a mere £6 as a yearling at Ballsbridge Sales.

From the 1940s onwards, the race has continued to grow in stature and glory. The great Irish chaser Prince Regent thrilled the Fairyhouse crowds in the early forties before attempting the major English chases following the Second World War, while the fifties and sixties saw the race dominated by trainer Tom Dreaper and jockey Pat Taaffe; the races in that era featured some of the finest chasers ever to have graced the sport, including Royal Approach, Flyingbolt and the mighty Arkle.

Modern times have seen the introduction of sponsorship to the great race, raising the race's status in terms of value and competition. The addition of sponsorship, first through Irish Distillers, and followed by both Jameson and Powers Gold Label, helped to attract high quality fields in the 1970s and onwards, with British interest also increasing. Indeed, following Rhyme 'N' Reason's victory in the 1985 Irish Grand National, four more British-trained horses in Omerta, Mudahim, Granit D'Estruval and the hugely popular grey, Desert Orchid, have won the Fairyhouse race.

With the race secure in its traditions and holding a romantic, respected and valuable place in the National Hunt calendar, it is hoped the future brings to Fairyhouse as many of the fascinating and inspiring moments that have helped to shape the definitive history of the Irish Grand National.

Above left: Papillon (left) and Bobbyjo at the final fence in 1998.

Above right: Desert Orchid jumps a fence in the 1990 race.

Left: The Fairyhouse stands in 1999

TOM DREAPER

No trainer in the entire history of the Irish Grand National has had as much impact on the race as that of Thomas William Dreaper. Born in 1898, Dreaper had been a useful amateur jockey and trained horses at his farm at Greenogue, Kilsallaghan for over forty years before handing the duties over to his son, Jim, in 1971. A cattle and sheep farmer by trade, Dreaper laid down his roots in County Meath throughout his career, resisting offers to go and train in England.

Dreaper's domination of the Irish Grand National began in 1942, and between that year and 1966, the trainer recorded an incredible ten victories in the race, a record that will surely never be broken. The run started with the great Prince Regent in 1942. Prince Regent was at the peak of his powers in the early 1940s, as he blossomed into a strapping chaser capable of carrying huge weight burdens to victory in the finest races. This the horse did in 1942, when, shouldering nearly a stone more than second-placed Golden Jack, the horse won the Irish Grand National. Prince Regent was also the horse that sent Dreaper on his way to becoming the current most successful trainer in Cheltenham Gold Cup history. With Irish runners staying at home during the Second World War, Prince Regent won the Gold Cup at his first attempt in 1946, and also ran fine races under top weight in the Aintree Grand Nationals of 1946 and 1947. One of the most popular chasers ever to thrill the crowds in Ireland, Prince Regent additionally ran very well in a number of other Irish Grand Nationals following his victory in 1942.

The next two Irish Grand National winners for Dreaper were packed with quality. The trainer saddled Shagreen (like Prince Regent, owned by Mr James V. Rank) to win in 1949. The horse was ridden by Eddie Newman, father to future leading jockey Gerry Newman. In 1954, it was the turn of the brilliant youngster Royal Approach to triumph. Rarely has a winner of the Irish Grand National oozed more class in victory, and a career at the highest level seemed certain for Royal Approach. Sadly, the horse broke down very badly after his victory at Fairyhouse and never recovered sufficiently. Royal Approach was ridden to Irish Grand National glory by Pat Taaffe, who shared a long-standing working relationship with Dreaper. The pair teamed up for many a famous success, with Royal Approach becoming the first of what would be a record six winning Irish Grand National rides for Taaffe. Of his first three Irish Grand National winners, Dreaper indicated that each were excellent horses in different ways, but refused to state which horse was the best.

Following the triumph of Royal Approach, the next five Irish Grand Nationals passed without joy for Dreaper, but this was merely an interlude to what amounted to an incredible domination of the race between 1960 and 1966. Beginning with the good mare Olympia, Dreaper amazingly won the next seven editions, a stunning achievement when one considers the feat was pulled-off courtesy of seven different horses. Following Olympia's win, Dreaper took the honours with the extraordinarily fast Fortria (also second in two Cheltenham Gold Cups), the mares Kerforo and Last Link, the incomparable Arkle, Splash and Flyingbolt, the second highest rated chaser of all time behind Arkle. The riders of the seven were, in order, Tos Taaffe, Pat Taaffe, Liam McCloughlin, Paddy Woods, Pat Taaffe, Paddy Woods and Pat Taaffe.

Arkle, of course, is considered the best chaser ever to have lived, and Dreaper prepared the horse to win three Cheltenham Gold Cups. The trainer added a fifth victory in that race in 1968 when Fort Leney won. Having passed the reigns over to son Jim, the Kilsallaghan stable would welcome home the winner of the Irish Grand National four more times. Colebridge won in 1974, preceding the triple champion Brown Lad, a horse that won the race in 1975, 1976 and 1978.

At one point, the six highest rated Irish Grand National winners of all time hailed from the Dreaper stable, each carrying 12st or more to victory. In order, they were Arkle, Flyingbolt, Prince Regent, Royal Approach, Fortria and Brown Lad. What Tom Dreaper achieved with his horses in the Irish Grand National is astounding, and will forever remain a cherished part of the history of the great race.

Tom Dreaper's Irish Grand National winners:

1942 Prince Regent
1949 Shagreen
1954 Royal Approach
1960 Olympia
1961 Fortria
1962 Kerforo
1963 Last Link
1964 Arkle
1965 Splash
1966 Flyingbolt

1942 – PRINCE REGENT

Without doubt, one of the biggest stars in steeplechasing in the first half of the twentieth century was the immensely popular Prince Regent, a bay gelding with an intimidating body frame, standing over seventeen hands high. Prince Regent dominated Irish racing during the 1940s, and but for the intervention of the Second World War that so disrupted racing in England, the horse surely would have enshrined himself as one of the top two or three horses of the century.

As it was, Prince Regent's career was magnificent. Owned by one of racing's most wealthy patrons of the time, Mr James V. Rank, the horse was sent into training at Tom Dreaper's farm at Greenogue, Kilsallaghan in County Dublin, with the trainer (when also an amateur jockey) partnering the horse to its first win in 1940. Dreaper was an unassuming man and never trained the quantity of horses at any one time that the likes of Nicky Henderson and Paul Nicholls do today, yet for over forty years he remained at the top of his profession, and in the Irish Grand National, his training record was unrivalled.

Developing into a powerful animal with great size and strength, Prince Regent quickly illustrated his brilliance over fences as a youngster, and was soon given the burden of carrying huge weights every time he raced, tasks he performed quite imperiously in his prime in the early forties. In 1942, when seven years of age, he contested the Irish Grand National for the first time. Allotted the maximum weight of 12st 7lbs, the already hugely popular Irish chaser was made a warm favourite on the day, starting the race at a price of 5/2. Taking the mount, as he did throughout most of Prince Regent's career, was Timmy Hyde. A former showjumper, Hyde had already tasted victory in the Fairyhouse race when winning aboard Clare County in 1938, while he had also won the Aintree Grand National on Workman a year later.

In a field of ten, those expected to give Prince Regent most to think about were Durbar, St Martin and Golden Jack. Receiving 2st from Prince Regent, the six-year-old Durbar had beaten the favourite at Leopardstown earlier in the season, but only after Prince Regent had suffered a rare fall. Second in the handicap, St Martin was a talented if error-prone chaser that had won a Galway Plate in his time, while the Dan Moore-ridden Golden Jack was owned by Miss Dorothy Paget, the lady who had owned the great chaser of the 1930s, Golden Miller, a horse that won five Cheltenham Gold Cups and an Aintree Grand National.

Indeed, it was to be Golden Jack that disputed the lead for much of the way, cutting out the running with the six-year-old British Raid on the first circuit. One of the striking features of the 1942 Irish Grand National was the state of the ground. Conditions were atrocious and the course had turned into a virtual quagmire. It was clear that the race would develop into a brutal examination of stamina, offering an even greater challenge to the heavily weighted Prince Regent.

As it was, Prince Regent was held up in the early stages by Hyde until being sent forward at the half way stage. It was then that the favourite began to display his class, regularly outjumping his rivals in a show of authority. Making his move, Prince Regent took the measure of most of the early leaders, with only Golden Jack able to stay with the powerful top weight.

The closing stages turned into a dour battle as Prince Regent fought hard to shake off the persistent challenge of Golden Jack. Hard ridden by Hyde but untouched with the whip, Prince Regent brought the crowd to their feet after jumping the last with the advantage. Churning resolutely towards the line with the conviction of a champion, Prince Regent shrugged off Golden Jack and drew a roar of approval as he crossed the line a brave and deserved winner, carrying the royal blue and primrose-quartered colours to his owner's biggest win to that point. Back in third came St Martin, ridden by Aubrey Brabazon.

Prince Regent had passed another stern weight-carrying test, this time in searching conditions. The fact that he possessed the required stamina for such a challenge came as little surprise with a brief study of his family. Prince Regent was by the excellent sire of staying chasers, My Prince, a sire also responsible for Aintree Grand National winners Gregalach, Reynoldstown and Royal Mail, as well as dual Cheltenham Gold Cup winner Easter Hero.

It was a first Irish Grand National success for Dreaper, but by no means the last, as he set about compiling a most enviable record in the race. A second victory in the race for Hyde also illustrated his fine relationship with Prince Regent, a horse he won on twelve times. Sadly, Hyde was paralysed in a fall in 1951 and was confined to a wheelchair for the rest of his life. Having won the 1942 Irish Grand National, Prince Regent continued to take on all before him in his homeland with great success, a fact all the more resounding considering the lack of racing in England in the early forties meant many top horses that would normally have been sold across the water stayed in Ireland to race.

It was a crying shame that by the time racing reconvened in earnest in England, Prince Regent was past his best, as age and years of excessive weight-carrying performances began to take their toll. Had he been able to contest Cheltenham Gold Cups or Aintree Grand Nationals as a younger horse, there is no telling where the horse may rank in the history of the great chasers. Although no longer able to dominate like he did as a younger horse, Prince Regent was still, however, a force to be reckoned with, and he captured the Cheltenham Gold Cup in 1946, albeit opposed by a mediocre bunch.

In his later years, Prince Regent was asked to compete in the Aintree Grand National, a race traditionally not kind to those at the top of the handicap. In both 1946 and 1947, Prince Regent was favourite for the race but had to carry 12st 5lbs or more both times, and though acquitting himself bravely, simply could not find the necessary reserves to come home in front, finishing third and fourth respectively. Prince Regent also ran at Aintree in 1948 aged thirteen, but that time he was carried out.

Prince Regent enjoyed a long career with tremendous success. He is considered one of the finest weight-carrying performers of all time and his efforts earned him widespread praise for his courage and class. He was the finest steeplechaser in Ireland during the period he raced and his place on the Irish Grand National roll of honour lends much credit and authority to the history of the race.

Tim Hyde (left) and J.V. Rank (centre) with their trophies following Prince Regent's win.

1942 IRISH GRAND NATIONAL RESULT

FATE	HORSE	AGE/WEIGHT	JOCKEY
1st	PRINCE REGENT	7.12.7	T. HYDE
2nd	GOLDEN JACK	7.11.9	D.L. MOORE
3rd	ST MARTIN	9.12.0	A. BRABAZON
4th	Bel Et Bon	a.11.7	J. Lenehan
5th	Knight Of Killala	6.9.11	H. Harty
6th	General Chiang	a.10.8	R.J. O'Ryan
7th	Waving Star	a.10.10	M.C. Prendergast
8th	Durbar	6.10.7	W.T. O'Grady
9th	British Raid	6.9.13	T. McNeill
10th	Dalmatian	a.9.7	M. Gordon

Weight is in stones & pounds
(a) – aged

6 April 1942
Winner – £740
Race Distance – three miles four furlongs
Time – 8mins
10 Ran
Winner trained by T.W. Dreaper
Winner owned by Mr J.V. Rank
Prince Regent, bay gelding by My Prince – Nemaea.

Betting – 5/2 PRINCE REGENT, 4/1 Durbar, 5/1 St Martin, 7/1 Golden Jack, 10/1 Bel Et Bon & British Raid, 100/8 Knight Of Killala & Waving Star, 100/6 General Chiang, 20/1 Dalmatian.

1943 – GOLDEN JACK

The first two horses home in the 1942 Irish Grand National dominated the betting for the 1943 renewal. Separated by 33lbs in weight, both Prince Regent and Golden Jack proved extremely popular both ante-post and on the day with the betting public. After their close duel of the year before, a big rivalry had developed between the two, owned respectively by Mr James V. Rank and Miss Dorothy Paget.

Now eight years of age and with his reputation as strong as ever, it was to be the defending champion Prince Regent that eventually won the battle for favouritism, beginning the race – as in 1942 – at 5/2. If the horse was to repeat his victory of twelve months before, he would have to put in an even greater weight-carrying performance, for he was asked once more to carry the maximum 12st 7lbs, whereas Golden Jack and Heirdom – both very good horses on their best form – were on 10st 2lbs and 9st 9lbs respectively. Originally, trainer Tom Dreaper was also to run the respected chaser Top O' The Mornin (also owned by Rank), but the horse was a late withdrawal.

Golden Jack's chances of victory seemed more realistic than in 1942. The bay was in good form and had long been a leading fancy for the race. Trained by Charlie Rogers and ridden by future leading trainer Dan Moore, Golden Jack was presented with a magnificent chance at the weights of beating Prince Regent, for Miss Paget's runner had run a bold race in 1942 and now was better off by 21lbs.

Of the others, Kilstar, Heirdom and Medoc II appeared the strongest challengers. Like Golden Jack, Kilstar was owned by Miss Paget, and although now an eleven-year-old, the horse retained plenty of pace, though his stamina was a question mark. Another eleven-year-old, Heirdom, was also strongly fancied and was a chaser of good quality that would enjoy plenty of success as he entered the twilight years of his career, while Medoc II was another classy animal although he was perhaps not the force of old. Owned by a wealthy and distinguished figure and a former Lord Mayor of Liverpool, Lord Sefton, the French-bred Medoc II started the Irish National as a 33/1 shot but carried 12st due to the fact the horse had won the Cheltenham Gold Cup in 1942.

It was well documented at the time of the 1943 Irish Grand National that transport facilities to Fairyhouse racecourse were poor, although the executive still hoped for a generous turnout on the big day, as in previous years. However, though those in attendance were in a vivacious mood, the crowd was smaller than expected after all. Still, the eight-runner field received rich encouragement as they lined up at the start.

As if to make a statement from flag-fall, Moore set off keenly aboard Golden Jack, setting a hot pace from Prince Regent, Medoc II, Kilstar, Baldonnell and Crickstown. Early on, one of the outsiders, Brown Joker, assumed last place.

The order remained more or less the same as the field passed the stands, Golden Jack still leading from Kilstar, Prince Regent and Medoc II, with Heirdom just beginning to get into the contest.

However, with much of the second circuit completed, the race had developed into a two-horse affair, and as the betting market indicated, the two involved were Golden Jack and Prince Regent. Entering the final straight, Golden Jack maintained a slender lead, but Prince Regent moved up elegantly alongside him, seemingly ready to overhaul the long-time leader and deliver yet another masterclass of a weight-carrying performance.

Prince Regent tried gamely to snatch the lead from Golden Jack but, on this occasion, it was the latter that held the upper hand and resisted the challenge of his rival. Drawing clear by two lengths jumping the final fence, the huge weight difference allowed Golden Jack to pull clear on the run to the line and record a memorable four-length success with Heirdom a length-and-a-half back in third. Seven of the eight had got round, with one of the outsiders, Baldonnell, being the only faller.

Despite the mismatch in weight, Golden Jack had won on merit and had led majestically from start to finish, bravely seeing off the resilient challenge of the great Prince Regent in the closing stages. Two of the great names in jump racing earned their first Irish Grand National wins courtesy of Golden Jack. Owner Miss Dorothy Paget added the Fairyhouse showpiece to her collection of big race glories with the great Golden Miller, while Dan Moore achieved his biggest success as a jockey.

Dan Moore would taste further success in the race four short years later, continuing a strong association with the race that is maintained to this day through his son Arthur, who subsequently rode the winner of the Irish Grand National in 1971 and trained the winner in 1996. After his successful career as a jockey, Moore set about becoming one of Ireland's leading trainers. He enjoyed further glory in that sphere in the Fairyhouse race with Tied Cottage in 1979 and is best remembered for training the brilliant chestnut L'Escargot, a horse that finished third in the 1971 Irish National (a race won by Arthur Moore aboard King's Sprite) and most memorably won two Cheltenham Gold Cups and an Aintree Grand National.

Dan Moore (pictured here on his 1947 winner Revelry) won the 1943 race on Golden Jack.

1943 IRISH GRAND NATIONAL RESULT

FATE	HORSE	AGE/WEIGHT	JOCKEY
1st	GOLDEN JACK	8.10.2	D.L. MOORE
2nd	PRINCE REGENT	8.12.7	T. HYDE
3rd	HEIRDOM	11.9.9	J.P. MAGUIRE
4th	Crickstown	a.9.7	P. Timmins
5th	Medoc II	9.12.0	J. Barrett
6th	Brown Joker	a.9.7	P. Sherry
7th	Kilstar	11.10.6	J. Brogan
Fell	Baldonnell	a.9.7	J. Cartwright

26 April 1943
Winner – £740
Race Distance – three miles four furlongs
8 Ran
Winner trained by C.A. Rogers
Winner owned by Miss D. Paget
Golden Jack, bay gelding by Goldcourt – Jacaru.

Betting – 5/4 Prince Regent, 5/2 GOLDEN JACK, 6/1 Heirdom, 100/8 Kilstar, 33/1 Baldonnell, Brown Joker, Crickstown & Medoc II.

1944 – KNIGHT'S CREST

Twenty-six horses were declared at the 29 March acceptance stage for the 1944 Irish Grand National, including eight between trainers Tom Dreaper and Charlie Rogers, successful in the previous two renewals with Prince Regent and Golden Jack respectively. Indeed, just twenty-four hours before the race on 17 April, Golden Jack remained one of the most fancied horses to win, but when his winning partner of the year before, Dan Moore, injured his knee, Rogers decided to withdraw the defending champion.

However, it was Prince Regent and not Golden Jack that had been race favourite since the publication of the weights, the horse's popularity as strong as ever. The horse was nine now, yet still in a class of his own, as was evident by the fact his allotted weight of 12st 7lbs was nearly 2st more than his nearest rival in the handicap for the Irish National.

With Golden Jack out of the way, the most serious challenges to Prince Regent seemed set to come from a pair of talented six-year-olds in Prince Blackthorn and Tiverton. Recently purchased by leading owner Lord Bicester, Prince Blackthorn was considered to have an excellent chance. The horse was a young improver and had looked like lowering the colours of Prince Regent recently at Baldoyle only to fall at the final fence. Second in the weights with 10st 9lbs to carry, Prince Blackthorn also held second place in the betting on 7/2. The real form horse coming into the 1944 Irish National was Tiverton. Partnered in the race by future trainer Danny Morgan, Tiverton had strung together a mightily impressive sequence of six wins over fences during the season and was a horse progressing rapidly. It was therefore no surprise when Tiverton's price began shortening rapidly in the days preceding the race, eventually settling at a starting price of 6/1.

In a field of thirteen, other interesting runners included Roman Hackle and Knight's Crest. Roman Hackle, a giant bay horse, had looked a champion of immense promise when easily winning the 1940 Cheltenham Gold Cup as a seven-year-old. But his form after Cheltenham took a serious dive, and his starting price of 25/1 off a weight of just 9st 7lbs in the Irish National served notice as to how far he had fallen from grace. Knight's Crest on the other hand was something of a dark horse. Just a seven-year-old, the horse was trained by Captain Cyril Harty and ridden by blossoming star Martin Molony. With consistent, if not always winning form prior to the big race, Knight's Crest emerged as perhaps the most intriguing outsider in 1944, eventually starting at 100/8.

From a smooth start, the early leading group consisted of Knight's Crest, Tiverton, Prince Regent and Erinox, but by the time the field came into the straight for the first time, HMS Sturgeon had emerged to shade the advantage over Prince Blackthorn, Ruby Loch and Prince Regent, with Erinox moving forward to make a leading group of five passing the stands.

It was to be a race featuring a number of catastrophic incidents and the first arrived shortly after passing the stands. Squeezed for room, Prince Blackthorn received an unexpected bump from another horse and fell to the ground on the flat. It was bitter luck for Prince Blackthorn, for he had been jumping and travelling extremely well, yet his chance evaporated in an instant, an example of the perilous nature of racing.

As the pace increased noticeably on the second circuit, the first to come under pressure was Erinox, and the horse quickly dropped back through the field. Conversely, Prince Regent improved his position slightly with his usual grace and powerful galloping, and with Knight's Crest and Ruby Loch for company, the favourite took command.

There was little incident or change in the running order until the third last fence. It was here that Prince Regent drew clear of Ruby Loch and Knight's Crest, bringing roars of encouragement from the crowd as he did so. Prince Regent was held in such high regard by all, and as he went for home, a second victory in the race appeared very likely.

Landing a length in front over the final fence, Prince Regent looked certain to win. But sizing up the situation from behind was a very talented young jockey in Molony, and realizing his horse had considerably less weight than the favourite, asked Knight's Crest to deliver a sustained drive to the line. Cutting back Prince Regent's lead with a devastating turn of foot, Knight's Crest was able to overhaul the leader and win by a length, somewhat stunning the crowd who had been convinced that Prince Regent was to be the hero of the day, although in many ways, he was, for he had given an incredible 3st to Knight's Crest and still very nearly won. Back in third, a mere length behind came Ruby Loch, owned by Mr C. Corbett. It was a bittersweet occasion for Mr Corbett, for although Ruby Loch had run with tremendous credit to take third place, his other runner, Mountain Loch, sadly dropped dead between the last two fences.

In a thrilling finish, the young Knight's Crest had won the day, with much praise falling on the shoulders of Molony, who was having his first ride in the race and Captain Cyril Harty, who was to enjoy his finest hour as a trainer in the race. Only recently, owner Corbett had been honoured by the Irish Army Prizejumping team, with whom he had won competitions the world over. Knight's Crest went on to compete at a high level for a number of years, returning to defend his title in the 1945 Irish National, and also braving the big Aintree fences in the Grand National of 1946, where he was a faller in a race where Prince Regent finished a gallant third.

1944 IRISH GRAND NATIONAL RESULT

FATE	HORSE	AGE/WEIGHT	JOCKEY
1st	KNIGHT'S CREST	7.9.7	M. MOLONY
2nd	PRINCE REGENT	9.12.7	T. HYDE
3rd	RUBY LOCH	a.9.7	E.J. KENNEDY
4th	Callaly	11.9.11	V. Mooney
5th	Sir Sen	a.9.7	D. Daly
6th	Erinox	a.9.7	J.P. Maguire
7th	Golden View II	9.10.5	T. McNeill
8th	Tiverton	6.10.2	D. Morgan
9th	Roman Hackle	11.9.7	R.J. O'Ryan
10th	H.M.S. Sturgeon	a.9.7	A. Brabazon
11th	Eastern Realm	a.9.13	P. Moylan
Fell	Mountain Loch	a.10.7	B. O'Connell
Fell	Prince Blackthorn	6.10.8	J. Brogan

17 April 1944
Winner – £810
Race Distance – three miles four furlongs
13 Ran
Winner trained by C. Harty
Winner owned by Mrs W. Mooney
Knight's Crest, bay gelding by Wavetop – Eerie.

Betting – 9/4 Prince Regent, 7/2 Prince Blackthorn, 6/1 Tiverton, 8/1 H.M.S. Sturgeon, 100/8 Erinox & KNIGHT'S CREST, 20/1 Golden View II, 25/1 Mountain Loch, Roman Hackle & Ruby Loch, 33/1 Eastern Realm, 100/1 Callaly & Sir Sen.

Above: Cyril Harty leads in Knight's Crest and jockey Martin Molony.

Right: Knight's Crest beats national hero Prince Regent in a tight finish.

1945 - HEIRDOM

Prince Regent was set to carry top weight for the fourth consecutive year in the Irish Grand National, again allocated a weight burden far exceeding his rivals. However, at the eleventh hour, Tom Dreaper's horse was withdrawn because of swelling on his back. This left a field of twelve to go to post, with the new top weight being the veteran chaser St Martin.

Most fancied of the dozen runners were the previous year's winner Knight's Crest and the talented youngster Happy Home. In good form according to his connections, the way Knight's Crest had finished the race the year before led many to believe he could again emerge victorious, especially given the horse's lightweight of just 9st 9lbs. However, in the days leading up to the race, all the talk was for the fast improving Happy Home, a bay six-year-old owned by Miss Dorothy Paget. Stamina was most definitely in Happy Home's arsenal, for his sire Cottage was also responsible for future triple-Cheltenham Gold Cup winner Cottage Rake, future Aintree Grand National winners Lovely Cottage and Sheila's Cottage, as well as future Welsh Grand National winner Bora's Cottage. With Dan Moore in the saddle and a good racing weight of 10st, money poured in for Happy Home before the race, sending the horse off as 3/1 joint-favourite with Knight's Crest.

Trainer Cecil Brabazon had two runners in the race, those being the outsider Historical Revue and the new top weight St Martin, a horse whose best form was of some years previously. However, there were plenty of appealing candidates, such as the good ex-hunter chaser Lovely Cottage, the Willie O'Grady-trained Callaly and the front-running Western Dandy. Well backed too was the six-year-old mare Alice Baythorn, owned and trained by Joe Osborne. Alice Baythorn had won the Maiden Plate over four miles at Punchestown the year before and was reported to be in tremendous heart beforehand by her trainer.

Respected yet hardly expected to win the race was the thirteen-year-old Heirdom, from the Kilkenny-based yard of John Kirwan. Two years previously at Leopardstown, Heirdom had received 3st from the great Prince Regent and beaten him by a head, a victory that remained Heirdom's most famous to date. Looking in magnificent physical condition before the race, Heirdom – a near black gelding – certainly seemed ready to do himself justice, yet at 100/7, he was far from the most fancied in the field.

As another big crowd gathered for the 1945 race, it was to be Happy Home and Western Dandy that emerged as the pacemakers, and the two dictated proceedings for the first mile. From a very early stage, the 1944 winner Knight's Crest tailed off, and the horse was to prove the race's major disappointment, never threatening in the contest and eventually finishing last.

As Happy Home and Western Dandy raced on, they were soon joined by St Martin, with Alice Baythorn and Callaly well placed just behind, and after two miles, this remained the leading group, with the veteran Heirdom lying in sixth position.

With two miles travelled, the pace suddenly increased dramatically, and this was through the efforts of another older horse, the twelve-year-old Callaly, ridden by Danny Morgan. Callaly surged into the lead with a mile to run, and this charge to the front caught out the likes of Happy Home and St Martin, both of whom began to fade out of contention, St Martin soon being pulled-up once his chance had gone.

With the majority of runners now coming under intense pressure, Callaly bounded towards the home straight. However, the one horse that had not been shaken off was Heirdom, the thirteen-year-old having received a very patient ride from jockey J.P. Maguire, and over the course of the last half-mile, the two horses engaged in a pulsating duel.

On the inside rails, Heirdom stripped Callaly of the lead as the two turned into the home straight and, from there, the battle intensified. Driven hard by Morgan, Callaly tried hard but simply could not overhaul Heirdom. Passing the post a length in front, Heirdom held on to win the National, with eight lengths back to the staying-on Lovely Cottage in third and then Happy Home in fourth. Nine of the twelve horses completed with the three others pulling-up.

The win for Heirdom came as something of a surprise, yet the horse had been produced at peak fitness, a testament to the training skills of Kirwan. It was a first Irish National win for Kirwan, Maguire and owner Mr H. Quinn, while at thirteen, Heirdom became the second oldest winner of the race, with the oldest being the fourteen-year-old Be Careful, the winner in 1923.

With Prince Regent missing, the form of the race initially seemed poor, but a number of horses emerged to have fine careers. Happy Home finished second in the Cheltenham Gold Cup in both 1947 and 1948 and finished fourth and sixth respectively in the Aintree Grand Nationals of 1948 and 1949, while Lovely Cottage, a horse that was transferred to the English yard of Neville Crump soon after the 1945 Irish National, went on to win the 1946 Aintree Grand National, with both Prince Regent and Heirdom in that particular field.

Martin Molony (centre) won the race three times and was ninth on Knight's Crest in 1945.

1945 IRISH GRAND NATIONAL RESULT

FATE	HORSE	AGE/WEIGHT	JOCKEY
1st	HEIRDOM	13.9.7	J.P. MAGUIRE
2nd	CALLALY	12.10.0	D. MORGAN
3rd	LOVELY COTTAGE	8.9.7	R.J. O'RYAN
4th	Happy Home	6.10.0	D.L. Moore
5th	Summer Star	a.9.7	D. McCann
6th	Western Dandy	a.10.5	M. Gordon
7th	Alice Baythorn	6.9.8	A. Brabazon
9th	Knight's Crest	8.9.9	M. Molony
Pulled-Up	Crickstown	a.9.9	P. Timmins
Pulled-Up	Historical Revue	7.9.7	J. Fitzgerald
Pulled-Up	St Martin	12.10.9	E. Newman

2 April 1945
Winner – £735
Race Distance – three miles four furlongs
Time – 7mins 9.8secs
12 Ran
Winner trained by J. Kirwan
Winner owned by Mr H. Quinn
Heirdom, brown or black gelding by Birthright – My Friend.

Betting – 3/1 Happy Home & Knight's Crest, 6/1 Callaly, 7/1 Alice Baythorn & Western Dandy, 100/7 HEIRDOM, 20/1 Lovely Cottage, 25/1 Summer Star, 33/1 African Collection, Crickstown, Historical Revue & St Martin.

1946 – GOLDEN VIEW II

Following the success of the thirteen-year-old Heirdom in the 1945 Irish Grand National, another veteran chaser caught the public imagination for the 1946 race, as St Martin was made 9/4 favourite. St Martin had, at one time, been one of the very best chasers in Ireland, but the horse had not won a race since 1942. However, St Martin had suffered a terrible time in that period with injuries, notably leg trouble, and his trainer, Cecil Brabazon, had exercised real patience in getting the horse fit to race again. St Martin was a popular horse among racegoers, and after a successful spell hunting, the thirteen-year-old was deemed fit to run in the big race. That St Martin was as low as he was in the betting was somewhat of a surprise, given his age and hefty weight of 11st 8lbs, yet sentiment often rules in betting, and the horse was a well-backed favourite on the day. St Martin was ridden by the stylish Aubrey Brabazon, also regarded as a top-class flat jockey having won Irish Classics in that sphere.

With perennial top weight Prince Regent not targeted at the race on this occasion (instead winning the only Cheltenham Gold Cup he contested before running a brave third in the first Aintree Grand National since 1940), it was the eleven-year-old chestnut Golden View II that carried the burden of top weight on 12st 7lbs. Trained in Rathcath by Dick O'Connell, Golden View II was an experienced chaser and one of the finest jumpers in Ireland. The horse had won his latest start – a three-mile chase at Baldoyle – yet it remained to be seen whether he was good enough to give weight away to a number of improving horses in the 1946 field.

Among those considered possible winners were Dunshaughlin, African Collection and Senria. Successful with Golden Jack in 1943, trainer Charlie Rogers this time ran the eight-year-old Dunshaughlin, a brown gelding owned by Miss Dorothy Paget. Dunshaughlin had been very well supported for the recent Aintree Grand National, and despite not distinguishing himself there (he fell), the horse was considered to be very good and had won at Fairyhouse the season before. Despite a liking for heavy conditions, which were absent at Fairyhouse in 1946, African Collection had run a fine race behind Prince Regent to finish fourth in the Cheltenham Gold Cup and was well supported, while the mare Senria had plenty of followers after a three-mile chase win at Naas in March. Senria was from the Tom Dreaper stable, and the mare had won a hunter-chase at Fairyhouse over three-and-a-quarter miles at the 1945 Irish National meeting.

Although the weather was dull and dreary, another big attendance was recorded, and with the ground riding fast, an exciting race looked likely. For much of the way, the favourite St Martin showed nicely among the leaders, together with the fancied mare Senria. But the going was against St Martin, a horse that preferred softer conditions, and just as he had done in the 1945 race, he began to fade out of contention in the last mile, as did Senria.

It was at the same point that St Martin and Senria drifted out of the picture that both Dunshaughlin and Golden Prince fell when travelling strongly, and this incident left three horses to fight out the remainder of the contest. The three in question were the six-year-old Klaxton, the held-up African Collection and the top weight, Golden View II. Jockey Jerry Fitzgerald had purposely kept the seven-year-old African Collection towards the rear early on, but as the race progressed, the horse made eye-catching movement through the field. However, when just starting to get into full flow, African Collection made a terrible mistake four fences from home, and this put pay to his chances of winning.

With Klaxton leading, it was to be Golden View II that came with a storming late burst inside the final half-mile, and roared on by the enthusiastic crowd, the chestnut flew up the run-in and proceeded to win easily by eight lengths from Klaxton with another eight back to African Collection. Only a six-year-old, Klaxton had run with great credit, and he would be another to try his luck in future Aintree Grand Nationals, running in that race three times, with his best effort coming when finishing tenth in 1948.

Despite bold runs from a number of runners, the 1946 Irish National belonged to Golden View II, and the horse proved a most popular winner. With Tote receipt records broken on the day (beating the previous record by £5000), the race was growing in status all the time. The first three home were all owned by ladies: Mrs L. Lillingston owned Golden View II (jointly with Capt. P.A. O'Reilly), Mrs K. Coonan owned Klaxton and Miss E. Shortiss owned African Collection. Mrs Lillingston's late husband had been a well-known amateur rider, and now she could enjoy the fact that her horse had joined the roll of honour of Ireland's most famous steeplechase.

1946 IRISH GRAND NATIONAL RESULT

FATE	HORSE	AGE/WEIGHT	JOCKEY	22 April 1946
1st	GOLDEN VIEW II	11.12.7	M. MOLONY	Winner – £740
2nd	KLAXTON	6.11.13	M. BROWNE	Race Distance – three miles four furlongs
3rd	AFRICAN COLLECTION	7.12.3	JERRY FITZGERALD	Time – 6mins 40.2secs
4th	Senria	a.11.0	E. Newman	11 Ran
5th	St Martin	13.11.8	A. Brabazon	Winner trained by R. O'Connell
6th	Skouras	6.10.0	D. McCann	Winner owned by Mrs L. Lillingston
7th	Erinox	a.11.10	P.J. Doyle	Golden View II, chestnut gelding by Johnny Roebuck – Rathview.
8th	Dunshaughlin	8.12.4	D.L. Moore	
Fell	Eiderlink	a.10.11	J. Brogan	Betting – 9/4 St Martin, 7/2 Senria, 7/1 African Collection, Dunshaughlin &
Fell	Golden Prince	a.11.9	J. Barrett	GOLDEN VIEW II, 100/8 Erinox, 100/6 Golden Prince, Klaxton & Lucky Time,
Pulled-Up	Lucky Time	a.10.0	T. McNeill	20/1 Eiderlink & Skouras.

Golden View II wins easily in 1946.

1947 – REVELRY

An open and competitive Irish Grand National looked on the cards in 1947, with a host of improving young horses lining up among a strong field of seventeen. Originally, Cool Customer – a future Cheltenham Gold Cup favourite – was set to carry top weight of 12st 7lbs, but the bay was a late withdrawal, leaving the seven-year-old Halcyon Hours to top the handicap on 12st. With new stands constructed at Fairyhouse in time for the 1947 race, an exciting renewal lay in wait.

Favourite was the seven-year-old brown gelding Cloncarrig, a great big strapping chaser trained at Naas by Joe Osborne. Improving all the time, Cloncarrig was considered a potential Gold Cup or Aintree Grand National horse of the future and had shot to prominence in the Irish National betting following a superb performance when winning the Leopardstown Chase in February. There were concerns over Cloncarrig, however, for despite his raw talent, he was prone to jumping errors. Furthermore, the horse had given a poor account of himself the year before at Fairyhouse when contesting the Maiden Chase. With Martin Molony booked to ride, Cloncarrig began the race well supported at 9/2.

Trainer Tom Dreaper had two runners in the field, the progressive Morning Star II and the big chestnut Roimond, the youngest horse in the race, while a number of horses that had enjoyed no luck in the recent Grand National at Aintree also lined-up, including Patrickswell, Handy Lad and the new top weight Halcyon Hours. It was another of the Aintree failures that took second spot in the betting behind Cloncarrig. Revelry had been well backed at Aintree, only to come a cropper at the very first fence. Trained by the 1946 winner Dick O'Connell, Revelry was a seven-year-old bay with good form in Ireland, and his partner for the Irish National was Dan Moore, a winner on Golden Jack in 1943 and a man that had greatly assisted O'Connell in the preparation of Revelry. When the pair had parted company at Aintree, Moore had received a nasty blow to the head, and it was only on the morning of the race that the jockey decided to take part. Moore obviously considered Revelry's chance a fine one, for the jockey lined-up at Fairyhouse with his neck heavily strapped and bandaged.

With sticky ground expected to make the race a thorough test of stamina, the runners were sent on their way, with Revelry, Morning Star II and Roimond the first to show. After the field lost Handy Lad early on, Revelry carved open a quick three-length lead, the horse jumping with real panache, clearly unaffected by his Aintree tumble.

Having been up with the pace early, the top weight Halcyon Hours soon found the going too tough and was pulled-up, while the favourite Cloncarrig had appeared to struggle from the outset and was never able to get going, as Revelry continued to lead on majestically from Skouras, Roimond, Lawabiding, Fuddle and the held-up African Collection.

Both Fuddle and Shaun Ogue had made good progress from the halfway point, but with half-a-mile left to run, the pair were overtaken in their pursuit of the leader Revelry by the mud-loving Highland Lad, African Collection, Skouras and Charles Edward, and the latter four were the only ones within touching distance of Revelry as the field swung into the home straight – many of the runners crying enough on the stamina-draining ground.

Revelry had never been headed throughout the race, but as Highland Lad came to join him at the top of the straight, the long-time leader looked to have drawn a real battle. However, it appeared that Moore had saved a bit on his horse coming to the last, and when Highland Lad made a dreadful error at that fence and nearly fell, the race was over.

Crossing the line in a canter, Revelry ran out a very easy winner by ten lengths to Highland Lad, with African Collection running into third place again, a further three lengths back. In fourth came the 100/1 outsider Charles Edward, a horse that had won the Ulster National at Downpatrick the previous Wednesday, but only seven of the seventeen starters completed, with the likes of Cloncarrig, Morning Star II and Roimond pulling-up. One of the more unlucky runners was Grange Silvia, who was well positioned and looked set for a place until coming down three fences out.

Revelry had led the entire way and despite Highland Lad's challenge, had never really looked in danger. One of the few worries presented to the winner during his round had come when the loose Handy Lad caused some interference at the third last. Revelry was very nearly carried out but, assisted skilfully by Moore, managed to dodge the bothersome Handy Lad and continue on his way to glory.

Moore received much credit for his brave decision to ride Revelry following his injuries from Aintree (George Wells, a good flat and hurdle jockey, had been on standby) and the win provided the second consecutive triumph for trainer O'Connell. Revelry had once changed hands for a mere 26 guineas but was eventually purchased by winning owner Mr J.T. Doyle from Lord Harrington for a fee of £10,000. Revelry went on to contest many important races the following year, finishing unplaced in the Cheltenham Gold Cup and twelfth in the Aintree Grand National.

1947 IRISH GRAND NATIONAL RESULT

FATE	HORSE	AGE/WEIGHT	JOCKEY	8 April 1947
1st	REVELRY	7.11.5	D.L. MOORE	Winner – £1,110
2nd	HIGHLAND LAD	8.9.7	A. POWER	Race Distance – three miles four furlongs
3rd	AFRICAN COLLECTION	8.11.0	J. BROGAN	Time – 7mins 36.8secs
4th	CHARLES EDWARD	8.10.5	T. ELLIS	17 Ran
5th	Skouras	7.10.5	D. McCann	Winner trained by R. O'Connell
6th	Lawabiding	9.9.11	R. McCarthy	Winner owned by Mr J.T. Doyle
7th	Fuddle	11.10.3	T. Shaw	Revelry, bay gelding by Rejoice – Amy Gay.
Fell	Grange Silvia	8.9.7	J. Doyle	
Fell	Handy Lad	12.9.7	W. Gilmour	
Pulled-Up	Barnhill	9.9.7	C. Sleator	Betting – 9/2 Cloncarrig, 6/1 REVELRY, 8/1 Morning Star II, 100/8 Fuddle,
Pulled-Up	Clonaboy	9.10.4	E. Dempsey	Lawabiding & Skouras, 100/7 Halcyon Hours & Highland Lad, 100/6 Grange
Pulled-Up	Cloncarrig	7.10.13	M. Molony	Silvia & Shaun Ogue, 20/1 African Collection, 25/1 Roimond, 33/1 Cooper Hill,
Pulled-Up	Cooper Hill	8.9.11	J. Fitzgerald	100/1 Barnhill, Charles Edward, Clonaboy & Handy Lad.
Pulled-Up	Halcyon Hours	7.12.0	M. Gordon	
Pulled-Up	Morning Star II	8.10.1	T. Hyde	
Pulled-Up	Roimond	6.11.0	E. Newman	
Pulled-Up	Shaun Ogue	9.11.7	D. Morgan	

Revelry jumps the final fence.

1948 – HAMSTAR

The Irish Grand National meeting at Fairyhouse was expanded to a two-day affair for the first time in 1948 and there could have been no better horse to advertise the attractions of racing than the brilliant and most recent Cheltenham Gold Cup winner, Cottage Rake. Another competitive field of seventeen lined-up, but it was the Gold Cup hero that stole all the attention beforehand.

A well-built, dark bay son of the prolific sire Cottage, Cottage Rake had won the Gold Cup in style, beating former Irish National runner Happy Home – a horse that subsequently finished fourth in the Grand National at Aintree – with a devastating late burst. Cottage Rake was the horse that put legendary trainer Vincent O'Brien, 'the Maestro', on the map. Cottage Rake became the flagship horse for the beginning of the young O'Brien's wonderful career, the horse having been bought by owner Mr Frank Vickerman, despite the concerns of numerous vets. Cottage Rake, not surprisingly, was top weight at Fairyhouse, a course where he had won before, and was made a red-hot 6/4 favourite.

Having trained the winner of the last two Irish Nationals, Dick O'Connell was doubly represented on this occasion, with his runners being the well-backed Fear Cruaid and the lightly-weighted Cap'n Andy, while previous Irish National runners African Collection, Grange Silvia and Handy Lad were again in the field. Among the leading contenders in the betting were the excellent jumper Arranbeg, the Joe Osborne-trained Green Dolphin, ridden by two-time winner Martin Molony, the surprise winner of the 1947 Aintree Grand National, Caughoo, and the eight-year-old Hamstar. From the County Tipperary yard of Willie O'Grady, Hamstar – bay with a big white face – had been well supported in the ante-post market, yet had been a doubt the morning of the race because of the ground. Hamstar was a horse with a history of leg trouble and would not have been risked on hard ground. Fortunately, conditions proved acceptable and Hamstar was allowed to take his chance. Nevertheless, his starting price of 6/1 seemed somewhat skinny, given the fact that Hamstar was little more than a novice chaser and had won just one other chase, that coming at Limerick a long time before the Irish National.

It was the 100/1 outsider Handy Coin that took them along in the early stages, and one of the first casualties was Wandering Wolf, who fell. However, Handy Coin was soon passed by Caughoo, and the Grand National winner was to lead for the next two miles, showing a welcome return to form absent since his shock win at Aintree the year before.

As Caughoo began to tire in the second half of the race, the lead would change hands a number of times. Jumping Ballyhack, the nine-year-old Balmy Breeze was the leader, with the likes of Fear Cruaid, Hamstar, Corry II, Cap'n Andy and the Gold Cup winner Cottage Rake all prominent. Indeed, it was after jumping the Ballyhack fence that Aubrey Brabazon sent Cottage Rake forward to dispute proceedings, and the horse remained in the picture until the finish.

Corry II had been travelling well, but the horse hit the fence after Ballyhack and was never able to regain his position thereafter, while the likes of Green Dolphin, African Collection and Arranbeg tried to make their stamina tell and came into contention inside the final mile.

After the mistake by Corry II, it was Hamstar and Cap'n Andy that emerged from the pack to dictate matters, and with the gallant Cottage Rake having to give 3st to both, the battle lay between the two lightweights. Hamstar had been jumping and travelling well the entire way for jockey E.J. Kennedy, but the run of Cap'n Andy had been a surprise one, and coming to the last fence, the two were locked together.

Rising neck and neck, Cap'n Andy made a terrible mistake and capsized on landing, shooting jockey Mick Gordon from the saddle and gifting the race to Hamstar. With his closest rival down, Hamstar came home as he liked, and was eased down to cross the line in a canter, receiving tremendous applause from the vast Fairyhouse crowd as he did so. Fifteen lengths away in second came the gallant Cottage Rake, who had been at a serious disadvantage at the weights yet had still performed with real credit. For Cottage Rake, legendary status lay in wait, for he was to win the next two Cheltenham Gold Cups to make it three in total. In third came Fear Cruaid, another that had run well under a big weight.

Both Kennedy and Gordon admitted it would have been a close run affair had Cap'n Andy not come down at the final fence, but unsurprisingly, both suggested they would have won. Even so, Hamstar had been mightily impressive in his victory, and it was a win all the more special given his history with injury. Owner Mr Blayney Hamilton had paid just 33 guineas for Hamstar as a yearling and the horse had been broken-in as a four-year-old when sent into training with O'Grady. Hamstar developed a bad leg in 1945 and O'Grady put him out to grass until 1947, patiently bringing the horse back to fitness. On a day when Tote receipts were up by nearly £9,000 on the previous year's meeting, setting a new record in Ireland, O'Grady's patience was rewarded in grand style, as Hamstar became the newest hero of the Irish Grand National.

1948 IRISH GRAND NATIONAL RESULT

FATE	HORSE	AGE/WEIGHT	JOCKEY
1st	HAMSTAR	8.9.7	E.J. KENNEDY
2nd	COTTAGE RAKE	9.12.7	A. BRABAZON
3rd	FEAR CRUAID	a.11.8	D.L. MOORE
4th	GREEN DOLPHIN	8.9.9	M. MOLONY
5th	Arranbeg	11.10.6	E. Newman
6th	Hottonea	9.9.7	D. McCann
7th	Stockman	6.9.11	B. Sheridan
8th	African Collection	9.10.6	J. Brogan
9th	Caughoo	9.10.9	E. Dempsey
10th	Corry II	a.9.7	B. O'Neill
11th	Balmy Breeze	9.9.7	M. Farrissey
12th	Handy Lad	13.9.7	M. O'Dwyer
Fell	Cap'n Andy	9.9.7	M. Gordon
Fell	Grange Silvia	9.9.11	W. Curran
Fell	Wandering Wolf	8.9.7	T. Shaw
Pulled-Up	Handy Coin	a.9.7	Mr F. Fitzsimons
Refused	Ballyfeighan	13.9.13	Mr A.O. Scannell

29 March 1948
Winner – £1,462
Race Distance – three miles four furlongs
Time – 6mins 45secs
17 Ran
Winner trained by W.T. O'Grady
Winner owned by Mr B. Hamilton
Hamstar, bay gelding by Noble Star – Home Again.

Betting – 6/4 Cottage Rake, 11/2 Fear Cruaid, 6/1 HAMSTAR, 100/8 African Collection, Arranbeg & Green Dolphin, 100/7 Grange Silvia, 20/1 Balmy Breeze, Cap'n Andy, Caughoo & Stockman, 25/1 Ballyfeighan, 33/1 Wandering Wolf, 40/1 Corry II, 50/1 Hottonea, 100/1 Handy Coin & Handy Lad.

Jumping a fence in the Irish National.

1949 – SHAGREEN

As far as the bookmakers were concerned, only three horses were given serious chances of winning the 1949 Irish Grand National. With the Cheltenham Gold Cup winner Cottage Rake a late withdrawal, the Vincent O'Brien stable was represented by Castledermot, a horse that arrived at Fairyhouse having run poorly at Aintree's Grand National meeting. However, remembering the horse's previous exploits when winning over four miles at Cheltenham, the seven-year-old bay Castledermot was made 9/2 favourite to give O'Brien his first Irish National winner.

The two other horses given serious consideration were Bricett and Shagreen. A brown twelve-year-old trained in England by Willie Stephenson, Bricett had run in four Aintree Grand Nationals, yet his best performance in that race had come most recently when finishing ninth. At a time when English challengers for the race were infrequent (mostly due to porous prize money), Bricett's presence added a welcome edge to the race, and the horse was a first Fairyhouse ride for Frenchie Nicholson. Owned, as Prince Regent was, by Mr James V. Rank, Shagreen was the representative of the Tom Dreaper yard. Although not as good as the great champion Prince Regent, Shagreen similarly had a touch of class. A grand-looking bay novice by the owner's stallion Epigram, Shagreen was blessed with rich stamina stemming from his dam Coleen (also owned by Rank), a mare that had finished second to Royal Mail in the 1937 Aintree Grand National and also finished fourth in two subsequent editions of that race. Warming up for the Irish National with a pleasing hurdles' win the week before, Shagreen was made 5/1 second favourite for the race, where he was partnered by Eddie Newman.

Others in the big field of twenty included race veterans African Collection, Caughoo and the 1948 runner-up Highland Lad, as well as fancied outsiders Stockman and Sadler's Wells. Winner of the important Leopardstown Chase, Stockman was trained by Cecil Brabazon and was top weight, while Sadler's Wells (not to be confused with the brilliant stallion of modern times) was trained locally by former winning jockey Dan Moore, and was a first Irish National ride for young Tommy Burns.

With Fairyhouse basking in glorious sunshine, the field were sent on their way. First to show were Shagreen, Castledermot and Result, but 100/1 shot Barney's Link was soon rushed up front to lead the field (which he did for nearly half the race), while the English raider Bricett was held up by Nicholson.

The race was not without its share of casualties. Point Of Law fell at the second fence, while both Arden Link and Lord Glenfield came down together at the tricky drop fence after the stands had been passed.

The first half of the race had been dominated by Barney's Link, Shagreen and Castledermot, but as the race progressed, the veteran Arranbeg began a bold challenge. Moving through the field in eye-catching style as they climbed to Ballyhack, Arranbeg soon took over the lead and appeared to be travelling strongly. It was after Ballyhack that Bricett began his move, picking off horses one by one, albeit from a long way back.

With three-quarters-of-a-mile to run, Barney's Link was beaten, and now it was Shagreen that hit the front, Newman moving his horse forward with confidence to take up the running from Arranbeg, Castledermot and Highland Lad. Newman had been sitting patiently prior to this, but when an opening appeared in front of him, he had no hesitation in asking Shagreen for his effort, and the response was instant.

Over the final three fences, it was a case of those left in contention trying to catch Shagreen. Castledermot had flattered to three out but weakened soon after, while Highland Lad made a mistake at the same fence and could not quicken sufficiently. Bricett had been left with too much ground to make up while Arranbeg's reward for a fine run was to fall two fences out, though neither he nor Stockman (also a faller at the second last) looked a danger at their points of exit.

With his rivals beaten off, Shagreen cleared the remaining fences in dashing style, and passing the post a comfortable four-length winner, Shagreen received warm applause from the crowd, for he was a most popular winner. In second place again came Highland Lad, with the beaten favourite Castledermot ten lengths away in third, with a head back to the fast-finishing Bricett.

Shagreen had never been out of the first five throughout the race, always jumping in the style of a fine chaser. It looked likely from some way out that Shagreen would have the beating of the 1949 Irish National field, and he emerged as the class horse of the contest, giving trainer Tom Dreaper his second Irish Grand National win in the process. Shagreen never ran in the Cheltenham Gold Cup, but he won a Grand Sefton Chase over the big Grand National fences at Aintree and ran twice in the big race itself. Although he fell on both occasions, he ran a fine race in the 1950 edition and, with his reputation enhanced, started joint-second favourite in 1951.

1949 IRISH GRAND NATIONAL RESULT

FATE	HORSE	AGE/WEIGHT	JOCKEY
1st	SHAGREEN	8.10.10	E. NEWMAN
2nd	HIGHLAND LAD	10.10.6	E.J. KENNEDY
3rd	CASTLEDERMOT	7.10.7	A. BRABAZON
4th	BRICETT	12.10.13	H. NICHOLSON
5th	Sadler's Wells	a.10.0	T.P. Burns
6th	Green Dolphin	9.10.0	M. Molony
7th	Caughoo	10.10.2	D. McCann
8th	Result	9.10.0	Mr H. Freeman-Jackson
9th	Rara Avis	a.10.0	B. Cooper
10th	Cottager	a.10.0	Mr A. Scannell
11th	African Collection	10.10.11	Mr J.R. Cox
12th	Cold Feet	a.10.5	T. Shaw
13th	Barney's Link	8.10.0	W. Curran
14th	Coupe	11.10.12	J. Brogan
15th	Corry II	a.10.0	B. O'Neill
Fell	Arden Link	a.10.0	C. Grassick
Fell	Arranbeg	12.10.0	A. Power
Fell	Lord Glenfield	a.10.0	M. Gordon
Fell	Point Of Law	7.10.0	M. Browne
Fell	Stockman	7.11.4	P. Crotty

18 April 1949
Winner – £1,480
Race Distance – three miles four furlongs
20 Ran
Winner trained by T.W. Dreaper
Winner owned by Mr J.V. Rank
Shagreen, bay gelding by Epigram – Coleen.

Betting – 9/2 Castledermot, 5/1 SHAGREEN, 8/1 Bricett, 100/7 Sadler's Wells, 20/1 Cold Feet, Result & Stockman, 25/1 African Collection, 28/1 Highland Lad, 33/1 Arranbeg, Coupe, Green Dolphin & Lord Glenfield, 50/1 Caughoo, Corry II, Cottager, Point Of Law & Rara Avis, 100/1 Arden Link & Barneys Link.

The elegant Shagreen beats Highland Lad in 1949.

1950 - DOMINICK'S BAR

Having missed the 1949 race, the great Cottage Rake was back to contest the 1950 Irish Grand National. Now eleven, Cottage Rake had won the Cheltenham Gold Cup for a third time in what was the most straightforward of his three wins in chasing's Blue Riband. Cottage Rake had surprisingly been beaten in the season's King George VI Chase at Kempton Park (a race he had won in 1948) by Finnure, a big, handsome, chestnut chaser owned by Lord Bicester, but at Cheltenham, under a tactically superb ride from Aubrey Brabazon, Cottage Rake gained his revenge on Finnure, cruising to a simplistic eight-length victory. His win at Cheltenham meant that Cottage Rake became only the second horse since Golden Miller to win the Gold Cup three or more times, the feat having been achieved since then by only two others: the legendary Arkle and the modern-day hero Best Mate. In the Irish National of 1950, as one would expect, Cottage Rake was asked to carry 12st 7lbs, nearly 2st more than Coupe – next in the handicap with 10st 10lbs. Cottage Rake was undeniably a fantastic horse, yet he had not been able to concede the weight two years previously when Hamstar won the Fairyhouse race. Through his achievements, Cottage Rake was the most popular chaser since Prince Regent, and a flood of money saw the horse start overwhelming favourite at even money.

The strongest competition to the favourite appeared likely to come from Coupe, Stormhead, Toy Glen and Dominick's Bar. The veteran staying chaser Coupe, fourteenth in the 1949 race, was a popular selection, mainly because of his win in the Leopardstown Chase, and the horse was ridden by Jimmy Brogan, while the Tom Dreaper-trained Stormhead (at six, half the age of Coupe) was a course winner and had displayed stamina in his chases, as well as deceptive speed in a number of recent outings over hurdles. Toy Glen (one of two in the race for trainer Dan Moore) was partnered by Tommy Burns, a jockey going for an unusual double, for he had recently won the Irish Lincoln on future Cheltenham Gold Cup winner Knock Hard, while also well supported was another six-year-old, Dominick's Bar. As a chaser, Dominick's Bar was more accustomed to running over shorter distances than that of the Irish National, but he was a useful horse from the stable of Tim Hyde. As a jockey, Hyde had twice won the race courtesy of Clare County in 1938 and Prince Regent in 1942, and his charge was partnered by Champion Irish Jockey Martin Molony, already twice an Irish National winner with Golden View II and Knight's Crest.

It was a most blustery day at Fairyhouse for the 1950 Irish National. A strong gale blew in gusts that sent hats flying in all directions. In addition, racegoers braved the rain and hail that also fell throughout the day, although despite these unwanted bursts there were also long periods of sunshine. Despite the changeable elements, a boisterous crowd cheered enthusiastically when Cottage Rake paraded on the course prior to the race, and the volume of noise increased once more as the twelve runners began their quest.

Statesman and Coupe were the first to show, and the race's only casualty occurred in the early stages when Amritsir crashed out at the third fence. Amritsir was partnered by the only amateur in the race, Mr Joe Osborne, whose father had been second aboard Ruby III in the 1928 Irish National.

It was not long before False Scent hit the front, and the horse raced away towards Ballyhack building up a strong lead. False Scent had not been given much consideration beforehand, but as the horse flew the Ballyhack regulation and surged into a dominant twelve-length lead, there was a feeling that the horse may yet cause a surprise.

However, in behind, the triple-Gold Cup winner Cottage Rake was making his move under Brabazon. As Cottage Rake moved up to stalk the suddenly under pressure leader five out, the crowd roared loudly once more, urging their hero onwards. Cottage Rake's move forward had been matched by Stormhead, and taking the fourth last together, the pair swiftly broke clear, setting up an apparent match between the two.

In receipt of a colossal 33lbs, Stormhead was able to quicken away, instantly putting six lengths between the pair as Cottage Rake fought valiantly to claw back his rival. In behind, Dominick's Bar – who had been with the leaders until halfway – began to stay on once more, chasing hard after the front two, while Toy Glen, prominent among the chasing pack, faded away tamely. Tiring at an even more alarming rate was False Scent. Having led the field for most of the way, the horse's effort evaporated rapidly from four out and he was eventually pulled-up.

Entering the straight with two fences to jump, Stormhead – a last minute ride for George Wells – held a distinctive advantage and looked likely to carry the colours of owner Mr James V. Rank to another Irish National success. However, blundering atrociously at the second last, Stormhead sprawled on landing and, although the horse miraculously recovered, vital momentum had been lost.

Stormhead had been comfortably clear before his mistake and was still in front after it, but the error allowed an opportunity for a rival to benefit and, unfortunately for Stormhead, Dominick's Bar was finishing with strength and power. Seizing his chance of glory, Molony urged Dominick's Bar over the final fence and on the run to the line, the partnership wrested the lead from Stormhead fifty yards from the post, battling through in thrilling style to take the race by two lengths. Coupe had found the early pace too hot but stayed on six lengths behind Stormhead to take third, with Cottage Rake fourth and Derrinstown (third in the following season's Aintree Grand National) fifth.

Somewhat fortunate they may have been, but the result gave a third respective Irish National win to Hyde and Molony, while providing a real tonic for the poorly owner of Dominick's Bar, Mrs P. Kiely, who was ill in bed at her home in Cork, sadly missing her horse achieve his biggest career win. Dominick's Bar – the first six-year-old to win the race since Alice Maythorn in 1936 – had been purchased as a yearling at Ballsbridge Sales for 100 guineas and was later passed on privately to Hyde. Dominick's Bar ran in two further Irish Nationals, carrying far more weight than in 1950, running with great credit on each occasion. The horse also ran in two Aintree Grand Nationals, tragically meeting his end through heart failure in the 1954 race.

Dominick's Bar powers past Stormhead to win.

1950 IRISH GRAND NATIONAL RESULT

FATE	HORSE	AGE/WEIGHT	JOCKEY
1st	DOMINICK'S BAR	6.10.6	M. MOLONY
2nd	STORMHEAD	6.10.2	G. WELLS
3rd	COUPE	12.10.10	J. BROGAN
4th	Cottage Rake	11.12.7	A. Brabazon
5th	Derrinstown	10.10.0	J. Mescall
6th	African Collection	11.10.3	M. Browne
7th	Stockman	8.10.2	P. Crotty
Fell	Amritsir	8.10.0	Mr J.A. Osborne
Pulled-Up	Colin Bell	7.10.0	M. Gordon
Pulled-Up	False Scent	8.10.6	F. Carroll
Pulled-Up	Michael Star	7.10.0	F. McKenna
Pulled-Up	Toy Glen	8.10.6	T.P. Burns

11 April 1950
Winner – £1,480
Race Distance – three miles four furlongs
Time – 7mins 1.6secs
12 Ran
Winner trained by T. Hyde
Winner owned by Mrs P. Kiely
Dominick's Bar, bay or brown gelding by Embargo – Dominick's Bell.

Betting – Evens Cottage Rake, 8/1 Coupe & DOMINICK'S BAR, 10/1 Stormhead
& Toy Glen, 100/6 False Scent, 20/1 African Collection, Amritsir, Colin Bell &
Stockman, 25/1 Derrinstown, 40/1 Michael Star.

1951 – ICY CALM

Because of recent poor weather, there were some doubts as to whether Fairyhouse could stage the 1951 Irish Grand National, but even though the ground was officially heavy, the course had been maintained in excellent shape, and running did indeed take place.

Top weight, form horse and favourite was the Tom Dreaper-trained Stormhead. Like Irish National winners Prince Regent and Shagreen before him, Stormhead was owned by Mr James V. Rank. The horse probably should have won the race in 1950, and certainly would have done but for his costly error two out, and despite the fact that he was asked to carry considerably more weight on this occasion (12st 7lbs), Stormhead had developed into one of the top chasers in the land. Stormhead won over three-and-a-half miles at Leopardstown before demonstrating his adaptability shortly before Fairyhouse with a tidy win over hurdles. With the previous year's winning rider, Martin Molony, in the saddle, Stormhead started a warm 100/30 favourite.

Vincent O'Brien was represented by the heftily weighted chestnut Royal Tan, a horse that would be narrowly beaten into second place in the Grand National at Aintree two weeks after Fairyhouse, while former jockey Willie O'Grady saddled both Red Snake and Icy Calm, of which the promising six-year-old Red Snake was the more strongly fancied in spite of disappointing on his latest start in the Leopardstown Chase. Dan Moore was responsible for three outsiders in Doctor Dandy, Inter Alia and Miss Steel. Dominick's Bar returned to defend his crown, while there was strong support for another six-year-old in the shape of Injunction, a grand type of mare with good recent form to her credit, trained by her owner, Mr A.C. Bryce-Smith.

It was Dominick's Bar and Red Snake that led over the first fence, before, on settling down into a rhythm, Inter Alia went on from Aaron's Rod, Result, Doctor Dandy and Dominick's Bar.

Passing the stands and going out into the country, the 25/1 shot Aaron's Rod opened up a clear lead from Inter Alia, Result, Dominick's Bar, Doctor Dandy, Lazylegs and Icy Calm, and by the time the field jumped the Ballyhack regulation, Inter Alia had moved up again to dispute the lead with Aaron's Rod.

It was at the Ballyhack regulation that the race began to get interesting. Starpool, well backed following a recent win at Leopardstown, crashed out of contention, while two fences later the second favourite Red Snake also hit the deck. Stormhead too was under pressure, and although Molony was hard at work to get him involved, the favourite was making little impact, and with less than a mile to go, it became obvious that Stormhead would not be taking a hand in the finish.

Inter Alia and Doctor Dandy remained in front inside the final mile, narrowly holding the initiative over Royal Tan and Dominick's Bar, while just behind this quartet, jockey Pat Doyle could be seen rousing Icy Calm, with the eight-year-old beginning to respond encouragingly to his pilot's urgings.

An exciting finish was apparent, for approaching three out, Doctor Dandy, Dominick's Bar and Royal Tan travelled abreast, tracked menacingly by Icy Calm, with Inter Alia's brave challenge beginning to deteriorate.

The first of the leaders to make their move was Royal Tan, the powerful chestnut swinging clear turning into the straight and coming clear under jockey Phonsie O'Brien. The Vincent O'Brien inmate looked to have the race won, for he was still in front jumping the last. However, Doyle had continued to ride with strength and determination aboard his horse and, in receipt of 23lbs, it was Icy Calm that was able to wear down Royal Tan, overhauling the chestnut on the run to the line and getting up to win by a length-and-a-half. Dominick's Bar ran another race of credit in taking third just a length back, with Miss Steel staying on for fourth despite having made mistakes. Of the more fancied runners, Injunction had been pulled-up, while the disappointing Stormhead was well back when he fell two out. Much credit rightly went to the runner-up Royal Tan. The horse developed something of a reputation as a 'nearly horse', for he always gave his all in many big races, often carrying huge weights yet so often denied true glory. Royal Tan twice finished in the frame in the Grand National at Aintree, but his finest moment arrived in that same race in 1954, winning the world's most famous steeplechase carrying 11st 7lbs under jockey Bryan Marshall.

It was a second Irish National success for trainer Willie O'Grady following Hamstar's victory three years previously, while Icy Calm carried the colours of County Tipperary sportsman Mr P.G. Grey. The winner was ridden admirably by young Pat Doyle, a jockey who had served his apprenticeship with the late John Kirwan, who had sent out Heirdom to win in 1945. For Icy Calm, the win was the peak of his career, for although the bay twice ran in the Grand National at Aintree, he was pulled-up in both the 1952 and 1954 editions.

1951 IRISH GRAND NATIONAL RESULT

FATE	HORSE	AGE/WEIGHT	JOCKEY
1st	ICY CALM	8.10.3	P.J. DOYLE
2nd	ROYAL TAN	7.11.12	MR A.S. O'BRIEN
3rd	DOMINICK'S BAR	7.11.7	P. TAAFFE
4th	MISS STEEL	7.10.0	T.P. BURNS
5th	Doctor Dandy	7.10.0	P. Norris
6th	Inter Alia	8.10.0	C. Sleator
7th	Jack The Ripper	9.10.0	C. Eddery
8th	Result	11.10.5	Mr H. Freeman-Jackson
9th	Little Trix	8.10.0	P.A. Farrell
10th	Tavoy	8.10.0	C. Grassick
11th	Lazylegs	7.10.0	P. O'Loughlin
12th	Starpool	9.10.8	E. Newman
Fell	Ardnacassa	13.10.0	T. White
Fell	Red Snake	6.10.4	G. Wells
Fell	Scottish Welcome	13.10.0	M. Mackin
Fell	Stormhead	7.12.7	M. Molony
Pulled-Up	Aaron's Rod	9.10.10	B. O'Neill
Pulled-Up	African Collection	12.10.7	D. McCann
Pulled-Up	Injunction	6.11.0	B. Cooper

26 March 1951

Going – Heavy

Winner – £1,500

Race Distance – 3miles

Time – 7mins 27.8secs

19 Ran

Winner trained by W.T. O'Grady

Winner owned by Mr P.G. Grey

Icy Calm, bay gelding by Dragonnade – Matchless Pride.

Betting – 100/30 Stormhead, 6/1 Red Snake, 7/1 Injunction, 8/1 Dominick's Bar, 10/1 Starpool, 100/8 Royal Tan, 100/6 ICY CALM, 20/1 Doctor Dandy, 25/1 Aaron's Rod, African Collection, Ardnacassa, Inter Alia, Jack The Ripper, Lazylegs, Little Trix, Miss Steel, Result, Scottish Welcome & Tavoy.

Mrs P.G. Grey holds her winner, Icy Calm.

1952 - ALBERONI

Favourite for the 1952 Irish Grand National, and justifiably so, was the Tom Dreaper-trained six-year-old, Ballymagillan. A fast-improving youngster, the horse had exhibited superb jumping ability over a circuit of the Grand National course most recently, taming the famous fences in tremendous style to win a two-mile-six-furlong chase from a very useful English horse, Little Yid. Prior to that, Ballymagillan had won a three-mile chase at Leopardstown and a pair of three-mile chases at Baldoyle. Dreaper reported the youngster to be in tremendous heart following his Aintree exertions, and although Ballymagillan picked up a 12lb penalty for that win, he was clearly a horse on the rise and would be unlikely to be as leniently treated in the Irish National again. Other pluses in support of the horse stemmed from the booking of jockey Pat Taaffe and also the fact that the horse had previous experience of Fairyhouse, winning a lesser race at the course the season before. With so much in his favour, it was no surprise Ballymagillan was sent off the red-hot 11/8 favourite.

Having fallen in the 1951 race, Red Snake had progressed and developed into one of the most improved chasers in the land. As a result of this, the Willie O'Grady-trained seven-year-old was allotted 2st more to carry than the year before, making him the race's top weight with 12st 4lbs. Red Snake – partnered at Fairyhouse by the previous year's winning jockey Pat Doyle – had displayed his well-being by impressively winning the Leopardstown Chase in February.

Others given strong chances of winning were Arctic Silver, ridden by Pat Taaffe's brother Tos, then an amateur, the ten-year-old bay Southern Coup, and the Vincent O'Brien-trained Alberoni. O'Brien had seen his previous Irish National runners Cottage Rake, Castledermot and Royal Tan all make the frame in the big race, but he was yet to win it. With Alberoni, he was represented by a chestnut nine-year-old that had won recently at Limerick, a result that persuaded the trainer to run Alberoni and not Royal Tan at Fairyhouse. Alberoni had been associated with the O'Brien stable since he was three years of age and had once finished runner-up in the Galway Plate. The horse was ridden in the Irish National by Len Stephens, a jockey who was based in England with Neville Crump and who was having his first experience of riding at Fairyhouse.

The eleven-year-old Barney's Link began the race at a cracking pace, hotly pursued by the favourite Ballymagillan. As it transpired, this pair would remain in the leading places for much of the race, the two horses setting a strong gallop.

It was at the drop fence past the stands when the race's only casualty occurred, although the incident would prove significant. The seven-year-old Lyrical Lady fell, and in doing so, seriously interfered with Arctic Silver. As a result, Arctic Silver was knocked right back towards the rear of the field and was left to fight an uphill battle for the rest of the race.

The 1950 winner Dominick's Bar, hopelessly out of form, had run well for a long way but began to weaken inside the final mile, while Red Snake had also performed satisfactorily, but he too was struggling to make an impact as the race got serious, and his challenge faded away tamely having jumped the fifth last.

Barney's Link, the oldest horse in the race at eleven, was not the most handsome of individuals, but possessed tremendous heart, and turning into the home straight with just two fences to jump, he was still in command together with his running mate Ballymagillan, who had done nothing wrong throughout. The pair were joined at the second last by Alberoni and the galvanised Arctic Silver, and although the latter made a dreadful mistake that nearly had him landing on his head, the horse somehow survived and took his place in a thrilling four-horse finish.

Barney's Link just led taking the last from Ballymagillan, with Alberoni on the inside and Arctic Silver on the stands side. After a short running rail following the final fence, the width of the course doubled on the run-in and it was here that Alberoni was able to thrust through and rip the lead from the gallant Barney's Link inside the last hundred yards. Holding off Barney's Link, Ballymagillan and the unlucky Arctic Silver in a fantastic battle, Alberoni crossed the line the winner of the Irish National. Barney's Link earned much credit for such a positive run, Ballymagillan had done all he could but had been beaten on merit, while Arctic Silver had done exceptionally well to finish as close as he did given his poor luck in running.

The Vincent O'Brien stable had been suffering a disappointing time in many of the recent big chases, but Alberoni's success emphatically ended that streak. The horse had earned no penalty for his recent Limerick win and he was able to take advantage and win off the minimum weight of 10st. It was that Limerick win that had been jockey Stephens' first ride in Ireland, and now he had carried the black and white colours of winning owner Mr Hugh Stanley to victory in the country's most prestigious race.

1952 IRISH GRAND NATIONAL RESULT

FATE	HORSE	AGE/WEIGHT	JOCKEY	14 April 1952
1st	ALBERONI	9.10.0	L. STEPHENS	Winner – £1,480
2nd	BARNEY'S LINK	11.11.11	MR W.E. ROONEY	Race Distance – three miles
3rd	BALLYMAGILLAN	6.10.12	P. TAAFFE	Time – 6mins 41.2secs
4th	Arctic Silver	8.11.0	Mr T. Taaffe	11 Ran
5th	Dominick's Bar	8.11.9	P. Breen	Winner trained by M.V. O'Brien
6th	Carey's Cottage	5.10.4	B. O'Neill	Winner owned by Mr H.H.M. Stanley
7th	Southern Coup	10.11.1	C. Sleator	Alberoni, chestnut gelding by His Reverence – Lady Pamela.
8th	Red Snake	7.12.4	P.J. Doyle	
9th	Starpool	10.10.1	E. Newman	Betting – 11/8 Ballymagillan, 6/1 ALBERONI & Red Snake, 9/1 Southern Coup,
10th	Point Of Law	10.10.5	J. Mescall	100/8 Arctic Silver, 100/7 Lyrical Lady & Starpool, 100/6 Barney's Link, 20/1
Fell	Lyrical Lady	7.10.8	T.P. Burns	Carey's Cottage, 33/1 Dominick's Bar & Point Of Law.

Owner, the Hon. Mr Hugh Stanley, trainer Vincent O'Brien (centre) and jockey Len Stephens with 1952 winner Alberoni at O'Brien's famous Ballydoyle stables.

1953 – OVERSHADOW

Of the fifteen jockeys that had rides in the 1953 Irish Grand National, only Eddie Newman and Pat Doyle had won the great race before. In an extremely open renewal of the race, both men appeared to hold solid chances of adding to their tally. Newman was on board the Pat Rooney-trained Arctic Silver, a horse somewhat unlucky to have finished only fourth the year before. Arctic Silver was a full-brother to the excellent but luckless favourite for the 1951 Grand National at Aintree, Arctic Gold, and the nine-year-old had warmed up for Fairyhouse with a promising performance over hurdles recently at Phoenix Park. Doyle's mount was the little brown gelding Lucky Dome, representing the powerful Vincent O'Brien yard that had been successful recently at Aintree with Early Mist in the Grand National. Lucky Dome had run in the big race at Aintree as well and had been well fancied beforehand, however, unable to cope with the enormous fences, the seven-year-old performed miserably and had been pulled-up. This was not to say that Lucky Dome was without talent, quite the opposite, for he was considered one of the leading chasers in Ireland, possessing tremendous heart. In fine form prior to Aintree, Lucky Dome's wins had included the important Leopardstown Chase, and despite shouldering top weight of 12st at Fairyhouse, the horse was well backed into 8/1 by the off.

Free Lancer, Gallant Wolf and In View took the three leading positions in the betting market. Free Lancer, a horse with an abundance of stamina, was a brother to the excellent Aintree Grand National winner of 1950, Freebooter, and in the current season, Free Lancer had finished runner-up to Lucky Dome at Leopardstown before winning over four miles at Hurst Park in March. The veteran Gallant Wolf had been recognised in England as a prominent staying hurdler. Since moving to the Irish stable of Tom Taaffe, Gallant Wolf had developed into a very useful chaser, one blessed with stamina, and the horse was considered to have a splendid chance of giving Pat Taaffe his first Irish National-winning ride. Favourite was the six-year-old In View, a half-brother to the 1946 Irish National winner Golden View II. Like Free Lancer, In View was trained locally by Dan Moore and was a horse thought to be approaching his best. In View became favourite for the Irish National following a second place at Cheltenham where, despite making jumping errors, he impressed in a race won by the future Gold Cup winner, Four Ten.

The oldest horse in the race at thirteen was the grey Overshadow, taking his place in the line-up following a highly creditable fourth behind Early Mist at Aintree. An hour before the race, connections were without a jockey for the horse. Pat Taaffe – who rode him at Aintree – was committed to Gallant Wolf, and for a while, a suitable pilot was nowhere to be found. However, when his intended mount at Mallow was declared a non-runner, Albert Power was re-routed to Fairyhouse.

Power had finished third aboard Derrinstown in the 1951 Aintree National, and when the experienced rider became available, he was quickly engaged by trainer Clem Magnier.

It was to be a race of little incident. Overshadow jumped off in front and assumed that position on settling down, tracked by former Galway Plate winner St Kathleen II, Limavaddy, Fort Wayne, In View and Lucky Dome. Gallant Wolf did not settle well early on, while Arctic Silver clubbed the third fence (where Gallant Gale fell) so hard it seemed to rock his confidence, and the horse was never a factor thereafter.

At the drop fence past the stands, St Kathleen II briefly edged in front, but Overshadow was thoroughly enjoying his run, showing no ill-effects from his Aintree effort, and the horse was soon in command again, leading from St Kathleen II, Cloncaw, In View, Southern Coup, Limavaddy and Carey's Cottage, with Gallant Wolf having to be pushed along aggressively by Taaffe to get competitive.

St Kathleen II was the next casualty, coming down at the Ballyhack regulation, where the seven-year-old Cloncaw joined Overshadow in front for a spell, but the thirteen-year-old went on again at the third last, finding reserves of energy, and it was left to the staying-on Gallant Wolf to give chase entering the straight, as the remainder began to tire.

Over the final two fences, Gallant Wolf tried valiantly to get on terms with the leader, but although he had made up considerable ground, his failure to settle early on had cost him, and Taaffe could only watch as Overshadow went clear again after the last, the grey drawing away to win by four lengths. With the winner aged thirteen and the runner-up twelve, a notable hat-trick was achieved for the veteran chasers when eleven-year-old Southern Coup rallied to take third place, meaning the three oldest horses in the race had filled the first three positions. The likes of Lucky Dome and Free Lancer had never threatened, while In View, though running well for some way, faded tamely into eighth.

With the exception of one short spell after passing the stands, Overshadow had led from start to finish, a fine achievement for a horse of his years, the grey displaying grit and courage in victory. Overshadow's win was a first Irish National success for both Power (second on Highland Lad in 1947) and trainer Magnier. It was the trainer's policy to keep his horses running regularly, and he had achieved much success through the method. Certainly Overshadow had defied more common trends by running fine races in both English and Irish Grand Nationals, separated by a mere nine days. Although out of luck with her other runner Lucky Dome, winning owner Mrs J.A. Wood (who had purchased the winner for £65) could now celebrate Overshadow joining Heirdom as the second oldest winner ever of the great race.

The veteran grey Overshadow beats Gallant Wolf.

1953 IRISH GRAND NATIONAL RESULT

FATE	HORSE	AGE/WEIGHT	JOCKEY
1st	OVERSHADOW	13.10.4	A. POWER
2nd	GALLANT WOLF	12.11.1	P. TAAFFE
3rd	SOUTHERN COUP	11.10.7	J. WALSHE
4th	Cloncaw	7.10.9	B. Cooper
5th	Carey's Cottage	6.10.2	M.E. Regan
6th	Limavaddy	10.10.0	J.V. Ahern
7th	Free Lancer	7.10.10	C. Grassick
8th	In View	6.10.1	R. Hamey
9th	Fort Wayne	9.10.12	T. Taaffe
10th	Lucky Dome	7.12.0	P.J. Doyle
11th	Ben Head	9.10.0	J. Mescall
12th	Arctic Silver	9.11.5	E. Newman
Fell	Gallant Gale	8.10.0	B. Merriman
Fell	St Kathleen II	10.10.0	A. Brabazon
Pulled-Up	Air Prince	9.10.0	E.L. McKenzie

6 April 1953
Winner – £1,480
Race Distance – three miles
Time – 6mins 41.6secs
15 Ran
Winner trained by C.L. Magnier
Winner owned by Mrs J.A. Woods
Overshadow, grey gelding by Overthrow – Tetrarchia.

Betting – 5/2 In View, 5/1 Free Lancer & Gallant Wolf, 8/1 Lucky Dome, 100/8 Arctic Silver, Cloncaw & Fort Wayne, 100/7 St Kathleen II, 20/1 Air Prince, Ben Head, Carey's Cottage, Gallant Gale, Limavaddy, OVERSHADOW & Southern Coup.

1954 – ROYAL APPROACH

Top weight for the 1954 Irish Grand National was Royal Approach, a comparative novice six-year-old trained by Tom Dreaper. A brilliant, near-black individual, Royal Approach arrived at Fairyhouse having won his last five races and was a horse considered to have the chasing world at his mercy. Certainly the best Irish chaser since Cottage Rake, Royal Approach held an unbeaten record over fences and had proved himself an exceptional performer, despite his lack of experience. The horse had that rare quality of jumping superbly without apparent effort, giving a glorious impression of an athlete in complete control of his task. He had exhibited some of his stratospheric potential with a most impressive recent win at Cheltenham, good enough to earn the horse a starting price of even money in the Irish National, despite the burden of 12st top weight. As well as the Dreaper connection and the fact that the horse was partnered by the popular Pat Taaffe, Royal Approach was owned by that great supporter of National Hunt racing, the veteran Lord Bicester, an owner who had previously won a Gold Cup with Silver Fame and been second in an Aintree Grand National with Roimond.

Chief market rivals to Royal Approach were Icelough and Sam Brownthorn. Both horses had won their last two starts, with Icelough taking the three-mile-five-furlong Leopardstown Chase, defeating many good horses in the process. A year older than Royal Approach, Sam Brownthorn already had the reputation as a proven stayer and sound jumper. Partnered at Fairyhouse by his owner, Mr H. Freeman-Jackson, Sam Brownthorn had shown his well-being, albeit unconventionally, by winning a mile-and-a-half flat race at Limerick a week before the Irish National.

Also in the field were the Dan Moore-trained stayer Pontage – a winner of the previous season's National Hunt Chase at Cheltenham over four miles – and the bay mare Kilkilogue, a fantastic jumper trained by her owner, Mr R.G. Patton. On going described as 'fairly good', a fast run race was to render the winner a wonderful chaser.

Directly from the start, Kilkilogue and Royal Approach broke into the lead, followed most prominently by Icelough, Limavaddy, Pontage and Colin Bell. It was clear that Pat Taaffe would have liked to have held his horse up, but so strongly was the horse travelling that the jockey made a quick decision to let the horse stride out and go on.

Taaffe's decision proved inspired. Out in the country and accompanied by only Kilkilogue, the leaders must have been a fence clear of their pursuers, of which the noseband-wearing Sam Brownthorn was struggling to go the pace on the first circuit. The only scare Royal Approach would receive came at the drop fence past the stands where he pecked slightly on landing but, apart from that, the horse delivered a faultless display, a display that impressed more the further he travelled.

Four fences from home, Kilkilogue was still hanging on to the procession constructed by Royal Approach, but it was clear there would be only one winner of that particular battle. In behind, Icelough had made up a lot of ground, but when he smashed through the third last, Tos Taaffe's saddle slipped, and the partnership did well to complete the race at all.

Turning into the home straight, Sam Brownthorn made a valiant attempt to get on terms with the leaders, devouring the ground with every stride. But this was to be a performance of genuine quality from Royal Approach, and safely negotiating the final two fences, Taaffe guided him home to an authoritative victory under top weight, the huge crowd showing their appreciation for an outstanding racehorse as Royal Approach crossed the line. With his jockey having lost his cap and helmet, Sam Brownthorn had blundered the second last, yet had finished with real power to take second, two lengths back, while Icelough was a further three lengths back in third, with Kilkilogue fourth. The mistake and subsequent ill-luck of Icelough had left Taaffe most frustrated, claiming he would have finished even closer to Royal Approach, possibly even beating him. That is, however, hard to imagine, for Royal Approach had delivered a near perfect display under a huge weight, giving the impression he would have had plenty more to offer if challenged.

It was a third win for Dreaper and a first for Pat Taaffe. The jockey was so impressed with Royal Approach that he proclaimed the horse to be the best he had ever ridden or was ever likely to ride. If only Taaffe had been able to glance ten years into the future. It was, however, a brilliant effort by Royal Approach and a performance that had many wondering if the horse could rise to the very highest levels. Sadly, the speculation was irrelevant. During his summer lay off, Royal Approach sustained a bad injury and never raced again, meaning one of the potential great champions was cut down in his prime.

1954 IRISH GRAND NATIONAL RESULT

FATE	HORSE	AGE/WEIGHT	JOCKEY
1st	ROYAL APPROACH	6.12.0	P. TAAFFE
2nd	SAM BROWNTHORN	7.10.6	MR H. FREEMAN-JACKSON
3rd	ICELOUGH	8.10.13	T. TAAFFE
4th	Kilkilogue	8.10.4	P. Crotty
5th	Inter Alia	11.10.0	E.J. Kennedy
6th	Nibot	7.10.6	M.R. Magee
7th	Colin Bell	11.10.3	E.L. McKenzie
8th	Limavaddy	11.10.7	J.V. Ahern
9th	Solwink	8.10.7	C. Sleator
10th	Statesman	8.10.1	E. Newman
11th	Pontage	8.10.8	P.J. Doyle

19 April 1954
Going – Fairly Good
Winner – £1,485
Race Distance – three miles
Time – 6mins 32.6secs
11 Ran
Winner trained by T.W. Dreaper
Winner owned by Lord Bicester
Royal Approach, brown or black gelding by King's Approach – Flotation.

Betting – Evens ROYAL APPROACH, 5/1 Icelough, 7/1 Sam Brownthorn, 15/2 Pontage, 100/7 Colin Bell & Solwink, 100/6 Kilkilogue, Nibot & Statesman, 40/1 Limavaddy, 50/1 Inter Alia.

Above right: Lord Bicester receives the trophy from Mrs Reilly. Behind is winning jockey Pat Taaffe who had changed colours for the presentation.

Below right: Royal Approach (dark colours, light sleeves) jumps the final fence first time round.

1955 – UMM

Never in history had a trainer won the Aintree Grand National and the Irish Grand National in the same season. Most recently, Vincent O'Brien had sent out Royal Tan to finish a close second in both races in 1951, partnered by Phonsie O'Brien on each occasion, while another jockey that almost achieved the double was Tim Hyde in 1939, winning at Aintree on Workman before finishing second on Sterling Duke at Fairyhouse. But the double remained elusive. Having won his third consecutive Aintree Grand National courtesy of Quare Times, O'Brien had high hopes of adding the Fairyhouse showpiece as well, with his representative, Oriental Way, strongly fancied. Pat Taaffe, who had partnered Quare Times to Aintree glory, was also chasing the double, his mount being the less fancied, but nonetheless capable, brown gelding, Umm. Trained by former jockey George Wells, Umm arrived at Fairyhouse a fresh horse, for his only run of the season had come in a recent Hurdle race at Mullingar.

Icelough, unlucky in the 1954 race, was favourite. The horse had been consistent throughout the season, although he had unfortunately been brought down in the Leopardstown Chase. That particular race was won by Copp, a big bay horse that had also won the season's Thyestes Chase at Gowran Park. His winning sequence projected Copp to the head of the betting for the Grand National at Aintree, where he only got as far as the seventh fence. That mishap aside, Copp was strongly fancied once more at Fairyhouse, taking his place in a field of sixteen that included the Thyestes Chase runner-up Ballyscaddane, and the Danny Morgan-trained mare Great Eliza, a splendid-jumping front runner.

On settling down it was, as expected, Great Eliza that took the field along on the yielding ground. It was not long before the mare had put a fair distance between herself and the chasing pack, headed by Southern Coup, Bold Buck, Nibot and Icelough.

Passing the stands, Great Eliza proudly marched on, with Nibot, Hunter's Folly, Pontage, Icelough, Southern Coup, Umm and Copp next. Although well positioned, Tos Taaffe was hard at work on Icelough, battling to keep the favourite among the leaders, while Copp and Oriental Way were not fluent with their jumping. Oriental Way in particular was not coping well. The horse had jumped on a fallen horse in the Grand National at Aintree, and now it appeared he was hesitating at his fences,

possibly scarred, as others had been before him, by the experience of Aintree. Whatever the reason for his poor display, Oriental Way never looked likely to win the race for O'Brien, thwarting the trainer's double bid.

Great Eliza was travelling smoothly heading out into the country and remained in front jumping the Ballyhack regulation, followed by Bold Buck, Nibot, Pontage, Hunter's Folly, Icelough, Umm and Inter Alia. But after jumping five out, the field, and most notably Bold Buck, began to close rapidly on the leader, and Bold Buck then took up the running turning into the straight, Copp and Umm giving chase with intent.

As, in behind, Copp made another mistake at the second last, Bold Buck surged on powerfully, looking most likely to win. However, Taaffe had ridden a very patient race on Umm, and with Copp shaken off, the jockey began his attack on the leader at the final fence. Bold Buck led over the last, but Umm was gaining on him with every stride, and although he was not overhauled until past the halfway point of the run-in, Bold Buck was run out of it by a perfectly timed challenge from Taaffe, as Umm won the Irish National by three-quarters-of-a-length. Copp, the top weight, kept on bravely, and despite numerous errors during the course of his round, was merely two lengths behind Bold Buck in third at the finish, with the gallant Great Eliza fourth. Copp's regular jockey, Tony Prendergast, had been suffering from illness and a high temperature and could not ride on the day, with amateur Bunny Cox – a future trainer – taking the mount. The likes of Ballyscaddane and Oriental Way had run poorly, but no horse was more disappointing than Icelough, the favourite running a most uncharacteristic race, fading meekly into fourteenth.

Taaffe had become the first person to win both Aintree and Fairyhouse Grand Nationals in the same season. It had looked a hard earned win, yet Taaffe – who could have sent his mount clear sooner yet wanted to ride a hold-up race – claimed the horse's victory was comfortable and perhaps slightly cosy. Umm carried the colours of Mr Con Rooney, the elated owner heaping all praise on the shoulders of Wells, who had advised Rooney to purchase Umm six months previously with a view to winning the Irish Grand National. It was a dream result for trainer Wells, the first big success of his career since taking out a license. Umm had looked fantastic in the paddock, and his finishing power had enabled him to win the Irish National, putting both Taaffe and Wells in the record books in the process.

1955 IRISH GRAND NATIONAL RESULT

FATE	HORSE	AGE/WEIGHT	JOCKEY
1st	UMM	8.10.5	P. TAAFFE
2nd	BOLD BUCK	a.10.3	C. FINNEGAN
3rd	COPP	11.11.4	MR J.R. COX
4th	GREAT ELIZA	a.10.4	B. COOPER
5th	Kilkilogue	9.10.13	P. Crotty
6th	Inter Alia	12.10.0	J. Lehane
7th	Nibot	8.10.0	F. Carroll
8th	Southern Coup	13.10.0	E.L. McKenzie
9th	Pontage	9.10.1	P.J. Doyle
10th	Boro's Pet	a.10.2	T. O'Brien
11th	Hannahstown	a.10.0	J. Gale
12th	Tutto	8.10.0	A. Power
13th	Ballyscaddane	a.10.3	M.R. Magee
14th	Icelough	9.11.0	T. Taaffe
15th	Oriental Way	7.10.1	E. Newman
16th	Hunter's Folly	a.10.0	B. O'Neill

11 April 1955
Going – Yielding
Winner – £1,485
Race Distance – three miles
Time – 7mins 4.73secs
16 Ran
Winner trained by G.H. Wells
Winner owned by Mr C. Rooney
Umm, brown gelding by Birikan – Ecilace.

Betting – 2/1 Icelough, 4/1 Copp, 8/1 Oriental Way, 10/1 Ballyscaddane, 100/8
Great Eliza, 100/7 UMM, 100/6 Boro's Pet, 20/1 Bold Buck & Hannahstown,
25/1 Pontage & Tutto, 50/1 Hunter's Folly, Inter Alia, Kilkilogue, Nibot &
Southern Coup.

Umm jumps a fence in the lead.

Umm comes home in front from Bold Buck and Copp.

1956 – AIR PRINCE

With nineteen runners, the 1956 Irish Grand National was once again a very open affair. Six or seven horses were given serious chances of winning, and there were more than a few outsiders of ability ready to spring a surprise.

Top weight and class horse in the field was the seven-year-old Roddy Owen, a powerfully built bay trained by former jockey Danny Morgan. Roddy Owen was owned by Lord Fingall and ridden by Matt Magee, and on his latest start at Cheltenham, Roddy Owen had finished second in the Mildmay of Flete Chase. Before Cheltenham, Roddy Owen had been impressive, winning twice at Leopardstown, and this form was good enough for him to start as low as 6/1 at Fairyhouse, together with the consistent Kilkilogue, fourth and fifth in the two previous Irish Nationals.

Eclipsing both Roddy Owen and Kilkilogue, however, at the top of the betting market was the now ten-year-old Icelough, running in his third Irish National. Trained at Rathcoole by Tom Taaffe and ridden by his son Tos, Icelough's recent form was poor, but many remembered his excellent third to Royal Approach and Sam Brownthorn in 1954, and hoped the course would again bring out the best in the horse.

An open race threw forward more questions than answers as punters were forced to work overtime in narrowing down their selections. The talented Fly Along had won easily on his latest start at Naas but had stamina doubts, Bobby Beasley's mount New Hope had been all set to win the Leopardstown Chase in February before falling at the last (Nibot won the race), while Air Prince was being targeted at the Aintree Grand National but had been scratched from that contest following a poor run at Leopardstown. Having first run in the Irish National in 1953, the chestnut Air Prince was a veteran at age twelve. Trained at Cahir in County Tipperary by Jimmy McClintock and owned by the trainer's wife, Air Prince was considered a decent stayer and was a half-brother to the excellent Aintree Grand National winner of 1952, Teal, but his recent form was less than encouraging, and his starting price of 20/1 fairly reflected his chance.

A record crowd looked on in excitement as the big field were sent on their way. It was not long before the action intensified, as Fly Along promptly fell at the first fence. However, it was to be a fairly incident-free race, with the only other casualty being the fancied New Hope, who fell at the first in the home straight on the first circuit.

What was a surprise was that it was the favourite Icelough that made the running under Taaffe and, passing the stands, he held command from Gallant Gale and Roddy Owen. At Ballyhack, the order remained the same, although both Air Prince and the Tom Dreaper-trained Camp Controller had moved forward to assume challenging positions.

From five fences out, the lead was to change hands many times. First, Roddy Owen edged in front, but as his big weight began to tell turning into the straight, it was Icelough that took it up again from the improving Air Prince.

Full of running, and with 18lbs less to carry than Icelough, Air Prince came to the final fence going very strongly in the centre of the course, and leaving Icelough in his wake having taken the last, the outsider produced a devastating turn of foot to scream up the run-in and win comfortably. From out of nowhere, another outsider in the shape of Richardstown finished very fast to take second, with the favourite Icelough not disgraced in third place. Filling sixth place on this occasion, it would be Roddy Owen that would emerge as the class horse of the race. In 1959, when ridden by Bobby Beasley (from possibly the greatest family of pedigree Irish horsemen in the history of the sport), Roddy Owen – having received his share of luck when the supreme-travelling English horse Pas Seul fell at the final fence – won the Gold Cup at Cheltenham, powering through the mud and up that famous finishing hill, displaying all the bravery and determination that made him one of the best chasers of the late 1950s.

A shock win it may have been, but in his finest hour, Air Prince had won with authority under jockey T. O'Brien, and the win was fully deserved. There were no hard luck stories, and led back following his victory, Air Prince was proudly acclaimed as the National hero of 1956.

1956 IRISH GRAND NATIONAL RESULT

FATE	HORSE	AGE/WEIGHT	JOCKEY
1st	AIR PRINCE	12.10.0	T. O'BRIEN
2nd	RICHARDSTOWN	8.10.0	J.J. RAFFERTY
3rd	ICELOUGH	10.11.4	T. TAAFFE
4th	SANDY JANE II	9.10.1	F. SHORTT
5th	Nibot	9.10.5	Mr G.W. Robinson
6th	Roddy Owen	7.11.8	M.R. Magee
7th	Kilkilogue	10.11.2	P. Crotty
8th	Art Master	7.10.0	Mr E.P. Harty
9th	Camp Controller	8.10.0	P. Taaffe
10th	Magic King	8.10.5	F. Carroll
11th	No Response	10.10.0	C. Sleator
12th	Gallant Gale	11.10.0	J. Magee
13th	Wicklow King	8.11.4	A. Power
14th	Brookling	7.10.0	D. Auld
15th	Tivvy Jack	8.10.0	J. Lehane
16th	Limavaddy	13.10.0	E. Newman
17th	Oriental Way	8.10.0	B. Cooper
Fell	Fly Along	8.11.7	C. Finnegan
Fell	New Hope	9.10.3	H. Beasley

2 April 1956
Winner – £1,485
Race Distance – three miles
19 Ran
Winner trained by J. McClintock
Winner owned by Mrs J. McClintock
Air Prince, chestnut gelding by Airway – Miltown Queen.

Betting – 11/2 Icelough, 6/1 Kilkilogue & Roddy Owen, 8/1 New Hope,
10/1 Magic King, 100/8 Fly Along & No Response, 100/7 Camp Controller,
Oriental Way & Sandy Jane II, 100/6 Art Master & Nibot, 20/1 AIR PRINCE &
Richardstown, 25/1 Gallant Gale & Wicklow King, 33/1 Brookling, Limavaddy &
Tivvy Jack.

Pictured here finishing third behind Royal Approach and Sam Brownthorn in 1954, the favourite Icelough again took third in 1956.

1957 – KILBALLYOWN

The 1957 Irish Grand National was perhaps the most open for many a year. With an enormous field of twenty-six runners, picking the winner appeared extremely difficult. The striking aspect of the 1957 race was that while there were a number of class horses at the top end of the handicap (notably Sam Brownthorn, Roddy Owen, Quita Que and Icelough), there were a huge number of horses saddled with, or close to, the minimum weight of 9st 7lbs, thus rendering the possibility of a lightly-weighted winner very realistic.

Of the class horses, Roddy Owen (a future winner of the Blue Riband) had yet to run in the Gold Cup at Cheltenham, but former Irish National runner-up Sam Brownthorn had, finishing an encouraging sixth most recently at Cheltenham behind the Michael Scudamore-ridden Linwell. Dan Moore's principal hope was the eight-year-old Quita Que, a very fast horse that two years later would win the inaugural running of what would become known as the Queen Mother Champion Chase at Cheltenham, while more of an outsider on this occasion, the popular Icelough was back to contest his fourth Irish National having recently run in the Grand National at Aintree where he was brought down.

Favourite though was one of the younger horses in the seven-year-old Sentina. Trained by Tom Dreaper, Sentina was a bay or brown gelding that was sired by the French-bred stallion Fortina, a horse that would establish a fantastic record in the Irish National with his progeny at the start of the next decade. Whether the sometime-risky jumping Sentina would be good enough to start that sequence remained to be seen, but the horse was certainly well respected in the market, starting the 6/1 favourite.

In a field where virtually no horse could be safely ruled out (including the now thirteen-year-old winner from the year before, Air Prince), others to attract attention were Gallerio, Fly Along, Tutto and Kilballyown. The youngest horse (together with stablemate Brenair II) in the race at six, Gallerio was trained by Charley Weld and had won his last two races, albeit over shorter distances than the Irish National. The nine-year-old Fly Along was even more fancied than in 1956 when he had fallen at the first fence, while Tutto had been Ireland's leading fancy for the recent Grand National at Aintree and had appeared to take to the fences well only to come down, somewhat unfortunately, at the eleventh fence. If Tutto had not been affected mentally by his Aintree experience, he was one of the classier animals in the field, and was well backed with Johnny Lehane on board. Kilballyown was a ten-year-old bay gelding by Last Of The Dandies, the stallion responsible for First Of The Dandies, second to Sheila's Cottage in the 1948 Grand National at Aintree. Kilballyown's recent form was good, the horse having won his last two races – a three-mile chase at Naas and a three-mile chase at Navan – and he was a first Irish National runner for ex-jockey Paddy Norris. The trainer stated that Kilballyown had never been in better form prior to Fairyhouse, and the horse was well backed to give Willie Robinson (who at the time rode predominantly on the flat) a first winner in the race.

It was to be a race that saw the majority of its action on the second circuit. First to show from the big group of runners were Copper Cottage, Spectacular Shot and the eleven-year-old Solwink, while the likes of Sentina and Kilballyown were held up towards the rear early on, their respective jockeys Pat Taaffe and Robinson prepared to ride patient races on their mounts.

The action really began to intensify at the Ballyhack regulation, eight fences from the finish. Among the horses going well at this stage were Solwink, Fair Gale, Gallerio, New Hope, Quita Que, Brookling and Pharamineux II, while creeping ever closer were Sentina and the cruising Kilballyown, with Royal Assent beginning to run on from further back. With many still in contention, the pressure was bound to tell on some, and at the Ballyhack regulation, Pharamineux II came down.

New Hope, a faller the year before when well fancied, struck the front from Fair Gale, but at the sixth last more drama unfolded. Solwink had been in the leading group from the start and was still going well when he hit the deck at the fence, while Quita Que – similarly travelling well – also fell. The two falls somewhat impeded Roddy Owen, a horse still in touch with the leaders at the time.

With two of the front-rank eliminated, Sentina began making rapid progress on the leaders but, misjudging the fifth last, became a further casualty, crashing out in frustrating fashion to the groans of favourite-backers. All the while, it was Robinson – guiding Kilballyown skilfully through the drama – that was sitting most comfortably of any of the jockeys, poised to make a challenge aboard his mount.

Overthrowing New Hope and Fair Gale turning into the straight, Kilballyown came to take up the running at the second last. Brookling, among the longer-priced horses, had made good headway from three-quarters-of-a-mile out and developed into the main challenger. But Kilballyown was strong and had plenty in reserve. With stamina on his side, Robinson eased the horse home over the remaining fences, Kilballyown running out a very comfortable winner by seven lengths from Brookling, with Royal Assent (putting his best work in once in the straight) third, New Hope fourth and Fair Gale fifth. Among the disappointments, Fly Along had never got involved, Sam Brownthorn had fallen and Tutto's jumping had been exaggerated, perhaps as a result of his experience at Aintree.

It was a fine triumph for Paddy Norris, the ex-jockey emphatically announcing his arrival on the training scene. Norris trained just ten horses at Deer Park near Phoenix Park, yet had done remarkably well since taking up a license the previous August. Norris had long had knowledge of Kilballyown's ability, for the trainer had been attached to Vincent O'Brien's stable when Kilballyown had been sold into that yard as a young horse, and indeed it was Norris that had broken the horse in. Kilballyown was next sent to be trained in England, but later returned to Ireland and was trained by Michael Connolly, but, when Norris got his trainer's license, the horse was sent to him. For Robinson, this was his biggest win to date over jumps. In 1958, Robinson finished an excellent second on Paddy's Point in the Derby at Epsom before turning his attention to becoming one of the finest riders in the National Hunt sphere. A tremendous career included successes on the great Mill House in the Cheltenham Gold Cup and aboard Team Spirit in

Kilballyown and jockey Willie Robinson win easily in 1957.

the 1964 Grand National at Aintree, both victories coming for legendary trainer Fulke Walwyn. As for Kilballyown, he was one of the better winners of the Irish National in the 1950s, and carried on racing for a number of years after, competing in the Grand National at Aintree in 1959, where he was unluckily brought down.

1957 IRISH GRAND NATIONAL RESULT

FATE	HORSE	AGE/WEIGHT	JOCKEY
1st	KILBALLYOWN	10.9.10	G.W. ROBINSON
2nd	BROOKLING	8.9.8	J. MAGEE
3rd	ROYAL ASSENT	9.9.7	D. AULD
4th	NEW HOPE	10.10.0	D. KINANE
5th	Fair Gale	7.9.7	C.F. McCormick
6th	Southern Dago	8.9.7	J.V. Ahern
7th	Roddy Owen	8.11.11	H. Beasley
8th	Icelough	11.11.1	Mr W. Taaffe
9th	Camo Cottage	8.9.7	Mr W. Deacon
10th	Richardstown	9.10.0	C. Kinane
11th	Gold Nugget II	8.9.7	P. Shortt
12th	Steel Friend	8.9.9	J. Morrissey
13th	Gallerio	6.9.13	W.J. Brennan
14th	Air Prince	13.9.9	T. O'Brien
15th	Tutto	10.11.2	J. Lehane
16th	Proud Charger	10.9.12	T. Taaffe
17th	Copper Cottage	7.9.7	Mr F. Fitzsimons
18th	Copper Palm	7.9.7	B. Cooper
Fell	Pharamineux II	9.9.7	M.R. Magee
Fell	Quita Que	8.11.9	J. Gale
Fell	Sam Brownthorn	10.12.0	J. Stapleton
Fell	Sentina	7.10.8	P. Taaffe
Fell	Solwink	11.10.7	C. Grassick
Fell	Spectacular Shot	8.9.7	F. Carroll
Pulled-Up	Brenair II	6.10.9	Mr E.P. Harty
Pulled-Up	Fly Along	9.10.9	C. Finnegan

22 April 1957
Winner – £2,043
Race Distance – three miles
Time – 6mins 57.29secs
26 Ran
Winner trained by P. Norris
Winner owned by Mrs M.A. Lynch
Kilballyown, bay gelding by Last Of The Dandies – Cringer.

Betting – 6/1 Sentina, 7/1 Quita Que, 9/1 Gallerio, 10/1 Fly Along & KILBALLYOWN, 100/9 Proud Charger, 100/7 Royal Assent & Tutto, 100/6 Copper Cottage, Richardstown & Roddy Owen, 20/1 Brenair II, Brookling, Camo Cottage & New Hope, 25/1 Solwink & Southern Dago, 28/1 Icelough & Sam Brownthorn, 33/1 Air Prince, Copper Palm, Fair Gale, Gold Nugget II, Pharamineux II, Spectacular Shot & Steel Friend.

1958 – GOLD LEGEND

Twenty-one runners faced the starter for the 1958 Irish Grand National, and much like the year before, the weight difference between those at the top and those at the bottom of the handicap was vast. The presence in the field of the classy Roddy Owen (running in his third Irish National) ensured the weights were kept down significantly, and apart from the top weight-carrying 12st and three others – Sentina, Quita Que and Lucky Dome – also shouldering significant weights, every other horse in the field raced off the minimum allocation of 9st 7lbs, a fact that seemed certain to guarantee a fast run race on ground that was to prove most testing courtesy of recent heavy rain that had fallen on the Fairyhouse course.

Despite his huge weight concession all round, Roddy Owen had proven himself the star of the chasing season in Ireland, and was beginning to look every inch the class horse that would win the following season's Cheltenham Gold Cup. If there was one horse in the field that had the ability to carry the weight successfully, it was Roddy Owen, for he had taken a number of important chases during the season. In fact, it had been his most recent performance that had been the most impressive, destroying many of the Irish National field in a scintillating victory in the Leopardstown Chase, where he was also giving 2st and an eight-length beating to a young chaser named Mr What. When Mr What came out a few weeks later and won the Aintree Grand National with consummate ease, Roddy Owen's star really shone prominently. His Leopardstown Chase win came on the back of another three-mile chase win at the same course, making him the very warm 9/4 favourite at Fairyhouse. Of course, the recent heavy rain and abundance of lightly-weighted rivals was against him, yet the horse seemed better than ever, and rightly stood atop the betting market.

Sentina, unlucky in the 1957 running, was again well supported for trainer Tom Dreaper and owner the Duchess of Westminster. The horse's form had been slightly topsy-turvy during the season, a disappointing run in the Leopardstown Chase being followed by a fine win in the competitive National Hunt Handicap Chase at the Cheltenham Festival. Most recently, Sentina had been well fancied for the Grand National at Aintree, only to be brought down at the first Becher's Brook, so the horse arrived at Fairyhouse a relatively fresh animal.

Former winners Air Prince and Kilballyown ran again (the latter having been targeted at the race all season), while others well backed included Quita Que, The Pegger, Knight Errant, Lucky Dome and Gold Legend. Quita Que was another to have run well in 1957 and Dan Moore's charge was in fine form having recently won the two-mile Cathcart Chase at the Cheltenham Festival, while the youngest horse in the race was the excellent hunter-chaser, The Pegger. Paddy Sleator's runner Knight Errant – a former Galway Plate winner – was considered to have good stamina and a strong finish, Vincent O'Brien again saddled Lucky Dome, third most recently in the Grand National Trial over four-miles-and-a-furlong at Hurst Park, while the eight-year-old chestnut Gold Legend represented County Meath trainer and ex-jockey, Jimmy Brogan.

Sentina was joined up front by the outsider Copper Cottage as the field settled down in the early stages, while tracking the two leaders most prominently were Gold Legend, Roddy Owen, Fair Gale and the chestnut Springsilver, and as they passed the stands after a circuit, the order remained the same with the field having lost The Pegger, a faller at fence number four.

Partnered by Johnny Lehane, Gold Legend was thriving, running off his light weight, and went up to join Sentina in the lead as the field raced on towards Ballyhack. It was here that the race began to get interesting. The previous year's winner, Kilballyown, had quietly been hunted round the first circuit by Willie Robinson, but as they came towards the Ballyhack regulation, the horse began to make smooth progress through the field. The horse was going as well as anything when Solwink came down at the fence, and with no way of avoiding the faller, Kilballyown was most unluckily brought down.

Leaving behind the incident at the Ballyhack regulation, Gold Legend, Springsilver and Sentina bounded on, Gold Legend in particular going very well. By four out, Sentina and Springsilver, together with Roddy Owen and Fair Gale – all prominent for a long way – began to weaken, and it was the two-mile specialist Quita Que that emerged as the biggest danger to Gold Legend.

Quita Que had made rapid progress on the inside and actually led jumping the third last, but Gold Legend was determined and matching Quita Que stride for stride, the two swung into the home straight locked together, seemingly set for a titanic duel to the death.

Coming to the last fence, there was nothing to choose between them. Gold Legend had jumped fantastically well all the way and had far less weight, but Quita Que was classy and brave, it was, in truth, too close to call. However, the question of which would win became irrelevant after the last, for meeting the fence all wrong, Quita Que crumpled on landing, falling in a heap in bitterly unlucky fashion allowing Gold Legend to race on unchallenged. Unchallenged that was until, from out of nowhere, Knight Errant delivered a devastating, last-gasp effort to snatch the race from the long-time leader. Knight Errant had been virtually unsighted in the race until jumping the last, but on the run to the line, he appeared to be scything down Gold Legend with every stride as he flashed home on the stands side. But having been in the front rank the entire way, Gold Legend hung on heroically, and despite needing the assistance of a photo, the judge called Gold Legend the winner by a head. Eight lengths back in third came Fair Gale, with Roddy Owen, somewhat disappointingly, fourth.

The first three home all carried the colours of lady owners, and it was a highly satisfying win for Brogan considering Gold Legend had been with the trainer since the horse was three. The win also came as a welcome return to form for jockey Lehane, whose last big winner had been aboard former Irish National runner Tutto in the 1957 Leopardstown Chase.

The eventual winner, Gold Legend, leads over a regulation fence in 1958.

1958 IRISH GRAND NATIONAL RESULT

FATE	HORSE	AGE/WEIGHT	JOCKEY
1st	GOLD LEGEND	8.9.7	J. LEHANE
2nd	KNIGHT ERRANT	8.9.7	C. FINNEGAN
3rd	FAIR GALE	8.9.7	C.F. McCORMICK
4th	RODDY OWEN	9.12.0	W.J. BRENNAN
5th	Springsilver	8.9.7	F. Shortt
6th	Southern Dago	9.9.7	J. Magee
7th	Camo Cottage	9.9.7	W. Deacon
8th	Air Prince	14.9.7	D. Kinane
9th	Sentina	8.10.10	P. Taaffe
10th	Royal Assent	10.9.7	D. Auld
11th	Lucky Dome	12.10.7	T. Taaffe
12th	Sandy Jane II	11.9.7	F. Carroll
13th	Richardstown	10.9.7	J. Morrissey
14th	Copper Cottage	8.9.7	A. Power
15th	Brookling	9.9.7	A. Redmond
Fell	Quita Que	9.10.8	J. Gale
Fell	Solwink	12.9.7	Mr James Cash
Fell	The Pegger	6.9.7	Mr G. Rooney
Pulled-Up	Dandybash	11.9.7	A. Duff
Brought Down	Kilballyown	11.9.7	G.W. Robinson
Brought Down	Wicklow King	10.9.7	P. Shortt

7 April 1958
Winner – £2,017
Race Distance – three miles
21 Ran
Winner trained by J. Brogan
Winner owned by Mrs J.P. Murphy
Gold Legend, chestnut gelding by Legend Of France – French Gold.

Betting – 9/4 Roddy Owen, 7/1 Sentina, 8/1 Quita Que, 9/1 Knight Errant, 10/1 Lucky Dome, 100/8 GOLD LEGEND, Kilballyown, Southern Dago & The Pegger, 100/7 Springsilver, 20/1 Richardstown, 25/1 Dandybash, 33/1 Air Prince, Brookling, Camo Cottage, Copper Cottage, Fair Gale, Royal Assent, Sandy Jane II, Solwink & Wicklow King.

1959 – ZONDA

Two winners of Championships races at the recent Cheltenham Festival lit up the card for the 1959 Irish Grand National. Of course, by now, both Roddy Owen and Quita Que were veterans of the race, yet they arrived for the 1959 contest having recently claimed the biggest victories of their respective careers. Roddy Owen, capitalising on a last-fence fall of the fine young English chaser Pas Seul (a fall that also badly hampered the 1957 Gold Cup winner Linwell), won the Gold Cup at Cheltenham, displaying bravery and fighting spirit up that famous finishing hill. After that race, most observers believed he was a lucky winner of the Blue Riband, and perhaps he was, yet he had jumped the fences at Cheltenham extremely well and had proved strong in the finish. It should also be noted that, in the 1960 Cheltenham Gold Cup, Roddy Owen came to the last fence full of running only to be badly impeded by the fall of Kerstin, and eventually had to settle for fourth behind none other than Pas Seul. As far as the Irish National went, 1959 would be the now ten-year-old Roddy Owen's fourth attempt at the race, the horse having finished sixth, seventh and fourth previously (although he never carried less than 11st 8lbs in any of those races). The perception was that – fine horse though he was – carrying 11st 12lbs on this occasion would again prove just beyond him, with the betting resembling those thoughts, Roddy Owen starting at 10/1. Quita Que, unlucky the year before, was joint-favourite at 4/1. The horse had won the newly formed Two Mile Champion Chase at the Cheltenham Festival and was a horse with class and obvious speed. Trained by Dan Moore, Quita Que arrived at Fairyhouse having been in fine form throughout the season, although as in past runnings of the race, some questioned whether the horse would have the necessary stamina to actually win an Irish National.

The previous two winners, Kilballyown and Gold Legend were once more in the line-up, while hotly fancied of the others included Knight Errant, Jonjo and Zonda. Trained by Paddy Sleator, Knight Errant ran again having been short-headed by Gold Legend in 1958. Knight Errant, ridden by Bobby Beasley, was an ex-hunter and, most recently, had run well under a big weight in a handicap hurdle at Naas in preparation for the Irish National, for which he was the race's other joint-favourite. Both the chestnut Jonjo and the Pat Taaffe-ridden Zonda entered the race in fine form, both being particularly good jumpers blessed with strong stamina. Zonda in particular was considered to be a horse on the rise. An eight-year-old bay, the horse had improved tremendously from the previous season, his biggest win coming in the season's Leopardstown Chase, where Roddy Owen finished behind him. Before Leopardstown, Zonda had finished second to the well-fancied Aintree Grand National prospect Slippery Serpent in the Thyestes Chase at Gowran Park. With regular rider Willie Robinson committed to riding Quita Que, Zonda was partnered by two-time winning jockey Pat Taaffe and began the race at 5/1.

With fifteen runners facing the starter, a good early pace was set, and on settling down, Sandy Jane II, Zonda, Quita Que and Mazzibell showed the way from Gold Legend and Fair Gale. Passing the stands, Quita Que had move forward to lead from Sandy Jane II and Zonda, while these three were followed by Mazzibell, Fair Gale, Gold Legend, Southern Dago, Steel Friend, Jonjo, Roddy Owen and Knight Errant, the lattermost being pushed along forcefully by Beasley just to keep his position, and it was clear the horse was under pressure.

One of the striking features of the 1959 Irish National was just how many horses stayed competitive for so long, with many still in with chances deep into the second circuit. One horse that began to weaken though was Knight Errant. Having been under pressure almost from the start, the horse did make some headway following the Ballyhack regulation, but it was not the horse's day, and his effort soon petered out as Quita Que led on from Zonda, Gold Legend and Fair Gale.

Five fences from home, Quita Que was still jumping very well, but in behind the challengers were mounting up, most notably Mazzibell, Jonjo and Zonda, while Gold Legend and Roddy Owen began to tire, the latter being ridden by amateur jockey Alan Lillingston who had received a pain-killing injection in his foot before the race.

Jonjo had moved forward with menace to four out, but his challenge proved deceptive, for no sooner had he joined the leaders than his effort came grinding to a halt, finding no extra as the contest intensified. Quita Que had run with great credit but the full distance of the race appeared beyond him, and he was engulfed at the third last fence by Mazzibell and the strong-running Zonda, and these two looked like battling out the finish.

For a race that had stayed competitive for so long, the finishing stages proved somewhat anti-climactic. Having been close to the leaders throughout, Taaffe suddenly sent Zonda clear turning into the home straight and it was to be a move that proved devastating. Forging ahead of the gallant Mazzibell, the race was all but over bar a fall from Zonda, and when the bay took the final two fences in style, he galloped home a most convincing winner by four lengths. The inexperienced chaser Knightsbrook (a future Cheltenham Gold Cup favourite) had made up a lot of ground from three out, and powering home at the finish, took second place under Pat's brother Tos, with Mazzibell having run a fine race to be six lengths away in third under young Liam McCloughlin. Only the pulled-up Uncle Whiskers had failed to complete, with Jonjo coming home fourth, Knight Errant seventh, Quita Que eighth, Roddy Owen eleventh and Gold Legend thirteenth.

The victory came for trainer M. Geraghty, and Zonda's win again illustrated the craft of Pat Taaffe around Fairyhouse. It was a third win for Taaffe, but a first in the race for owner Peggy St John Nolan, who had helped prepare the horse for the Irish National. Together with her husband, the owner had been a fine supporter of National Hunt racing in Ireland for many years and in later years would own Drumroan, third in the 1978 Grand National at Aintree. Zonda, a future favourite for the Hennessy Gold Cup at Newbury, had been given as a gift to the owner when the horse was only three, and now the bay had responded by becoming one of the most convincing of Irish Grand National winners of the 1950s.

The 1959 winner Zonda, pictured here leading in another of Ireland's most important races, the Thyestes Chase.

1959 IRISH GRAND NATIONAL RESULT

FATE	HORSE	AGE/WEIGHT	JOCKEY
1st	ZONDA	8.10.5	P. TAAFFE
2nd	KNIGHTSBROOK	7.9.7	T. TAAFFE
3rd	MAZZIBELL	6.9.7	L. McCLOUGHLIN
4th	Jonjo	9.9.7	W.J. Brennan
5th	Sandy Jane II	12.9.7	F. Shortt
6th	Kilballyown	12.9.7	E.L. McKenzie
7th	Knight Errant	9.10.3	H. Beasley
8th	Quita Que	10.11.7	G.W. Robinson
9th	Steel Friend	10.9.7	J. Morrissey
10th	Fair Gale	9.9.7	P. Crotty
11th	Roddy Owen	10.11.12	Mr A. Lillingston
12th	Southern Dago	10.9.7	J. O'Brien
13th	Gold Legend	9.9.11	F. Carroll
14th	Brookling	10.9.7	R. Coonan
Pulled-Up	Uncle Whiskers	7.9.7	C. Finnegan

30 March 1959
Winner – £1,878
Race Distance – three miles
Time – 6mins 56.1secs
15 Ran
Winner trained by M.Geraghty
Winner owned by Mrs G. St John Nolan
Zonda, bay gelding by Dornot – Zanthene.

Betting – 4/1 Knight Errant & Quita Que, 5/1 ZONDA, 7/1 Jonjo, 10/1 Roddy Owen, 100/6 Gold Legend & Mazzibell, 22/1 Fair Gale & Knightsbrook, 25/1 Kilballyown & Southern Dago, 28/1 Brookling, Sandy Jane II & Steel Friend, 50/1 Uncle Whiskers.

1960 – OLYMPIA

The 1960 Irish Grand National was one of the strongest renewals of the race for some time, with most of the sixteen-strong field having a good chance of victory. Top weight with 12st was Zonda, a horse that had won in great style in 1959 and had delivered some fine performances since then. A grand nine-year-old trained by M. Geraghty and ridden on this occasion by Willie Robinson, Zonda had finished second in the season's Leopardstown Chase and third most recently behind the brilliant Pas Seul in the Gold Cup at Cheltenham. Prior to those runs, Zonda – admirable and consistent – had also been placed in the respected Thyestes Chase at Gowran Park, as well as in a chase at Manchester. With such creditable form behind him, Zonda looked certain to run a big race at Fairyhouse, and if it were not for his huge weight, the horse would certainly have started shorter than his final price of 100/8.

Favourite, and something of a dark horse, was the eleven-year-old Blue Moth. The horse had been a very good animal a few seasons previously, only for injuries to curtail his very promising career. Since his injury problems, Blue Moth had been switched to the yard of Paddy Sleator, and the horse had just begun to show glimpses of his former excellence. Having gained a stylish win in the Thyestes Chase, Blue Moth had stayed on strongly to finish third in the Leopardstown Chase, a performance of such promise that it sparked a day-of-race gamble on the horse that eventually saw him start as low as 7/2.

In 1958, when still a comparative novice, Mr What had run his rivals ragged to win the Grand National at Aintree in fantastic style. The horse had certainly become a specialist over those big Aintree fences, and would ultimately run in that race six times (finishing third in 1959 and 1962). His victory at Aintree in 1958 had come for trainer Tom Taaffe, but the horse had since moved to the yard of Danny Morgan and remained a fine jumper and stayer. Trying the Irish National for the first time, Mr What was ridden by the very good amateur Eddie Harty who, as a professional, would win the Grand National at Aintree in 1969 aboard the Toby Balding-trained Highland Wedding.

Zonda, Blue Moth and Mr What provided plenty of class for the 1960 race, and plenty of extra interest and competitiveness was assured from the presence in the field of the likes of former runner-up Knight Errant (a stablemate of Blue Moth) and the good stayer Kilmore, a horse that would also win the Grand National at Aintree in time. Nic Atkins, Take Time, Double Crest and Olympia were others to attract significant support. Sired, like future Aintree National winner Nicolaus Silver, by Nicolaus, Nic Atkins was a regular in all of the top chases in Ireland, having been second in the Thyestes and seventh in the Leopardstown, while former hunter-chaser Take Time was a first Irish National ride for promising youngster

Paddy Shortt. As well as the eight-year-old Double Crest, ridden by Pat Taaffe, Tom Dreaper also saddled the improving six-year-old mare Olympia, ridden by Tos Taaffe. Twelve months previously, Olympia had won a hunter-chase at Fairyhouse when ridden by owner Lord Donoughmore's son, the Honourable Mark Hely-Hutchinson. Olympia was considered to have come on tremendously at Dreaper's yard in the past year and, despite her age and relative inexperience, held second place in the betting at 6/1.

In what was the richest Irish Grand National to that point, the race was dominated for much of the way by the gallant Zonda. Trying to win the race for the second year in a row, Zonda led early and, despite his big weight, was able to hold a position amongst the leaders throughout the race.

It was to be a very fast run race, and many of the leading contenders beforehand were unable to get on terms to strike a blow. Most notable of these was the favourite Blue Moth, and despite the pre-race hype, the horse was never close enough to threaten, eventually finishing a disappointing ninth. When their respective careers were over, both Mr What and Kilmore had been crowned Grand National winners at Aintree, but at Fairyhouse in 1960 the pace was too hot, and both finished well down the field.

Zonda had set a strong gallop, and although the well-backed Mountnorris improved after the Ballyhack regulation to challenge until the home straight, and Knight Errant again ran an Irish National of promise, it was left to two of the lightly-weighted horses, Olympia and Take Time, to throw down the challenge to Zonda.

Zonda's run had been majestic, but the weight eventually told, and skipping past the long-time leader in the straight, it was to be the mare Olympia that finished best of all, fulfilling her potential in graceful style, she bounded home a six-length winner from Take Time, with Zonda an honourable third just two-and-a-half lengths back.

It was a fourth Irish National win for Tom Dreaper following the victories of Prince Regent, Shagreen and Royal Approach, while it was the first for Tos Taaffe. It was clear that Olympia (the first mare to win since Pontet in 1937) had developed into a top class horse under the guidance of Dreaper, and she competed in many of the top races during her career, finishing fifth behind Saffron Tartan in the 1961 Cheltenham Gold Cup and fourth behind Mandarin in the 1961 Hennessy Gold Cup at Newbury. Olympia was a bay mare and the first of four Irish National winners for the excellent sire Fortina. The victory of Olympia also began an incredible run in the race for Tom Dreaper, and the success he enjoyed in the race over the next seven years will surely never be matched in any major steeplechase in Great Britain or Ireland.

Tom Dreaper's fine mare Olympia wins easily in 1960.

1960 IRISH GRAND NATIONAL RESULT

FATE	HORSE	AGE/WEIGHT	JOCKEY
1st	OLYMPIA	6.9.11	T. TAAFFE
2nd	TAKE TIME	9.10.2	P. SHORTT
3rd	ZONDA	9.12.0	G.W. ROBINSON
4th	KNIGHT ERRANT	10.10.4	C. FINNEGAN
5th	Jonjo	10.9.11	W.J. Brennan
6th	Mountnorris	11.9.11	Mr G. Rooney
7th	Double Crest	8.10.7	P. Taaffe
8th	Kilmore	10.10.10	C. Kinane
9th	Blue Moth	11.11.6	H. Beasley
10th	Mr What	10.11.8	Mr E.P. Harty
11th	Knoxtown	10.9.12	F. Carroll
12th	Knockanacunna	10.9.11	R. Coonan
13th	Gentle Colein	9.10.3	T. O'Brien
Fell	Gay Navarree	8.9.11	J.J. Rafferty
Fell	Uncle Whiskers	8.9.11	E.L. McKenzie
Pulled-Up	Nic Atkins	9.10.3	F. Shortt

18 April 1960
Winner – £2,256
Race Distance – three miles
Time – 6mins 39.9secs
16 Ran
Winner trained by T.W. Dreaper
Winner owned by Lord Donoughmore
Olympia, bay mare by Fortina – Lady Lucinda.

Betting – 7/2 Blue Moth, 6/1 OLYMPIA, 8/1 Take Time, 10/1 Gay Navarree,
Kilmore & Mountnorris, 100/8 Knight Errant & Zonda, 100/7 Double Crest, 100/6
Mr What, 20/1 Nic Atkins, 25/1 Jonjo & Nic Atkins, 33/1 Uncle Whiskers, 40/1
Knockanacunna, 50/1 Gentle Colein.

1961 – FORTRIA

The defending champion, Olympia, was a late withdrawal from the 1961 Irish Grand National, yet the field of fourteen remained stocked with class, potential and big race winners, fuelling the prospect of a magnificent renewal. Topping the handicap on 12st were Zonda and Fortria. Despite his big weight, Zonda was expected to run really well. After an enforced absence of a couple of months, Zonda had returned to action and had run well to be second to Jonjo in the Leopardstown Chase, following that up with a decent performance in a hurdle race at Phoenix Park. Despite having gone up considerably in the weights since winning the Irish National in 1959, Zonda remained one of the most resilient chasers in Ireland, and was expected to be hard to beat. Fortria, on the other hand, was something of an unknown over the distance of the Irish National. Full of class and trained by the imperious Tom Dreaper, Fortria was renowned for being a brilliant horse between two and two-and-a-half-miles, distances in which the horse had already won a pair of Two Mile Champion Chases at Cheltenham (1960 and 1961) and also a Mackeson Gold Cup at Cheltenham in 1960 (the horse would win the same race in 1962). A bay gelding by Fortina, sire of Olympia, Fortria was out of the mare Senria that had finished fourth in the Irish National of 1946. Few doubted the exceptional quality of Fortria, but many questioned the horse's stamina for such a race, and as such, Fortria started behind three others in the betting market, joint-fourth favourite with Zonda at 17/2.

The three at the top of the betting were Solfen, Owen's Sedge and Solitude. Favourite at 4/1 was the bay gelding Solfen, a horse trained by Willie O'Grady that had suffered a training setback in the autumn but had returned to action in the weeks leading up to Fairyhouse, pleasing connections mightily by running well for a long way in the Leopardstown Chase. The long-time ante-post favourite for the race had been the grey eight-year-old, Owen's Sedge. Second on his most recent run in the National Hunt Handicap Chase at the Cheltenham Festival, Owen's Sedge was smart and consistent, while Solitude was carrying the minimum weight of 9st 7lbs, but was an improving animal that had won over three miles at Leopardstown in February. Old favourites Roddy Owen and Knight Errant ran again, while there was an Irish National debut for the resolute stayer Team Spirit, trained close to Fairyhouse by Dan Moore.

Although ultimately it would prove to be an exceptionally fast-run race, the gallop on the first circuit was little more than sedate, as the ten-year-old Fredith's Son made the running, with the veteran Roddy Owen prominent together with the Charley Weld-trained, and Christy Kinane-ridden, Highfield Lad.

It was passing the stands that the race really began to heat up, the pace quickening dramatically as Fredith's Son led on. Roddy Owen was jumping so well that he made his way forward under amateur Alan Lillingston to join the leader. Not all the horses were travelling so well, however, including Solfen. The favourite never looked like justifying the support for him, while the likes of Knight Errant and Kilrory were both struggling as the tempo increased, and Liam McCloughlin's mount Moyrath totally tailed off.

Approaching the Ballyhack regulation, Fredith's Son and Roddy Owen remained in dispute of the lead, and with Owen's Sedge, Highfield Lad, Solitude and Fortria all travelling with serious intent in behind, the prospect of a great finish looked assured.

It was noticeable how Pat Taaffe was saving Fortria's questionable stamina through the first circuit-and-a-half, and with the horse moving with such confidence, a legitimate challenge looked likely. That challenge arrived at the fourth last fence as Fortria rapidly improved his position up the inside, and sent through the tiniest of gaps by Taaffe at the fence, the combination suddenly seized the lead. Of the chasing pack, Roddy Owen began to weaken while Solitude – in a great position under Frank Carroll at the fourth last – was taken off his feet by the devastating attack of Fortria.

A fence later, Fortria had come clear, and turning smoothly into the home straight with a decisive advantage, the race was his bar a fall. Owen's Sedge and Fredith's Son valiantly gave chase, but the former had crashed through the third last and was making no impression on the leader while Fredith's Son similarly had run his race. Sailing over the final two fences with grace and precision, Fortria crossed the line a very good four-length winner from Owen's Sedge, with Fredith's Son half-a-length back in third. Although all fourteen completed, Solfen could only manage seventh place, Zonda tenth and Solitude eleventh.

Those two Irish National specialists, Tom Dreaper and Pat Taaffe, had done it again, winning for the fifth and fourth time respectively. Because of the stamina doubts, some had doubted Fortria's ability to see out the Irish National trip, but the horse had done it with class, and in the process covered the distance in race-record time, opening the possibility of further success at longer distanced-races. Indeed, Fortria would prove one of the very best horses of the decade, for as well as his previous successes in the Two Mile Champion Chase and Mackeson Gold Cup, Fortria would go very close to winning the Gold Cup at Cheltenham. Leading over the final fence in the 1962 race, Fortria was eventually beaten by a mere length by the great warrior Mandarin, and it was another Fulke Walwyn-trained horse that denied Fortria the crown at Cheltenham in 1963, with Mill House the victor, this time by twelve lengths.

Fortria, pictured here at Cheltenham, was another Irish National winner for trainer Tom Dreaper.

1961 IRISH GRAND NATIONAL RESULT

FATE	HORSE	AGE/JOCKEY	JOCKEY	3 April 1961
1st	FORTRIA	9.12.0	P. TAAFFE	Winner – £2,301
2nd	OWEN'S SEDGE	8.11.1	J. MAGEE	Race Distance – three miles
3rd	FREDITH'S SON	10.10.13	F. SHORTT	Time – 6mins 35.1secs
4th	Highfield Lad	9.10.2	C. Kinane	14 Ran
5th	Clipador	10.10.4	H. Beasley	Winner trained by T.W. Dreaper
6th	San Marco	8.9.7	R. Coonan	Winner owned by Mr G. Ansley
7th	Solfen	9.11.6	J.J. Rafferty	Fortria, bay gelding by Fortina – Senria.
8th	Team Spirit	9.10.10	G.W. Robinson	
9th	Knight Errant	11.10.10	C. Finnegan	
10th	Zonda	10.12.0	Mr A. Cameron	Betting – 4/1 Solfen, 11/2 Owen's Sedge, 8/1 Solitude, 17/2 FORTRIA & Zonda,
11th	Solitude	8.9.7	F. Carroll	10/1 Clipador, 100/8 Highfield Lad, 100/7 Kilrory & Knight Errant, 18/1 San
12th	Moyrath	8.9.7	L. McCloughlin	Marco, 22/1 Fredith's Son, 25/1 Roddy Owen & Team Spirit, 28/1 Moyrath.
13th	Roddy Owen	12.11.5	Mr A. Lillingston	
14th	Kilrory	8.10.7	Mr F. Prendergast	

1962 – KERFORO

Having narrowly been beaten in the Gold Cup at Cheltenham in March, Fortria returned to Fairyhouse in April to defend the Irish National crown he had won so majestically in 1961. Fortria was top weight with 12st and also the last-gasp favourite at 4/1, but if the horse was going to win a second Irish National, he would be achieving what only four others had done previously and would be breaking a long standing trend. Since the first Irish National in 1870, Scots Grey (1872 and 1875), The Gift (1883 and 1884), Little Hack II (1909 and 1913) and Halston (1920 and 1922) had won the race twice, with only The Gift able to win the race in consecutive years. Fortria was far and away the classiest horse in the race (Fredith's Son was next in the handicap on 10st 10lbs), but the horse's task was immense, especially considering the hard race he had endured at Cheltenham, where he had led at the final fence only to be run out of it up that punishing finishing hill by Mandarin.

The race's two grey horses, Loving Record and Owen's Sedge, figured as the most likely threats to Fortria. The eight-year-old Loving Record, ridden by Tos Taaffe, was a horse that would run in many major chases throughout his career, and had long been ante-post favourite (a position he held until shortly before the off) for the Irish National despite a fall in the season's Thyestes Chase. Owen's Sedge had run so well in the 1961 race and had enhanced his reputation as a superb jumper by recently taming the big Aintree Grand National fences when finishing a pleasing fourth in the Topham Trophy.

Of the others, Kilcullen trainer Paddy Murphy saddled the fancied seven-year-old Brown Diamond – the mount of Willie Robinson – as well as the front-running Fredith's Son, a horse that had run extremely well, jumping with real panache and finishing fifth in the recent Grand National at Aintree. Another that had run in the Aintree spectacular was the eight-year-old mare Kerforo, trained, like Fortria, by Tom Dreaper and partnered at Fairyhouse by twenty-eight-year-old Liam McCloughlin. Considered one of the most consistent chasers in Ireland, Kerforo had been well fancied at Aintree and had just been creeping into contention when coming down at the fence before Becher's Brook second time around. Enhancing her claims at Fairyhouse was the fact that Kerforo was a winner of two of Ireland's biggest chases, the Thyestes Chase and the Leopardstown Chase.

With both gate receipts and Tote receipts higher than they had ever been before, the popularity of Irish Grand National day at Fairyhouse was in glorious evidence as the big crowd settled down to watch the action unfold. It was a smaller field than usual, but a race of high excitement was expected nevertheless.

Fredith's Son, as expected, jumped to the front at the first fence, but his usual trailblazing tactics – which had been adopted at Aintree – were not employed on this occasion, with jockey Francis Shortt content to let Frank Carroll's mount, Brown Knight, take up the running at the second fence.

Passing the stands after a circuit, Brown Knight continued to show the way to Fredith's Son, Brown Diamond, Last link, Kerforo and Team Spirit, but after the Ballyhack regulation, Fredith's Son resumed his customary position at the head of affairs, as Brown Knight's run began to peter out. The most dangerous-looking of the pursuing pack were Kerforo, Brown Diamond, Team Spirit and the improving favourite, Fortria.

Running a near identical race to the year before, Taaffe asked Fortria for his challenge at the fourth last. However, after the 1962 Irish National, many of the jockeys reported the ground to be 'patchy', and conditions underfoot seemed to affect Fortria, for he was not able to quicken in the same way as he did the year before. Finding no extra, Taaffe could only watch as the lightly weighted pair of Kerforo and Team Spirit overthrew Fredith's Son for the lead at the third last, and from there, engaged in their own private battle.

Willie Robinson had elected to ride Brown Diamond in the race, and so it was a young Tommy Carberry that had come in for the ride on Team Spirit, and attacking the fences in the home straight, the jockey knew his horse would not fail on the category of stamina. But Kerforo was a very good horse, with more speed than Team Spirit at the race distance, and after a tough head-to-head battle over the last two fences, it was the mare that edged in front and held on for victory by a length-and-a-half. Four lengths back in third came Brown Diamond, with Fredith's Son fourth, Court Taster (a back marker for most of the way until making up late ground) fifth, the gallant Fortria sixth and the grey Owen's Sedge seventh. The most disappointing performance came from Loving Record, with the horse never able to get competitive and eventually pulling-up before the second last. Team Spirit was recognised in Ireland as a dour stayer, and his crowning moment would arrive in 1964. Having been switched to the yard of Fulke Walwyn in England, the horse displayed his fine stamina by outlasting Purple Silk in a thrilling finish to the Grand National at Aintree.

But it was Kerforo that had won the day at Fairyhouse, and in doing so had given Tom Dreaper a sixth win in the race and an incredible third in succession. The victory for McCloughlin was a popular one with the crowd, for the jockey hailed from Ratoath, a mere stone's throw from Fairyhouse racecourse. McCloughlin had been attached to the Dreaper stable for six years and was regarded as a deeply underrated rider. Indeed, it had been McCloughlin that had been aboard Kerforo when the mare had won the Thyestes and Leopardstown Chases, and now the jockey could enjoy the celebrations as Kerforo won Ireland's most prestigious steeplechase.

Kerforo leads at the last fence from Team Spirit.

1962 IRISH GRAND NATIONAL RESULT

FATE	HORSE	AGE/WEIGHT	JOCKEY
1st	KERFORO	8.10.3	L. McCLOUGHLIN
2nd	TEAM SPIRIT	10.9.12	T. CARBERRY
3rd	BROWN DIAMOND	7.9.10	G.W. ROBINSON
4th	Fredith's Son	11.10.10	F. Shortt
5th	Court Taster	8.9.7	C. Finnegan
6th	Fortria	10.12.0	P. Taaffe
7th	Owen's Sedge	9.10.5	J. Magee
8th	Last Link	6.9.7	P. Woods
9th	Brown Knight	8.9.13	F. Carroll
10th	San Marco	9.9.7	R. Coonan
Pulled-Up	Loving Record	8.10.1	T. Taaffe

23 April 1962
Winner – £2,245
Race Distance – three miles
11 Ran
Winner trained by T.W. Dreaper
Winner owned by Mr F.J. Stafford
Kerforo, bay mare by Foroughi – Kerlogue Steel.

Betting – 4/1 Fortria, 9/2 Loving Record, 7/1 Owen's Sedge, 15/2 Brown Diamond, 9/1 KERFORO, 100/8 Fredith's Son, 100/7 Team Spirit, 100/6 Brown Knight, 20/1 Last Link, 25/1 San Marco, 40/1 Court Taster.

1963 – LAST LINK

Having won the previous three Irish Grand Nationals courtesy of Olympia, Fortria and Kerforo, Tom Dreaper saddled three very good horses in 1963 as he searched for an incredible seventh victory in the race. According to Dreaper, it was his 1961 hero Fortria that was his principal hope, although the betting market suggested he was the outsider of the three, largely due to unsuitably testing ground and the burden of again carrying top weight of 12st. Illustrating his good recent form, Fortria had again finished second in the Gold Cup at Cheltenham the month before, although he was firmly put in his place by the new chasing sensation in England, Mill House.

Without the class of their illustrious stablemate, both Willow King and Last Link were talented horses that were well fancied in the betting. Willow King had run poorly behind Team Spirit in the National Hunt Handicap Chase at the recent Cheltenham Festival, but before that had won at Naas in tremendous style. Last Link was a seven-year-old bay mare with the same parentage as Fortria. The horse had run without distinction in the previous year's race, but had improved in the current season and had finished runner-up in his previous two races, including when chasing home fellow Irish National participant, My Baby, in the Thyestes Chase at Gowran Park.

There were two English challengers on this occasion, Duke Of York and O'Malley Point. Duke Of York had good form in England and was owned and trained by Mr John Tillings. The horse was ridden by the fine English jockey Tim Brookshaw, for whom the 1963 Irish National was a first ride in the country. Duke Of York was another that had succumbed to the mighty Mill House in the Cheltenham Gold Cup, but he had performed well to finish third, having finished fourth in the same race in 1962. O'Malley Point, a bay twelve-year-old, was an out-and-out stayer trained by Derek Ancil. The horse's best performance had come at Aintree in 1961 when third behind Nicolaus Silver in the Grand National, and in that same race recently he had again jumped round the most difficult of courses, although he finished some way back of the winner Ayala in nineteenth spot. O'Malley Point was partnered at Fairyhouse by a former winner of the race, Tos Taaffe.

With the likes of the Dan Moore-trained grey Flying Wild, the previous year's third Brown Diamond and the Joe Osborne-trained mare Height O' Fashion in the field, the race was certain to be competitive, and as usual, a huge crowd had assembled to watch the richest ever running of the Irish Grand National.

It was an Irish National that saved much of its incident for the closing stages. Brown Diamond led the race for much of the way, with Willow King always holding a prominent position. Duke Of York was always a danger, but the horse was clearly struggling to cope with the drops of some of the big fences at Fairyhouse, and lost vital ground every time he did so.

Willow King lost ground with a bad mistake at the Ballyhack regulation, but was soon back in the thick of the action under a determined ride from Liam McCloughlin. With Fortria a surprise faller during the race, the likes of Flying Wild and Four Aces jumping well but unable to truly handle the testing conditions, and Duke Of York ruining his hopes when botching the third last fence, it appeared that four horses had a chance by the final fence. Brown Diamond was already weakening at the last, but both Willow King and Last Link were strongly in contention. It appeared the mare Height O' Fashion was going best of all, but when the six-year-old took a most unlucky tumble at the last (hampering the trailing Brown Diamond and Flying Wild), it was left to Last Link and Willow King to fight it out. Last Link had only been fourth jumping the last fence, but had met the obstacle full of running under jockey Paddy Woods, and though Willow King was spirited and gave his all, Last Link outstayed her stablemate, powering onto the line and passing the post a six-length winner. Willow King had run his heart out in second, with Brown Diamond third again, three lengths away. The English horses had disappointed by and large. Duke Of York had spoiled his round with shoddy jumping, while O'Malley Point – though jumping well enough – had never been close enough to the lead to challenge.

Clearly, Height O' Fashion had been unlucky, even Dreaper doubting whether Last Link would have beaten her, yet Woods was convinced his horse was travelling strongest coming to the last, and was adamant Last Link would have won anyway. While Dreaper now seemed to own the patent for winning Irish Nationals, it was a first success in the race for thirty-one-year-old Woods, and the jockey proved a most popular victor. Woods was born a mere stone's throw from Fairyhouse racecourse and had been working at Dreaper's yard for seven years as travelling head-lad and second jockey to Pat Taaffe. Now Woods could bask in some glory of his own, as Last Link (the third mare of Dreaper's seven Irish National winners and the third horse sired by Fortina to win the Fairyhouse steeplechase) became the latest winner of Ireland's great race.

Left: *Paddy Woods, pictured here in 1994 with dual Irish National-winning son Fran, rode the 1963 winner Last Link.*

Opposite: *The grey Flying Wild, one of the few horses to beat the mighty Arkle, finished fourth in the 1963 Irish National.*

1963 IRISH GRAND NATIONAL RESULT

FATE	HORSE	AGE/WEIGHT	JOCKEY
1st	LAST LINK	7.9.7	P. WOODS
2nd	WILLOW KING	8.9.10	L. McCLOUGHLIN
3rd	BROWN DIAMOND	8.10.1	F. SHORTT
4th	Flying Wild	7.9.9	T. Carberry
5th	Duke Of York	8.11.7	T. Brookshaw
6th	My Baby	8.9.7	A. Redmond
7th	Four Aces	7.9.11	J.J. Rafferty
8th	O'Malley Point	12.10.0	T. Taaffe
Fell	Fortria	11.12.0	P. Taaffe
Fell	Height O' Fashion	6.9.8	R. Coonan

15 April 1963
Winner – £2,870
Race Distance – three miles
Time – 7mins 22.5secs
10 Ran
Winner trained by T.W. Dreaper
Winner owned by Mr A. Craigie
Last Link, bay mare by Fortina – Senria.

Betting – 4/1 Duke Of York, 6/1 Brown Diamond & Flying Wild, 7/1 Four Aces & LAST LINK, 9/1 Willow King, 10/1 Height O' Fashion, 100/9 Fortria, 20/1 My Baby & O'Malley Point.

1964 – ARKLE

No steeplechaser in history has ever had the impact that Arkle had on racing, and it is highly unlikely that any chaser will reach such glorious heights again. To say that Arkle was a once in a lifetime horse probably is an understatement, for he was a horse for all time. Arkle raced with rare grace and an almost arrogant sense of belief that he was the best. He was a horse that had everything: speed, stamina, fluent jumping, toughness, charisma and, above all, pure class. He won almost every major chase in England and Ireland, including the Thyestes Chase, Leopardstown Chase, King George VI Chase, Whitbread Gold Cup, Hennessy Gold Cup and Cheltenham Gold Cup. He never ran in the Aintree Grand National, but only because his owner Anne, Duchess of Westminster, dare not risk the horse known as 'Himself' in that race. He was a weight-carrying extraordinaire and captured the hearts and imagination of all those that flocked in their droves to see him at the racecourse. He was, quite simply, the best ever.

Arkle had been a dominant novice chaser the season before, winning the race at the Cheltenham Festival now known as the Royal & SunAlliance Chase. Unbeaten over fences, Arkle travelled from his yard at Tom Dreaper's to England for the 1963 Hennessy Gold Cup at Newbury where he faced his first clash with the Cheltenham Gold Cup winner, Mill House. A mistake late on meant Arkle was beaten, but neither Dreaper nor jockey Pat Taaffe were unduly concerned and fully expected to turn the tables when Arkle met Mill House again in the Gold Cup in March 1964. In England, defeat for Mill House was not even considered, yet the vast army of Irish supporters had full faith in Arkle, and it was to be the Irish youngster that announced himself the number one chaser by stunning Mill House in breathtaking style to win the Gold Cup. The result turned the chasing world on its head, and so began the dominance of the mighty Arkle. Before Cheltenham, Arkle had also won the Christmas Chase at Leopardstown, the Thyestes Chase at Gowran Park and the Leopardstown Chase, and he arrived at Fairyhouse, as one would expect, considered a near-certainty to win on his first attempt at the Irish Grand National. With 12st to carry, Arkle had 2st more than his nearest rival at the weights, the grey Flying Wild, but backed according to his status, Arkle began the race a heavy odds-on shot, despite the fact that terrible weather in the days leading up to the race had left the ground very testing. In fact, the course had been saturated, so much so that the course's Raheen car park had been closed.

There were just six horses facing Arkle, but among them were some fair performers, including the versatile mare Height O' Fashion, unlucky in the 1963 race and a lover of soft ground. Flying Wild was again fancied, but had fallen in both the season's Leopardstown Chase and Aintree Grand National (first fence), while Loving Record had run well in many of Ireland's important chases during the season, and Ferry Boat was a free-running seven-year-old that jumped well and had fine stamina. Of the outsiders, the brown gelding Baxier (owned by Lord Fermoy) was trained by former jockey Phonsie O'Brien and had run well to finish eighth in the recent Grand National at Aintree behind Team Spirit.

Despite the poor weather in the days preceding the race, a huge crowd was on hand at Fairyhouse, everyone wanting to catch a glimpse of the outstanding Arkle. For the first time, a helicopter was used to help police in their efforts to keep the crowd flowing smoothly. Arkle, unsurprisingly following his supreme performance at Cheltenham, was cheered ecstatically from the paddock to the start of the race, as the fans at Fairyhouse provided a rich welcome for their new hero.

In the race, Taaffe got Arkle to settle very well, as Ferry Boat and Loving Record showed the way from the great horse, and the order remained the same passing the stands – the remainder headed by Flying Wild. Despite all the rain, the strong winds present at the course had acted positively on the going, and the surface was far less treacherous than had been anticipated.

Ferry Boat and Loving Record still held the lead jumping the Ballyhack regulation, with Pat Taaffe unconcerned when they soon extended their advantage. As the race developed, it was clear that Taaffe was sitting pretty on Arkle. At the third last, Taaffe tried to squeeze Arkle through a narrow gap, but when that was closed by the jockey's brother Tos aboard Loving Record, Arkle was forced to switch sides to deliver his challenge.

It made no difference however, for Loving Record soon weakened and surging into the home straight with his devilish speed unleashed, Arkle was able to overthrow Ferry Boat with consummate ease and took up the running at the second last. Jumping the final fences majestically, Arkle looked to be heading for an easy victory, but Height O' Fashion came with a late run that, momentarily, had Taaffe worried. However, despite the big difference in weight, Taaffe asked his horse for extra, and responding courageously, Arkle strode out to win by a length-and-a-quarter from the game Height O' Fashion, with Ferry Boat (having fenced tremendously) eight lengths away in third.

It was a memorable performance, and the cheers rung out for the champion long after Taaffe had steered Arkle back into the winner's enclosure. It was now five in a row for Dreaper and eight overall. It would be hard to imagine any trainer having trained a better collection of chasers in their career than Tom Dreaper. He had already guided the likes of Prince Regent, Royal Approach and Fortria to glory, and there would be many more stars to pass through his Kilsallaghan yard yet. None, however, could match Arkle, and the horse emphatically made his only ever appearance in the Irish Grand National a winning one.

Arkle jumps the final fence in front from Height O' Fashion.

1964 IRISH GRAND NATIONAL RESULT

FATE	HORSE	AGE/WEIGHT	JOCKEY
1st	ARKLE	7.12.0	P. TAAFFE
2nd	HEIGHT O' FASHION	7.9.12	T.F. LACY
3rd	FERRY BOAT	7.9.7	F. SHORTT
4th	Loving Record	10.9.7	T. Taaffe
5th	Flying Wild	8.10.0	T. Carberry
6th	Baxier	8.9.7	R. Coonan
7th	Greatrakes	9.9.7	F. Carroll

30 March 1964
Going – Soft
Winner – £2,555
Race Distance – three miles
Time – 7mins 5secs
7 Ran
Winner trained by T.W. Dreaper
Winner owned by Anne, Duchess of Westminster
Arkle, bay gelding by Archive – Bright Cherry.

Betting – 1/2 ARKLE, 13/2 Height O' Fashion, 15/2 Flying Wild, 17/2 Loving Record, 20/1 Ferry Boat, 25/1 Baxier & Greatrakes.

1965 – SPLASH

1965 may well have been the richest running yet of the Irish Grand National, but the fact that just four horses (a record low for the event) turned out was a major disappointment. Seven runners had been declared at the final acceptance stage, but one of Ireland's most promising young stars, the future Cheltenham Gold Cup winner Fort Leney, was withdrawn having pulled himself up in the recent Scottish Grand National at Bogside; the horse was subsequently found to be suffering from a heart problem. Also pulled out late on were the 1964 runner-up and top weight, Height O' Fashion, and the outsider Cavendish. One of the chief reasons for the incredibly small field was the coughing epidemic that tore through Irish yards around the time of the 1965 Irish National. In fact, even some of those that did line-up had not escaped the bug.

Of the four runners, the most heralded names were those of Zonda and Duke Of York. Winner of the race way back in 1959, Zonda was now a fourteen-year-old and was understandably considered to be some years past his best. Yet in a poor renewal, even the veteran stood a fair chance of winning the Irish National, and Zonda's warm-up race had seen him finish second in the Grand Military Gold Cup at Sandown. One stable that had been seriously affected by the cough had been that of Charley Weld, who ran Duke Of York. As a precaution, Weld had isolated Duke Of York in a stable about a mile-and-a-half from his own for over a week in attempt to steer his charge clear of the epidemic. At one point in his career, Duke Of York had been labelled a possible Cheltenham Gold Cup winner. Indeed, the horse finished third in that race in 1963, but having met with setback after setback when trained in England, his owner had sent him to Weld's yard in Ireland. Duke Of York's latest run had been most promising, the horse finishing third behind Rondetto and Fort Leney in the National Hunt Handicap Chase at the Cheltenham Festival. This performance (Rondetto and Fort Leney were both exceptional horses) was good enough to see Duke Of York installed as even money favourite for the Irish National, yet the horse had performed miserably on his previous run in the race, and there was some doubt over his ability to handle the big Fairyhouse fences.

Completing the quartet were Devon Breeze and Splash. Devon Breeze was the outsider of the group. The horse was a seven-year-old hunter-chaser and had been another to suffer from coughing recently, first being diagnosed with the bug before running in a hunter-chase at Navan a couple of weeks before Fairyhouse, although the horse had recovered sufficiently to take his place in the Irish National field. With Fort Leney an absentee, Tom Dreaper set his sights on a sixth consecutive win courtesy of the seven-year-old chestnut Splash. A magnificent jumper with a huge heart and blessed with the stomach for a battle, Splash had won his previous two races and was considered to be in super form. Taking the ride on Splash was Paddy Woods, the jockey successful aboard Last Link in the 1963 race.

On good ground, the pace was steady early on, but the tempo really increased passing the stands to start the second circuit. Splash had lost ground by jumping to his left at the drop fence past the stands, but his determination had soon got him back with the pack, as Devon Breeze and Duke Of York led on. As he had the last time he ran in the Irish National, Duke Of York seemed to be having trouble handling some of the drop fences at Fairyhouse, and despite his prominent position, the horse never seemed at ease on the course.

At the fourth last, Devon Breeze was bowling along merrily in the lead, with Duke Of York close by, but Splash had responded with extra effort every time Woods asked him, and even though the jockey was working furiously to keep his mount in contention, Splash was emerging as a serious threat to the leading two.

Woods' efforts began to reap rewards as the leading two began to come back to Splash, and entering the straight with two to jump, Duke Of York cried enough. Devon Breeze had run a bold race of real credit under Timmy Hyde, but now the long-time leader was in for a real battle with Splash. Making tremendous progress on the stands side, Splash poached a length lead jumping the final fence, and grinding all the way to the line, the chestnut was able to score by three lengths to Devon Breeze. Duke Of York finished third, ten lengths back, but returned feeling very sore. The horse had a long history of leg troubles and the problem had surfaced once more, it emerged after the race that Duke Of York had gone lame again. Zonda ran with great pride and finished only a head back from Duke Of York in fourth place.

The amazing winning streak of trainer Tom Dreaper continued. Six in a row and nine overall, and despite requiring plenty of driving and pushing, Splash had fully earned his place on the roll of honour. Admitting to feeling exhausted after the race, Woods could now relax, safe in the knowledge that he had helped to extend the trainer's fabulous run of results in the Irish National, and could also take great pride from recording his second personal success in the race.

The 1965 winner Splash is led in.

1965 IRISH GRAND NATIONAL RESULT

FATE	HORSE	AGE/WEIGHT	JOCKEY
1st	SPLASH	7.10.13	P. WOODS
2nd	DEVON BREEZE	7.9.7	T.E. HYDE
3rd	DUKE OF YORK	10.11.6	R. COONAN
4th	Zonda	14.9.12	T. Carberry

19 April 1965
Going – Good
Winner – £4,237
Race Distance – three miles
Time – 6mins 57.4secs
4 Ran
Winner trained by T.W. Dreaper
Winner owned by Mr A. Craigie
Splash, chestnut gelding by Fortina – Tackler.

Betting – Evens Duke Of York, 6/4 SPLASH, 15/2 Zonda, 100/9 Devon Breeze.

1966 – FLYINGBOLT

Almost unbelievably, the Kilsallaghan yard of Tom Dreaper housed the two top rated steeplechasers of all time at the same time. There would be no disputing – then or now – that Arkle was number one, yet also tucked away among the army of warriors at Dreaper's yard was the huge chestnut Flyingbolt, a horse of immense ability. He was a seven-year-old that seemed destined to take the place of Arkle in Cheltenham Gold Cups when that great horse's career came to an end in the King George VI Chase later in 1966. Flyingbolt was tremendously versatile, almost a freak of a horse, and had all the qualities required to become a true champion. It had been at the recent Cheltenham Festival where Flyingbolt had displayed his sensational adaptability. Showing his fine speed and flare for fast, fluent jumping, Flyingbolt took the Two Mile Champion Chase in wonderful style. Then, amazingly, the horse was back at Cheltenham twenty-four hours later to compete in the Champion Hurdle where, despite a most determined challenge, he was denied first place by under four lengths, finishing third behind the winner Salmon Spray. To even attempt two such races in consecutive days was quite an achievement, to get so close to winning both was altogether remarkable, and the performances portrayed Flyingbolt as a magnificent horse. It was no secret that Flyingbolt was held in the highest regard by Dreaper, but the horse naturally was targeted with venom by the handicapper. At Fairyhouse he was allotted the maximum 12st 7lbs for the 1966 Irish Grand National, and although only six horses from the ten declared faced the starter, there were some useful handicappers included, and Flyingbolt would have to concede close to 3st to them all. Compounding the difficulty of the task set for Flyingbolt was the heavy going, as a period of unsettled weather in Ireland had left the ground extremely testing. Despite these concerns, Flyingbolt had won the Thyestes Chase at Gowran Park before Cheltenham and was backed as if defeat was out of the question, the hoards of punters that braved the elements at murky and muddy Fairyhouse sending their new hero off as the 8/11 favourite.

Among the outsiders were Brown Diamond, twice placed in the race, and the seven-year-old Mydo, while Height O' Fashion, Splash and Great Lark were expected to give Flyingbolt most to think about. A true stayer, Height O' Fashion had been soundly beaten by Flyingbolt in the Thyestes Chase, but had then run the mighty Arkle close in the Leopardstown Chase, albeit receiving much weight. Having been second in the race before, the mare looked best equipped to challenge the hot favourite. A stablemate of Flyingbolt's, the 1965 winner Splash was again in the line-up, while the improving mare Great Lark, trained by Willie O'Grady, had won her last two races, including a three-mile chase at Naas.

With visibility poor and a heavy mist hanging over the course, the race got under way. The very first fence brought drama, as the well-backed Great Lark came down, and it was Brown Diamond that led for the majority of the first circuit from Flyingbolt, Splash, Mydo and Height O' Fashion, although Flyingbolt had pulled his way to the front in the home straight on the first lap, with very little ground covering the five still standing.

On the long climb towards the Ballyhack regulation, the 33/1 shot Mydo dropped out of contention, but at the famous fence at the top of the course, there was nothing to separate Brown Diamond, Flyingbolt and Splash, with Height O' Fashion being eased smoothly into contention.

Pat Taaffe on Flyingbolt had been in front sooner than he ideally wanted, yet he was travelling so strongly and the horse had taken him there, but it was to be Height O' Fashion that came to tackle the favourite five fences out, and just headed Flyingbolt until the mare made a mistake at the third last that temporarily knocked her backwards.

With the remainder beaten, the battle was on between Flyingbolt and Height O' Fashion. Flyingbolt had veered slightly to the left in the home straight, and this had allowed Height O' Fashion a route back into the contest. Jumping the last with the crowd in a frenzy, the mare edged slightly in front on the run-in, but Flyingbolt was brave and ever so strong. Taaffe had to drive the white-faced chestnut hard, but Flyingbolt possessed tremendous heart, and clawing back the gallant mare got up in time for the post with two lengths to spare. Splash had landed awkwardly after jumping the third last, but stayed on well to take third place four lengths back with Brown Diamond fourth and Mydo fifth. Height O' Fashion had again run her heart out in the Irish National, yet she had now been beaten in the race by only Arkle and Flyingbolt (with the exception of her fall in 1963), so for her to finish second once more was a praiseworthy achievement.

His win in the Irish National was perhaps Flyingbolt's best ever performance, for he had given nearly 3st to Height O' Fashion on heavy ground, been headed on the run-in and still found the necessary extra to win a thriller. Taaffe had always been confident of victory, but admitted the mare was a very tough opponent. It was hoped that Flyingbolt would win the Gold Cup at Cheltenham in 1967 (he would have been a certain favourite in that race), but a rare viral infection severely disrupted his career, and he would never run in chasing's Blue Riband event.

It was now seven wins in a row in the race for Dreaper and ten overall. Such a record is almost unfathomable and will surely never be duplicated in any major chase. It is worth noting that Dreaper only ever trained around thirty to forty horses at one time, but he preached quality and his horses were always extremely well educated and ready to do themselves justice. It would be the last time the great trainer would taste victory in the Irish National, but he still had more Cheltenham glory to come courtesy of Fort Leney in the 1968 Gold Cup. A few years later, Dreaper handed over the task of training the Kilsallaghan string to his son Jim, and watched as Colebridge and Brown Lad carried on the winning tradition in the Irish National, while Ten Up also won the Gold Cup at Cheltenham for the stable in 1975. Not long after Ten Up's victory, Tom Dreaper passed away, leaving behind a legacy of one of the finest trainers to have graced the sport.

1966 IRISH GRAND NATIONAL RESULT

FATE	HORSE	AGE/WEIGHT	JOCKEY
1st	FLYINGBOLT	7.12.7	P. TAAFFE
2nd	HEIGHT O' FASHION	9.9.9	T.F. LACY
3rd	SPLASH	8.9.7	P. WOODS
4th	Brown Diamond	9.9.7	F. Shortt
5th	Mydo	7.9.7	F. McKenna
Fell	Great Lark	7.9.7	B. Hannon

11 April 1966
Going – Heavy
Winner – £4,470
Race Distance – three miles
Time – 7mins 7.4secs
6 Ran
Winner trained by T.W. Dreaper
Winner owned by Mrs T.G. Wilkinson
Flyingbolt, chestnut gelding by Airborne – Eastlock.

Betting – 8/11 FLYINGBOLT, 3/1 Height O' Fashion, 5/1 Great Lark, 8/1 Splash, 100/6 Brown Diamond, 33/1 Mydo.

Rated the second best chaser of all time after Arkle, the magnificent Flyingbolt jumps a fence in the 1966 Irish National.

1967 – VULPINE

For the first time in eight years, a trainer other than Tom Dreaper would win the Irish Grand National. The Kilsallaghan trainer would likely have saddled the favourite in 1967, but he was forced to withdraw top weight Thorn Gate late on when the horse was found to be lame. Without Thorn Gate, the race had a very open look to it, with twelve runners going to post, and the richest ever running of the race seemed sure to be competitive and exciting.

Replacing Thorn Gate as both top weight and favourite was the talented eight-year-old San Jacinto. Trained by Paddy Sleator, San Jacinto had been running a very big race in the recent Leopardstown Chase behind future Gold Cup winner Fort Leney before a last fence fall ended his race. His jumping remained a concern, as did his hefty weight burden, but San Jacinto had plenty of potential, although there were many others that were considered, including Corrie-Vacoul, Talbot, Greek Vulgan and Vulpine. Corrie-Vacoul was owned by the Duchess of Westminster, trained by Willie O'Grady and ridden by Stan Murphy, and the horse had finished second in the Thyestes Chase before disappointing at Cheltenham. Talbot, representing trainer Danny Morgan, was considered a most promising youngster having won at Naas earlier in the season before finishing third in the Thyestes Chase, while Greek Vulgan was trained by former winning jockey Tos Taaffe and ridden by future trainer Ben Hannon. Greek Vulgan had won the Thyestes Chase yet had disappointed in the Leopardstown Chase. Only a six-year-old, Vulpine represented trainer Paddy Mullins, and following an indifferent spell hurdling, the horse had returned to the chasing sphere and had recently run well to finish fifth in the Leopardstown Chase. A bay gelding by the terrific sire of staying chasers, Vulgan, Vulpine had won the Power Gold Cup at Fairyhouse on Irish National day the season before and was ridden in the big race by young Matt Curran – his first Irish National ride.

The inconsistent Blue Blazes and dual-runner-up Height O' Fashion were others with their fair share of supporters, and on good ground, the field were sent on their way. Talbot was the early leader from Babysnatcher III and Reynard's Heir, and passing the stands for the first time, the order was Greek Vulgan, Talbot, Fort Ord and Vulpine. However, it was to be a race marred by numerous falls and incidents that occurred on the second circuit, just as the race was heating up.

At Ballyhack, Talbot was suddenly pulled-up by Francis Shortt. It transpired that Talbot had broken a joint in his off-foreleg and subsequently, the horse was sadly put down. Leaving the tragedy behind them, it was now Fort Ord – ridden by Eamon Prendergast – that led from Greek Vulgan, Vulpine, Corrie-Vacoul and Reynard's Heir, with the favourite San Jacinto beginning to creep into contention.

Vulpine had been prominent throughout and appeared to be relishing being back running over fences after his unsatisfactory spell hurdling, and turning into the straight, there was nothing to choose between the Mullins runner and the strong-travelling Corrie-Vacoul. All the time, San Jacinto was getting closer to the leaders, seemingly poised to make his challenge.

Corrie-Vacoul had left his disappointing run at Cheltenham behind him and still held every chance when jumping the second last. But a mistimed leap sent the horse to the ground, and a fence later, the only remaining threat to Vulpine also hit the deck, as the frustrating San Jacinto fell at the last for the second consecutive race, this time the groans of favourite backers accompanied the tumble.

Matt Curran had lost an iron at the second last, but now he received his share of luck through the falls of Corrie-Vacoul and San Jacinto, and despite his mount veering over to the stands side on the run-in, the jockey was able to drive Vulpine home strongly for a three-length win. In second came Reynard's Heir, the chestnut well ridden by Tommy Kinane, and this was a partnership that would go on to finish eighth in the following season's Grand National at Aintree. Fort Ord had run well for a long way, and the horse owned and trained by Cyril Harty was a mere half-length down on Reynard's Heir when taking third place, with fifteen lengths back to the well-fancied Greek Vulgan. Besides the unfortunate non-finishers, Height O' Fashion ran a poor race and never looked like challenging as she had done in previous years.

It turned out to be an all-County Kilkenny victory, for Vulpine was owned and bred by Mr T.W. Nicholson, while both Mullins and Curran were from the area. Curran was having his first ride at Fairyhouse, and had impressed many with his calmness and determination aboard Vulpine, having lost an iron two out. There would be further Irish Grand National success in future years for the young jockey. Further success would also await trainer Paddy Mullins. The handler had a relatively small string, but he would enjoy more glory at Fairyhouse and even greater glory at Cheltenham, where in 1986, he would saddle the unforgettable mare Dawn Run to victory in the Gold Cup, as she became the first horse to win both the Champion Hurdle and Gold Cup.

1967 IRISH GRAND NATIONAL RESULT

FATE	HORSE	AGE/WEIGHT	JOCKEY	27 March 1967
1st	VULPINE	6.11.6	M. CURRAN	Going – Good
2nd	REYNARD'S HEIR	7.9.13	T. KINANE	Winner – £4,537
3rd	FORT ORD	7.9.8	E. PRENDERGAST	Race Distance – three miles
4th	Greek Vulgan	10.10.13	B. Hannon	12 Ran
5th	Blue Blazes	8.10.3	F. Carroll	Winner trained by P. Mullins
6th	Babysnatcher III	8.9.7	T. Finn	Winner owned by Mr T.W. Nicholson
7th	Height O' Fashion	10.11.4	T.F. Lacy	Vulpine, bay gelding by Vulgan – Queen Astrid.
8th	Vulgan's Girl	8.9.7	T. Carberry	
Fell	Corrie-Vacoul	7.11.7	T.S. Murphy	
Fell	San Jacinto	8.11.12	R. Coonan	Betting – 5/2 San Jacinto, 11/2 Greek Vulgan, 7/1 VULPINE, 8/1 Blue Blazes, 9/1
Pulled-Up	Robenco	8.9.7	Mr A. Kavanagh	Reynard's Heir, 10/1 Corrie-Vacoul, 100/9 Height O' Fashion & Talbot, 100/6 Fort
Pulled-Up	Talbot	6.9.13	F. Shortt	Ord, 20/1 Vulgan's Girl, 25/1 Babysnatcher III, 100/1 Robenco.

Vulpine, third from left, about to jump a fence in the 1967 race.

1968 – HERRING GULL

Trainer Paddy Mullins had won the previous year's Irish Grand National with the six-year-old Vulpine, and in 1968 he had another youngster to go to war with, a horse perhaps even more talented than Vulpine. The horse was the brilliant, if somewhat inconsistent, six-year-old novice Herring Gull. It was true that the young chestnut had fallen twice in his five races during the season, but his ability shone through gloriously when he managed to stand up, for the other three races of his season had ended in victory. Most impressively, Herring Gull had won the Totalisator Novices' Chase at the recent Cheltenham Festival (jumping impeccably), thrashing a future Aintree Grand National winner and very good horse in Gay Trip in the process. Although only a novice, Herring Gull had all the credentials. His age was of no detriment, as Vulpine and others had proved, he had won on the course in a Hurdle race, had won over the Irish National distance at Cheltenham, and was definitely a horse on the rise. Ultimately, neither the fact that jockey John Crowley was having his first ride in the race nor the horse's big weight of 11st 13lbs deterred punters from sending off Herring Gull the 5/2 favourite.

The fine sire Fortina, winner of the Cheltenham Gold Cup in 1947, had already sired four winners of the Irish Grand National (and would in time also be responsible for two Gold Cup winners in Fort Leney and Glencaraig Lady), and he was represented on this occasion by Splash and Knockaney. In the 1966 Irish National, Splash had only carried 9st 7lbs due to the presence in the field of the great Flyingbolt, but on this occasion, he was burdened with top weight of 12st, due to his 1965 Irish National win and the fact that he was such a consistent horse. Conversely, Knockaney was a most inconsistent chaser and had fallen at Fairyhouse in February. However, at his best, Knockaney was a very good horse, and the horse was well weighted against the likes of Splash, Herring Gull, former placed horses Height O' Fashion and Reynard's Heir, and the lightly-raced nine-year-old Blue Blazes.

Despite the presence of good ground, four horses – Greek Vulgan, Trick O' The Loop, Ferry Boat and Bravada – were non-runners, and on settling down, the twelve-runner field was taken along by the Dan Moore-trained Collierstown.

It was to be a race where most of the horses jumped very well throughout the race, and there were to be no fallers. Collierstown set a scorching pace for a long way before he tired approaching the fourth last, where the main players came to the fore. Herring Gull had looked in superb condition in the paddock before the race and was clearly a horse ripe with confidence following his superb run at Cheltenham. Coming to the third last, it was Herring Gull and Knockaney (ridden by Ben Hannon) that had the race between them, although Herring Gull was merely cantering.

Turning into the straight, the battle was on in earnest, and jumping the final two fences locked together, the pair engaged in a thrilling duel to the line. Knockaney was in receipt of 23lbs and had three years more experience than Herring Gull, but the combat was as even as could be. Halfway up the run-in, the older horse edged in front and looked set to confirm his status as the race's dark horse, but Herring Gull was extremely brave, and with Crowley conjuring up one final drive from his charge, the youngster got up on the line, stretching out his head at the vital moment to win the day in one of the most exciting finishes to the Irish National of all time. Knockaney was a very good horse in his own right, but he had simply been denied by a horse at the top of his game. Eight lengths away in third came the former winner Splash, with Reynard's Heir fourth.

As at Cheltenham, Herring Gull had jumped with grace and power and had fully deserved his win. Prior to Cheltenham, there had been suggestions that Herring Gull was bereft of true stamina, but his performance at Prestbury Park's severely undulating track and now under a big weight at Fairyhouse had fully dispelled that theory, giving trainer Mullins his second consecutive Irish National win and handing a dream debut to jockey Crowley, whose part in the triumph was major.

Herring Gull had amassed over £12,000 in prize money over the course of the season and was naturally viewed as an ideal candidate for the 1969 Cheltenham Gold Cup. Herring Gull never made it to Cheltenham in 1968, but he did run in the race in 1970 and 1971. After a number of somewhat inferior editions of that particular race, Herring Gull was unlucky enough to come up against another Irish chaser, the Dan Moore-trained L'Escargot, just as that horse was turning into a powerhouse in the sport. Herring Gull – confusing after his richly promising younger days – was unable to affect the result on either occasion, as L'Escargot became the first horse since Arkle to record consecutive wins in chasing's Blue Riband event.

1968 IRISH GRAND NATIONAL RESULT

FATE	HORSE	AGE/WEIGHT	JOCKEY
1st	HERRING GULL	6.11.13	J. CROWLEY
2nd	KNOCKANEY	9.10.4	B. HANNON
3rd	SPLASH	10.12.0	P. WOODS
4th	Reynard's Heir	8.11.2	T. Kinane
5th	Valouis	9.9.8	S. Barker
6th	Peccard	7.10.2	A. Redmond
7th	Silvertrix	8.10.8	P. Black
8th	Height O' Fashion	11.11.5	J.P. Sullivan
9th	Good Mop	9.10.1	C. Finnegan
10th	Collierstown	7.9.12	T. Carberry
11th	Gypsando	9.10.10	J.P. Harty
12th	Blue Blazes	8.11.4	F. Carroll

15 April 1968
Going – Good
Winner – £4,758
Race Distance – three miles
Time – 6mins 59secs
12 Ran
Winner trained by P. Mullins
Winner owned by Mrs G.A.J. Wilson
Herring Gull, chestnut gelding by Devonian – Lonely Wings.

Betting – 5/2 HERRING GULL, 6/1 Splash, 7/1 Knockaney, 8/1 Collierstown, Reynard's Heir & Silvertrix, 10/1 Peccard, 100/9 Blue Blazes, 100/7 Valouis, 100/6 Gypsando, 20/1 Good Mop & Height O' Fashion.

Right: Mrs J. Wilson leads in Herring Gull.

Below: Herring Gull (left) beats Knockaney.

1969 – SWEET DREAMS

In 1969, there may well have been no true superstar chaser that had enlightened many of the recent runnings of the Irish Grand National, such as Arkle, Flyingbolt or Herring Gull, yet among the eighteen-strong field were a collection of highly capable, seasoned chasers, and once again the race looked set for a most competitive and exciting renewal.

Favourite was the eight-year-old bay son of Vulgan, King Vulgan, a horse ridden by Tim Hyde, whose father Timmy had won the race in previous years aboard Clare County and Prince Regent. King Vulgan was nicely weighted with 10st 9lbs to carry, yet much of the race day attention focused on the event's winning-most trainer, Tom Dreaper. The main representative from the yard on this occasion was the strapping nine-year-old, Crown Prince. As a novice, Crown Prince had been held in the highest regard, yet had gone to Cheltenham in 1966 for the Totalisator Novices' Chase only to flop confusingly behind the excellent Different Class. Soon after that Cheltenham disappointment, Crown Prince went wrong and was forced off the track for over two years. Despite his problems, Dreaper maintained unwavering faith in the horse, and after Crown Prince had returned to action a few weeks before Fairyhouse in a Hurdle race at Navan, the trainer confidently claimed Crown Prince to be in grand fettle, remarks that saw the horse backed down to 8/1 joint-second favourite with the previous year's runner-up, Knockaney. Riding Crown Prince was the multiple Irish National winner Pat Taaffe, the jockey opting for the mount rather than the unreliable ten-year-old Prince Tino, who was subsequently partnered by Paddy Woods.

The 1967 winner Vulpine was back again under jockey Matt Curran, Aintree Grand National tenth Miss Hunter ran under a light weight, and jockey Sean Barker, a good understudy to Taaffe at Dreaper's yard, got the ride on recent Cheltenham faller, Vulture. The surprise winners of two of Ireland's biggest chases during the season took part in the shapes of Greek Vulgan (Thyestes Chase) and Gypsando (Leopardstown Chase), while the good amateur jockey, Mr John Fowler, rode Kilburn, a faller in the recent Grand National at Aintree, an incident that left the horse's regular jockey, Tommy Carberry, with fractured vertebrae. Quietly fancied, especially by her trainer, was the eight-year-old bay mare Sweet Dreams. Trained on the Curragh by Kevin Bell and owned by bookmakers' wife Mrs Paddy Meehan, Sweet Dreams had been unlucky on her last run in the Ulster National, for she was going well when she had to be pulled-up because of a slipped saddle. Sweet Dreams was ridden by the very capable jockey Bobby Coonan, whose previous rides in the race had included race favourites Duke Of York and San Jacinto.

There was glorious weather at Fairyhouse for the 1969 Irish Grand National, helping to attract a huge crowd to the course. Whereas the year before Collierstown had set a cracking pace in leading for the majority of the way, on this occasion, the long-time leader was the mare Miss Hunter, although the pace was somewhat more conservative than in the 1968 race.

Despite her exertions from running and completing the course in the Grand National at Aintree just nine days earlier, Miss Hunter put up a fine performance, boldly leading the field until she was joined by the favourite King Vulgan at the fifth last, and it was here that those who would have a hand in the finish came to make their respective challenges.

The crowd roared their approval as King Vulgan hit the front independently at the fourth last, chased by Miss Hunter, Kilburn and Sweet Dreams, while further back, previous winner Vulpine was being stoked along furiously by Curran. Of those in the leading group, Sweet Dreams in particular appeared full of running, and it was no surprise when she pulled alongside the favourite soon after jumping the third last.

Sweet Dreams and King Vulgan remained together until approaching the final fence, but in receipt of a stone, the mare began to come clear, and only a fall would stop her now. Jumping the fence in fine style, Sweet Dreams pulled further and further away from the beleaguered favourite King Vulgan on the run-in, and in the end, was a most convincing and comfortable winner. Devouring the ground late on was Vulpine, carrying 12st. The 1967 winner had been impeded by another horse at the fourth last, but had roared up the home straight and was a fast finishing second in front of King Vulgan, Kilburn and Miss Hunter. The big disappointment of the race was obviously Crown Prince, with the Dreaper inmate never able to get competitive, eventually finishing twelfth of the thirteen that completed.

Trainer Kevin Bell had always been quietly confident that Sweet Dreams could win the Irish National, stating beforehand that the horse had been in fine form since her unlucky performance at Downpatrick, while the win was a first in the race for Coonan who, despite putting up 2lbs overweight having dieted all week, timed the mare's challenge to perfection and proved the horse had both stamina and class. Sweet Dreams was sired by the very good stallion, Arctic Slave, and was originally bought by trainer Paddy Sleator for her owner for less than 400 guineas at Ballsbridge Sales, before going into training with Bell.

1969 IRISH GRAND NATIONAL RESULT

FATE	HORSE	AGE/WEIGHT	JOCKEY
1st	SWEET DREAMS	8.9.8	R. COONAN
2nd	VULPINE	8.12.0	M. CURRAN
3rd	KING VULGAN	8.10.8	T.E. HYDE
4th	KILBURN	10.11.2	MR J.FOWLER
5th	Miss Hunter	8.9.7	F. Shortt
6th	Brown Boy	10.10.5	T. Casey
7th	Blue Blazes	10.10.1	F. Carroll
8th	Greek Vulgan	12.10.13	C. Finnegan
9th	Knockaney	10.10.3	B. Hannon
10th	Kilcoo	10.10.1	Mr A.S. Robinson
11th	Vulture	7.10.2	S. Barker
12th	Crown Prince	9.11.9	P. Taaffe
13th	Prince Tino	10.11.9	P. Woods
Fell	Gypsando	10.10.12	J.P. Harty
Pulled-Up	Battle Dust	9.9.7	T. Finn
Pulled-Up	Bold Fencer	8.11.10	J. Crowley
Pulled-Up	Old Times	8.10.7	D.T. Hughes
Pulled-Up	Rosinver Bay	9.9.7	E. Prendergast

7 April 1969
Going – Good
Winner – £5,047
Race Distance – three miles
Time – 7mins 20.4secs
18 Ran
Winner trained by K. Bell
Winner owned by Mrs P. Meehan
Sweet Dreams, bay mare by Arctic Slave – Halador.

Betting – 6/1 King Vulgan, 8/1 Crown Prince & Knockaney, 10/1 Bold Fencer,
SWEET DREAMS & Vulture, 100/8 Kilburn, 100/7 Blue Blazes, Gypsando, Prince
Tino & Vulpine, 20/1 Brown Boy, Greek Vulgan & Miss Hunter, 25/1 Kilcoo, 33/1
Old Times & Rosinver Bay, 50/1 Battle Dust.

Sweet Dreams jumps a fence during the 1969 race.

Mrs P. Meehan with Sweet Dreams after the race.

1970 – GAROUPE

The 1970 running of the Irish Grand National was, in retrospect, one of the classiest renewals of the race to be run in the seventies. In fact, the decade as a whole ranks among the strongest periods class-wise in the history of the race, with many Cheltenham Gold Cup winners, Champion Chase winners and countless other big race winners from England and Ireland taking their chances in the event.

Two horses fresh from running in the Cheltenham Gold Cup, won by the Dan Moore-trained chestnut L'Escargot, were among the thirteen-strong field, although Herring Gull and French Tan had suffered quite contrasting fortunes at Prestbury Park. Herring Gull had won the Irish National in 1968 but had never quite scaled the heights expected of him when a youngster, and the horse, at the time of the 1970 race, seemed some way off his best. A fall in the Gold Cup had done little to improve his confidence, yet he remained a class chaser, and despite carrying 11st 5lbs, was made fourth favourite at 5/1. Conversely, the brown eight-year-old French Tan was a horse fresh from running the race of his life in the Gold Cup. Having run up a sequence of wins during the season, French Tan had battled L'Escargot to the death at Cheltenham but had just been outlasted up that final, punishing hill, and had finished second under Pat Taaffe. However, despite his hard race at Cheltenham and the fact that he carried top weight of 11st 11lbs, French Tan proved extremely popular, starting the race 9/2 joint-second favourite for jockey Bobby Coonan. On the same price was the chestnut mare Glencarrig Lady, a very talented novice partnered by Tommy Carberry. Glencarrig Lady arrived at Fairyhouse having looked all set to win the Totalisator Novices' Chase at the Cheltenham Festival only to fall at the final fence. That effort, however, had proved she was a horse capable of landing a major contest, and the fact that Vulpine and Herring Gull had won their Irish Nationals when Glencarrig Lady's age (six) was further encouragement for punters wishing to back the mare.

But favourite for the race was yet another from the endless stream of star chasers from the Tom Dreaper yard. The trainer had bypassed Cheltenham with his seven-year-old challenger Stonedale specifically to run in the Irish National. A fresh horse and a great jumper, Stonedale was a horse full of promise and had displayed rare speed for a staying chaser when carrying 12st 7lbs in a race at Navan a few weeks prior to Fairyhouse. In that race at Navan, Stonedale was caught late on by a high-class novice in No Other (receiving 2st from Stonedale), and when No Other went on to beat the Thyestes Chase winner Smooth Dealer (also an Irish National runner) at Limerick, Stonedale's Navan form looked outstanding. Stonedale was a horse that normally took a strong pull in his races, but with Pat Taaffe in the saddle, the horse was sent off the rock-solid 15/8 favourite.

Two English challengers were present in the forms of The Inventor and Fearless Fred; both had previously won hunter chases over three-and-a-half miles at Fairyhouse, while the latter, trained by Fred Rimell, had also started second favourite for the 1969 Grand National at Aintree, only to fall early on. The previous year's favourite, King Vulgan, was back having won the season's Leopardstown Chase, while the progressive Garoupe was another six-year-old thought to have a decent chance. Like Glencarrig Lady, both a novice and trained by Francis Flood, the bay had finished unplaced on his last two runs, despite running well, and a late

surge of money for the horse saw the gelding start at 10/1 for veteran jockey Cathal Finnegan, who had been riding in the Irish National since the mid 1950s.

It was, by almost double, the richest Irish Grand National ever run, and with a fine field of thirteen sent on their way on good ground, the crowd watched in excitement. Stonedale had been made the strong favourite for the race following the late withdrawal of Kinloch Brae, the star chaser trained by Willie O'Grady that had been favourite for the Gold Cup at Cheltenham only to fall when in contention three out, and it was Stonedale – in his usual hard-pilling style – that tanked along at the head of affairs.

It was noticeable very early on, however, that Stonedale was not jumping with the normal boldness that had made him a horse of such promise, and try as he might, he was never able to truly dominate nor shed the chasing pack of Smooth Dealer, Baby Snatcher, Money Boat, Garoupe and Cnoc Dubh.

It was to be a race that really came to life inside the last half mile. Stonedale still led but other leading fancies such as Herring Gull and French Tan were under heavy pressure. The English pair of The Inventor and Fearless Fred had moved through smoothly to challenge, while young Garoupe was looking most dangerous of all.

At the fifth last Stonedale cracked, suddenly going backwards, and before long his race was over, eventually pulled-up by Taaffe. Fearless Fred was next to come under pressure as The Inventor took up the running, tracked by Cnoc Dubh, Garoupe and the improving Glencarrig Lady, and turning into the home straight, these four had the race between them.

It was the two novices, Glencarrig Lady and Garoupe, that pulled clear approaching two out, and although the mare had held a slight lead approaching the fence, Garoupe ranged alongside taking the fence. From there, there appeared little doubt as to which horse would win. Coming away from his stablemate, jumping the last, Garoupe stayed on strongly up the run-in to score by five lengths from Glencarrig Lady, with Cnoc Dubh eight lengths away in third, just edging out The Inventor.

The same age, and separated by just 6lbs in weight at Fairyhouse, it appeared trainer Francis Flood had two fine steeplechasers to tackle future top prizes with. The mild surprise was that it was Glencarrig Lady and not Garoupe that became the true superstar. Garoupe did eventually run in a Gold Cup at Cheltenham, but only finished fifth behind The Dikler in 1973, however Glencarrig Lady was well in contention before falling late on behind L'Escargot in the 1971 Gold Cup, and duly gained her revenge when winning by a narrow margin from the English horse Royal Toss in the same race twelve months later.

But it was Garoupe that enjoyed the glory at Fairyhouse in 1970, providing a long overdue first Irish National win for Finnegan, who had been forced to forgo riding arrangements at Cheltenham because of a shoulder injury. Garoupe was from the second crop of the sire Escart III (the first having produced L'Escargot), and the horse was bred by the winning trainer's brother, Jim. Francis Flood had only set up as a trainer in County Wicklow some three years previously, and there could have been no better outcome for his first ever Irish Grand National runners than finishing first and second in 1970.

*Former winners
Herring Gull and
jockey John Crowley.*

1970 IRISH GRAND NATIONAL RESULT

FATE	HORSE	AGE/WEIGHT	JOCKEY	30 March 1970
1st	GAROUPE	6.9.9	C. FINNEGAN	Going – Good
2nd	GLENCARRIG LADY	6.10.1	T. CARBERRY	Sponsor – Irish Distillers
3rd	CNOC DUBH	7.9.7	M.A. BRENNAN	Winner – £9,656
4th	The Inventor	9.9.8	J.P. Bourke	Race Distance – three miles
5th	Herring Gull	8.11.5	J. Crowley	Time – 7mins 18.2secs
6th	French Tan	8.11.11	R. Coonan	13 Ran
7th	King Vulgan	9.10.7	B. Hannon	Winner trained by F. Flood
8th	Baby Snatcher	9.10.6	P. Woods	Winner owned by Mrs F. Williams
Pulled-Up	Fearless Fred	8.11.1	K.B. White	Garoupe, bay gelding by Escart III – Treanmore.
Pulled-Up	Money Boat	6.9.7	A.L.T. Moore	
Pulled-Up	Rodragusa	7.9.7	Mr J. O'Riordan	Betting – 15/8 Stonedale, 9/2 French Tan & Glencarrig Lady, 5/1 Herring Gull,
Pulled-Up	Smooth Dealer	8.9.7	T. Kinane	10/1 GAROUPE, 20/1 Baby Snatcher, Fearless Fred, King Vulgan & The Inventor,
Pulled-Up	Stonedale	7.11.9	P. Taaffe	33/1 Cnoc Dubh & Smooth Dealer, 40/1 Money Boat, 66/1 Rodragusa.

1971 – KING'S SPRITE

The 1971 Irish Grand National was another renewal of tremendous quality. It was with real excitement that news was broken of trainer Dan Moore's intention to run the brilliant chestnut L'Escargot, twice a winner of the Cheltenham Gold Cup. L'Escargot had been a surprise winner of the Cheltenham showpiece in 1970, but returning to the course twelve months later in grand form, 'The Snail' easily got the better of another Irish raider, Leap Frog, to win his second Gold Cup. With L'Escargot in fantastic heart following his Cheltenham success, Moore decided to let the horse take his chance at Fairyhouse, despite having the enormous burden of carrying top weight of 12st 7lbs. However, L'Escargot had strength, stamina and above all class, and if there was a horse in training at that point capable of defying such a weight, it was L'Escargot.

Next in the weights, and clear favourite at 3/1, was the English raider Spanish Steps. Not since 1928 had an English-trained horse won the Irish Grand National, but in Spanish Steps the country had a horse of true quality, one that had won the Hennessy Gold Cup at Newbury in super style in 1969, when only six-years-old, and had followed up that performance by finishing third to L'Escargot in the 1970 Gold Cup. A beautiful looking bay horse out of the grand-staying mare Tiberetta, that had been placed in three Aintree Grand Nationals, Spanish Steps was owned and trained by Mr Edward Courage, and was ridden by John Cook, a jockey fresh from securing a thrilling victory aboard Specify in the Grand National at Aintree.

In a big field of nineteen, many horses fitted the profile of a possible Irish National winner, including the consistent and durable Proud Tarquin, trained by race specialist Tom Dreaper, No Other, Cnoc Dubh and Vulture – all three-mile chase winners around Fairyhouse in their respective careers, another good English horse, The Pantheon, trained by Fred Rimell, former winner Herring Gull, and the likeable, seven-year-old, Francis Flood-trained mare, Money Boat, a horse that had run well before coming down at the second Becher's Brook in the Grand National. Also well fancied were Dim Wit and King's Sprite. Trainer Paddy Mullins had previously been successful with Vulpine and Herring Gull, and in Dim Wit, he had a most intriguing six-year-old novice. Well-weighted and going from strength to strength, Dim Wit had won his last three races, including over three miles at Naas and over a shorter distance at Fairyhouse in February, beating Alpheus in the process, a horse that then came out and won the Arkle Chase at the Cheltenham Festival. The nine-year-old King's Sprite was something of a dark horse. Trained by George Wells and ridden by Dan Moore's son Arthur, the lightly-weighted King's Sprite had finished second in the season's Leopardstown Chase, with L'Escargot third, and had also been narrowly beaten by the progressive Black Secret at Naas in January. Since those races, L'Escargot had trounced his opponents in the Gold Cup while Black Secret had been denied, by the narrowest of margins, by Specify at Aintree, marking King's Sprite down as a most dangerous horse for the Fairyhouse feature.

Despite the presence of quick ground, the early pace was steady as Proud Tarquin disputed the lead with No Other and the outsider Craobh Rua. L'Escargot was held up in the early running by jockey Tommy Carberry, and after a circuit had been completed, Proud Tarquin still held command from Craobh Rua, Vulture, Secret Vulgan and Cnoc Dubh, the field in general being closely bunched, with No Other a faller at the halfway stage. Sadly, The Pantheon broke down and was pulled-up with a circuit to run.

There were plenty of horses in with chances as the second circuit developed, Secret Vulgan moving forward behind Proud Tarquin, with Esban, Craobh Rua and Cnoc Dubh well to the fore, while from the rear, L'Escargot and King's Sprite began to make eye-catching progress.

With the race heating up intensely, the drama began to unfold. Spanish Steps was under real pressure when he fell five fences out, bringing down Herring Gull in the process, while Dim Wit appeared to be travelling well and looked primed for a strong challenge when clouting the fourth last and tumbling to the ground together with the five-year-old Deirdre's Joy. Next to go a fence later was Cnoc Dubh, although he was losing ground at the time.

With a string of casualties behind him, Proud Tarquin – jumping tremendously throughout – remained in front at the third last, and with the field strung out by this time, it was L'Escargot and King's Sprite that emerged as the chief dangers. But at the second last, the outlook was to change dramatically. Two lengths up, a terrible blunder when taking the fence saw Proud Tarquin lose ground, and the horse came away from the fence two lengths behind King's Sprite.

It was now King's Sprite that had the advantage at the last, but even though jumping the fence in front, L'Escargot was now looming as a major threat on the inside, while the game Proud Tarquin was once more putting in an asserted challenge. In a thrilling finish, King's Sprite proved strongest, holding on defiantly to edge Proud Tarquin by a length-and-a-half, with the gallant L'Escargot a mere three-quarters-of-a-length back in third. Both Proud Tarquin and L'Escargot had given their all in trying to peg back King's Sprite and both emerged with real credit, especially L'Escargot, who was deemed the hero in trying to emulate the likes of Prince Regent and Flyingbolt in carrying 12st 7lbs to victory, narrowly failing to give 36lbs to the winner. The great L'Escargot would enjoy a most fruitful remainder of his career, culminating with glorious victory at Aintree in the 1975 Grand National. Only eight horses completed the course – including Esban, winner in 1973 of the Scottish Grand National – and the narrowness of the course came in for criticism from the jockeys. In later years, the course would be widened.

So Arthur Moore joined his father in riding the winner of the Irish Grand National. Dan had ridden Golden Jack and Revelry to victory in the 1940s, and the win of King's Sprite gave a second race win to trainer George Wells, following the success of Umm in 1955. It had been the richest race in Irish steeplechasing history, and the big crowd at Fairyhouse had been treated to yet another wonderful spectacle as the name of King's Sprite was added to the illustrious roll of honour.

1971 IRISH GRAND NATIONAL RESULT

FATE	HORSE	AGE/WEIGHT	JOCKEY
1st	KING'S SPRITE	9.9.13	A.L.T. MOORE
2nd	PROUD TARQUIN	8.11.1	P. McCLOUGHLIN
3rd	L'ESCARGOT	8.12.7	T. CARBERRY
4th	CRAOBH RUA	7.9.7	T. KINANE
5th	Secret Vulgan	9.10.1	J.P. Bourke
6th	Dead Beat	9.9.7	J. Crowley
7th	Esban	7.9.7	C. Finnegan
8th	Money Boat	7.10.7	F. Berry
Fell	Beauair	7.9.7	P. Kiely
Fell	Cnoc Dubh	8.9.11	M. Ennis
Fell	Deirdre's Joy	5.9.7	P. Black
Fell	Dim Wit	6.10.5	M. Curran
Fell	No Other	8.11.6	R. Coonan
Fell	Spanish Steps	8.11.9	J. Cook
Pulled-Up	Sarejay Day	9.9.7	F. Carroll
Pulled-Up	Serpentine Lad	9.9.7	J.P. Harty
Pulled-Up	The Pantheon	8.10.5	T.W. Biddlecombe
Pulled-Up	Vulture	9.9.7	S. Barker
Brought Down	Herring Gull	9.11.1	H. Beasley

12 April 1971
Going – Good
Sponsor – Irish Distillers
Winner – £9,985
Race Distance – three miles
Time – 7mins 19.6secs
19 Ran
Winner trained by G.H. Wells
Winner owned by R. McIlhagga
King's Sprite, chestnut gelding by Pampered King – Imps Link

Betting – 3/1 Spanish Steps, 7/1 KING'S SPRITE, 8/1 Dim Wit & L'Escargot, 9/1 The Pantheon, 10/1 No Other, 11/1 Proud Tarquin, 14/1 Esban, 20/1 Herring Gull, 22/1 Secret Vulgan, 28/1 Cnoc Dubh & Money Boat, 33/1 Dead Beat, 50/1 Vulture, 66/1 Beauair, 100/1 Craobh Rua, Deirdre's Joy, Sarejay Day & Serpentine Lad.

Proud Tarquin and jockey P. McCloughlin finished second in 1971.

The great Irish Champion, L'Escargot, won two Cheltenham Gold Cups and one Aintree Grand National, but could never land the Irish National, despite a brave effort in 1971.

Right: *Race favourite Spanish Steps.*

1972 – DIM WIT

The two horses at the head of the handicap for the 1972 Irish Grand National had been the recent Cheltenham Gold Cup heroine, Glencarrig Lady, and the good Jim Dreaper-trained chaser, Leap Frog. However, the former had gone lame the Friday before the race and the prevailing heavy ground at Fairyhouse was totally against Leap Frog, so both horses were withdrawn. The absence of those two high-class horses meant that the giant bay horse, The Dikler, topped the weights on 11st 9lbs. From the powerful yard of Fulke Walwyn in Lambourn, The Dikler – a hard-pulling son of the excellent sire Vulgan – was an absolutely enormous animal, and had come mightily close to winning the Gold Cup at Cheltenham recently, just lacking the turn of foot to better Glencarrig Lady. That performance was sufficient to earn The Dikler favouritism at Fairyhouse, starting at 7/2 for jockey Barry Brogan.

Even without Glencarrig Lady and Leap Frog, it was an Irish National with plenty of class, for as well as The Dikler, the likes of Kinloch Brae, 1971 hero King's Sprite, and former Power Gold Cup winner No Other all took part. Kinloch Brae was a particularly interesting contender. Having been a fantastic novice three seasons before – winning the Cathcart Chase at Cheltenham – Kinloch Brae had been hot favourite for the Cheltenham Gold Cup in 1970 when trained by Willie O'Grady, and jumping like the proverbial stag for most of the way, looked certain to win until a mistimed jump three fences out landed him on the deck. Thereafter, the horse was never quite the same, developing leg trouble before being sent to Toby Balding's in England. Owned by the Duchess of Westminster and ridden, as in that Gold Cup, by Tim Hyde, there was some doubt as to whether Kinloch Brae was back to anywhere near his best, despite narrowly failing to concede 10lbs to the good handicapper The Ghost in the Kim Muir Chase at Cheltenham. Still, Kinloch Brae was extremely well treated on his best form, and began the race well backed at 5/1.

Others of interest included the novices Bahia Dorada and Shaneman, and the second-season chaser Dim Wit. Frank Berry had won the Gold Cup on Glencarrig Lady, and in that horse's absence, switched to the mare's stablemate at Francis Flood's yard, Bahia Dorada. As a hurdler, Bahia Dorada had proved that stamina was his forte, and although he had, at times, looked uncomfortable jumping fences in fast-run two-mile chases, the longer trip of the Irish National looked certain to play to the horse's strengths. Trained by Tos Taaffe and ridden by future flat trainer Ben Hannon, Shaneman had formerly been one of the leading hurdlers in Ireland. Adjusting very well to fences, Shaneman had impressed most recently when thrashing his opposition, including the subsequent Aintree Grand National third Black Secret, over three miles at Naas. Behind only The Dikler in the weights, Dim Wit had been one of the leading novice chasers of the previous season. Trained by Paddy Mullins and ridden by Matt Curran, the chestnut was a previous Fairyhouse winner over two-miles-two-furlongs on heavy ground, and also a race distance winner on soft and heavy ground, so the course and conditions seemed ideal for a bold challenge. Despite pulling-up, having jumped uncharacteristically poorly

in the recent Cheltenham Gold Cup, Dim Wit had won over three miles at Naas earlier in the season, and was well supported at 15/2.

On heavy ground, it was understandable that the pace was steady as the runners endeavoured to conserve vital stamina for what was sure to be a gruelling test. Passing the stands with a circuit to go, No Other led from Bahia Dorada, Highway View, Kinloch Brae, Dim Wit and The Dikler, before Kinloch Brae smoothly jumped through into second place early on the second lap, until passed by the resurgent Highway View eight out.

Having made steady, determined progress throughout the second circuit, the outsider Beggar's Way came through and jumped to the front five fences out from Highway View and Kinloch Brae. Here, another outsider, Khan, fell, interfering with Shaneman as he did so and leaving Hannon most frustrated post-race, the jockey adamant his mount would have gone close bar the incident.

Beggar's Way had shot four lengths clear going to the next fence, but now Veuve and jockey Tommy Carberry loomed up as real contenders. Although Beggar's Way still led narrowly jumping three out, Veuve was going far better, and approached the second last looking the likely winner, with Dim Wit beginning a challenge from further back.

But the second last fence was to decide the 1972 Irish National. Jumping the fence well, Veuve crumpled agonisingly on landing, coming down to the groans of those that had backed the 16/1 shot, leaving Carberry to curse his ill-luck. The trailing Highway View, ridden by Pat Black, was hampered by the fall, although that horse's chance had surely gone by then.

Left clear by the unlucky departure of Veuve, it was Dim Wit that was able to cut down the tiring Beggar's Way on the run to the final fence, sail the last and come home an easy eight-length winner. Beggar's Way took second with Bahia Dorada (having spoiled his round with poor jumping) staying on for third, half-a-length back. Of the others, The Dikler's hard race at Cheltenham and the heavy ground had taken their toll, and the horse was pulled-up four out, while Kinloch Brae had been unable to quicken when the leaders pulled away at the fourth last. Also pulled-up was the Mick O'Toole-trained Red Candle, and that horse would go on to win the Hennessy Gold Cup at Newbury in 1973 when trained in England by Ricky Vallance.

Dim Wit had proved himself a very good horse given the right conditions, and despite what had happened to the likes of Veuve and Shaneman during the race, Curran was adamant his horse would have won anyway, stating he had a dream run down the inside, keeping Dim Wit behind the leaders, for he was a horse that tended to get lazy when hitting the front. Dim Wit gave Kilkenny trainer Paddy Mullins a third Irish National following those of Vulpine and Herring Gull, and provided the thrill of a lifetime for the horse's owner, veterinary surgeon Jeremiah O'Neill, who had purchased Dim Wit for the bargain price of 90 guineas as a foal.

1972 IRISH GRAND NATIONAL RESULT

FATE	HORSE	AGE/WEIGHT	JOCKEY
1st	DIM WIT	7.10.13	M. CURRAN
2nd	BEGGAR'S WAY	8.9.7	P. KIELY
3rd	BAHIA DORADA	7.9.12	F. BERRY
4th	Highway View	7.10.10	P. Black
5th	Shaneman	7.9.11	B. Hannon
6th	Kinloch Brae	9.10.10	T.E. Hyde
7th	French Alliance	10.9.7	S. Shields
Fell	Khan	8.9.11	F. Carroll
Fell	Veuve	8.10.1	T. Carberry
Pulled-Up	Kildrum	8.9.7	J.P. Bourke
Pulled-Up	No Other	9.10.6	Mr J. Fowler
Pulled-Up	Red Candle	8.9.7	F. Leavy
Pulled-Up	The Dikler	9.11.9	B. Brogan
Brought Down	King's Sprite	10.10.0	A.L.T. Moore

3 April 1972
Going – Heavy
Sponsor – Irish Distillers
Winner – £9,162
Race Distance – three miles
Time – 7mins 53secs
14 Ran
Winner trained by P. Mullins
Winner owned by J.J. O'Neill
Dim Wit, chestnut gelding by Star Signal – Miss Wise.

Betting – 7/2 The Dikler, 5/1 Kinloch Brae, 7/1 Bahia Dorada, Highway View & Shaneman, 15/2 DIM WIT, 15/1 Red Candle, 16/1 Veuve, 20/1 King's Sprite, 33/1 Beggar's Way, Khan & No Other, 100/1 French Alliance & Kildrum.

Dim Wit, winner in 1972.

The giant bay The Dikler, favourite in 1972.

1973 – TARTAN ACE

Of all the renewals in the 1970s, the Irish Grand National of 1973 was perhaps the highest quality race. The 1973 edition was stocked with classy individuals, some that were young horses on the rise, and some that were veterans attempting to rekindle their careers. With horses such as Inkslinger, Argent, L'Escargot, Dim Wit, Sea Brief, Garoupe, Skymas, King's Sprite and French Tan in the field, it made for an intriguing contest.

Top weight and favourite was the brilliant young American chaser, Inkslinger. A six-year-old sent over from the United States into training at Dan Moore's yard, Inkslinger had been given just two warm-up races over Anglo-Irish fences before taking his chance at the recent Cheltenham Festival. There, Inkslinger showed off his brilliance and enormous potential by first winning the Two Mile Champion Chase and then, two days later, the Cathcart Chase. Inkslinger had settled well in both his races at Cheltenham, quickening well up that famous finishing hill, and was quickly talked about as a possible Gold Cup winner of 1974. Quick ground was deemed necessary for Inkslinger to be at his best, for despite winning over 2m 6f in America, he was used to running over shorter distances, and naturally for a race like the Irish National, stamina was a concern, as was the big weight of 12st 2lbs. As well as Inkslinger, Moore also saddled dual Gold Cup winner L'Escargot. Recently coming fourth behind former Irish National favourite The Dikler at Cheltenham in the Gold Cup, L'Escargot subsequently finished third behind the brilliant Aintree horse Red Rum in the Grand National.

Of the three former Irish National winners in the field, both Garoupe and King's Sprite had been out of form recently but could not be discounted given their previous exploits at Fairyhouse, while, as he had proved in 1972, Dim Wit was at his best on soft or heavy going, a far cry from the firm ground present at Fairyhouse in 1973. Former Cheltenham Gold Cup runner-up French Tan, now eleven, took his chance under jockey Pat Black, while of the younger horses, Skymas, Sea Brief, Argent and Tartan Ace all had their followers. Skymas was another horse apparently better suited for shorter distances, but was of a high-class. Skymas, as it turned out, would eventually prove something of a Cheltenham specialist, winning the Mackeson Gold Cup later in 1973 before, as an older horse, winning the Two Mile Champion Chase in 1976 and 1977. Sea Brief, now a dual winner of the Leopardstown Chase, had gone to Cheltenham for the previous year's Festival touted as the 'new Arkle', having enjoyed a breathtaking novice chase campaign, and although he did not win that year's Totalisator

Champion Novice Chase, the horse was tough and durable, and carried the Arkle colours of Anne, Duchess of Westminster for trainer Jim Dreaper. Argent too had been a high-ranking novice, falling when favourite for the Totalisator Champion Novice Chase in 1971, yet retained plenty of ability, finishing third in the season's Leopardstown Chase, and was partnered by former winning jockey Bobby Coonan. Tartan Ace was a promising six-year-old chestnut trained by Tom Costello. The horse had won three chases in a row earlier in the season but had been defeated on his two most recent starts. With a low handicap mark in Ireland, Costello resisted the temptation of sending Tartan Ace to Cheltenham for the Totalisator Champion Novice Chase, instead electing to run him off a light weight in the Irish National.

Setting off in front, it was Skymas that dictated the early pace, tracked by Sea Brief and Inkslinger. By the time the stands were passed after one circuit of action, Skymas and Sea Brief were in control, chased by Inkslinger, Doonbeg and Garoupe, with Argent bringing up the rear.

Eight fences from home, Skymas and Sea Brief pulled well clear of Inkslinger (jumping immaculately throughout) and Doonbeg, but a fence later, the youngster Tartan Ace had made rapid progress and loomed up to challenge the two leaders.

Sea Brief made a terrible mess of the fifth last, and from there, the race developed into a battle between Skymas and Tartan Ace. In truth, Tartan Ace had looked the likely winner from the third last, but it was not until approaching the final fence that he was able to shake off the brave and versatile Skymas. As soon as he did so, it was a case of popping the last fence, which he did, and having been expertly and patiently guided round by jockey Jackie Cullen, Tartan Ace then came well clear up the run-in to win by eight lengths from Skymas. Ten lengths further back in third place was Sea Brief, just edging out the staying-on Inkslinger. The lattermost was aimed at and ran in the 1974 Cheltenham Gold Cup, where unfortunately he fell behind the brilliant Irish horse Captain Christy.

Tartan Ace was purchased by Costello as a foal from breeder Mr John Twomey from North County Cork, and the horse had proved hard to break before being put to showjumping, where he won three competitions. Tartan Ace was then sold as a four-year-old to Mrs Sean Graham, the wife of the well-known Belfast bookmaker. It was a first ride in the race for Cullen, and Tartan Ace had responded with a superb round of jumping to become the comfortable Irish Grand National winner of 1973.

Inkslinger, favourite in 1973.

1973 IRISH GRAND NATIONAL RESULT

FATE	HORSE	AGE/WEIGHT	JOCKEY	23 April 1973
1st	TARTAN ACE	6.9.7	J. CULLEN	Going – Firm
2nd	SKYMAS	8.10.3	T.S. MURPHY	Sponsor – Irish Distillers
3rd	SEA BRIEF	7.11.6	S. BARKER	Winner – £9,305
4th	Inkslinger	6.12.2	T. Carberry	Race Distance – three miles
5th	Garoupe	9.10.13	F. Berry	Time – 6mins 54.2secs
6th	Doonbeg	8.9.7	T. Kinane	14 Ran
7th	Shaneman	8.9.7	P. Kiely	Winner trained by T. Costello
8th	L'Escargot	9.11.9	A.L.T. Moore	Winner owned by Mrs S. Graham
9th	French Tan	11.10.2	P. Black	Tartan Ace, chestnut gelding by Ace Of Clubs – Auld Laid Shawl.
10th	King's Sprite	11.9.7	F. Leavy	
Fell	Arklow	8.9.7	J. Bracken	
Pulled-Up	Argent	9.11.9	R. Coonan	Betting – 7/2 Inkslinger, 5/1 Sea Brief, 6/1 Shaneman, 7/1 Argent, 8/1 Garoupe,
Pulled-Up	Dim Wit	8.11.7	J.P. Harty	9/1 L'Escargot & Skymas, 10/1 TARTAN ACE, 20/1 Dim Wit, French Tan & King's
Pulled-Up	On Straight	8.9.7	J. Brassil	Sprite, 66/1 Arklow, Doonbeg & On Straight.

1974 – COLEBRIDGE

The Irish Grand National of 1974 was blessed with the presence of the brilliant winner of the recent Cheltenham Gold Cup. A seven-year-old bay trained by multiple Irish National winner Pat Taaffe, the superb but somewhat eccentric Captain Christy had become the first novice since Mont Tremblant twenty-two years previously to capture chasing's Blue Riband, surviving a monumental last-fence blunder at Cheltenham to power past The Dikler and win by five lengths. As a young horse, Captain Christy had proved particularly hit-and-miss, occasionally showing his enormous potential but too often proving frustrating, either not completing in his races or demonstrating an almost mad side to his temperament during his homework. Despite this, the horse was an outstanding hurdler, good enough to finish third in the 1973 Champion Hurdle at Cheltenham behind Comedy Of Errors, before embarking on a novice chase season. As a novice, Captain Christy had proved most unreliable, although undoubtedly eye-catching when on his game, yet it remained a huge risk when the horse was asked to compete against modern-day greats such as Pendil and The Dikler at Cheltenham. But rising to the challenge under jockey Bobby Beasley, the horse was able to switch off towards the rear of the field before making a devastating late challenge and winning in breathtaking style. It was a surprise when Captain Christy was not made favourite at Fairyhouse, but the horse did have to carry a stone more than his nearest rival, and it was noted that no horse apart from Arkle had won the Cheltenham Gold Cup and Irish National in the same season.

Considered most likely to give Captain Christy a race of real menace were Colebridge and L'Escargot. Since his memorable Gold Cup wins at the start of the decade, trainer Dan Moore and owner Mr Raymond Guest had aimed L'Escargot principally at the Grand National at Aintree, a race in which he was again placed in 1974 behind the incomparable Red Rum. Although now eleven, the much-loved chestnut had slid down the handicap a little, offering a fair chance of Fairyhouse glory. Colebridge, sired by Vulgan and related to Arkle, was the representative of the Kilsallaghan stables that had so dominated the race for many years. Jim Dreaper had not long been in charge at the yard having taken over for his father Tom, and the handler certainly had his charge in prime form, the bay recently carrying 12st 7lbs to victory in a three-mile handicap chase at Naas. This performance shot Colebridge to favouritism at Fairyhouse, where he was partnered by Dreaper's stable jockey, Eddie Wright.

With the diminutive but consistent Highway View – trained by Bunny Cox – and the seven-year-old Naas winner Southern Quest providing a degree of strength in depth, the ten runners were sent on their way on officially good ground. Recognised as a front-runner, it was indeed Southern Quest that set off at a good, sensible gallop, one that he would maintain for much of the race. The horse was tracked for much of the first lap by Slaney Gorge, Colebridge, Highway View and Hillhead VI, with Captain Christy, as at Cheltenham, settled towards the rear.

Then came the big shock of the race. As the runners approached the downhill seventh fence, the leaders were able to clear it without incident. But merely biding his time at the back, Captain Christy met it wrong and toppled over on landing, bringing huge gasps from the crowd. Captain Christy was a most talented racehorse, and his ability probably merited one more Gold Cup title, but having already shown a severe dislike for heavy ground, he was pulled-up at Cheltenham in 1975 behind the mudlark Ten Up. However, Captain Christy did win a pair of King George VI Chases at Kempton Park, in 1974 and 1975 (the second time thrashing the very good horse Bula in course record time), but tendon trouble after that 1975 race led to his retirement. After the Irish National, Taaffe was philosophical in defeat, merely saying 'that's racing'. None the worse for his premature departure, Captain Christy came out the next day and jumped his rivals ragged at Fairyhouse to win the Powers Gold Cup.

With Captain Christy out of the race, Southern Quest bounded on, pulling six lengths clear at the start of the second lap from Highway View, Hillhead VI and Slaney Gorge. Meanwhile, Wright was displaying bold nerve, patiently guiding Colebridge through from the back of the field to challenge with intent at the final regulation fence.

Southern Quest began to tire approaching four out, and it was little Highway View that took up the running, but Hillhead VI, L'Escargot and, most significantly, Colebridge, chased the new leader ominously. Although Highway View led over the third last, Colebridge quickly loomed alongside, and going on in the home straight, the Dreaper-trained horse soon put daylight between himself and his rivals, winning the race comfortably by five lengths, with L'Escargot out-fighting Highway View for second place.

Colebridge had shown fine stamina and jumping ability, and had dominated the closing stages of the race. The horse's dam, Cherry Bud, was a half-sister to Arkle, and the family class enabled Colebridge to one day finish third in a Cheltenham Gold Cup (behind Royal Frolic in 1976). Stable jockey Eddie Wright had ridden a perfectly judged race on the winner, and paid a suitable compliment to the newest Irish National winner by claiming Colebridge to be the best horse he had ever ridden.

Cheltenham Gold Cup winner Captain Christy, second favourite for the 1974 Irish National.

1974 IRISH GRAND NATIONAL RESULT

FATE	HORSE	AGE/WEIGHT	JOCKEY
1st	COLEBRIDGE	10.11.2	E. WRIGHT
2nd	L'ESCARGOT	11.10.8	T. CARBERRY
3rd	HIGHWAY VIEW	9.9.8	M. MORRIS
4th	Hillhead VI	10.9.7	T. Kinane
5th	Doonbeg	9.9.7	P. Kiely
6th	Vibrax	7.9.7	J. Donaghy
7th	Slaney Gorge	7.9.7	R. Shortt
8th	Southern Quest	7.9.7	J. Bracken
Fell	Captain Christy	7.12.2	H.R. Beasley
Pulled-Up	Kobuk	12.9.7	F. Berry

15 April 1974

Going – Good

Sponsor – Irish Distillers

Winner – £8,916

Race Distance – three miles four furlongs

Time – 7mins 50.1secs

10 Ran

Winner trained by J.T. Dreaper

Winner owned by Mrs P.E. Burrell

Colebridge, bay gelding by Vulgan – Cherry Bud.

Betting – 11/5 COLEBRIDGE, 3/1 Captain Christy, 4/1 Highway View & L'Escargot, 17/2 Southern Quest, 33/1 Hillhead VI, 40/1 Vibrax, 50/1 Slaney Gorge, 66/1 Doonbeg, 100/1 Kobuk.

1975 – BROWN LAD

One of the most striking performances at the recent Cheltenham Festival had come from the Jim Dreaper-trained Brown Lad. A confirmed mudlark that had been aimed at the Sun Alliance Chase following an exceptional year of novice chasing, Brown Lad was re-routed to run in the Lloyds Bank Hurdle on the Wednesday at Cheltenham after Tuesday's card had been abandoned because of treacherous weather. On extremely heavy ground, Brown Lad showed what an adaptable and genuine horse he was by winning with ease, exuding class as he did so. Although he was only a novice, Brown Lad had, earlier in the season, been a most impressive winner of the highly regarded Reynoldstown Novice Chase at Ascot, and was already being mentioned in some quarters as a possible Cheltenham Gold Cup winner of 1976. If such talk was to be believed, the 10st 5lbs that Brown Lad was allotted for the 1975 Irish Grand National seemed a very lenient weight, and the horse was unsurprisingly made the red-hot 6/4 favourite for the race. Jim Dreaper (who also ran the useful bay Lean Forward) was fresh from sending out his first Cheltenham Gold Cup winner, with the equally mud-loving Ten Up triumphing the month before, and now the trainer hoped Brown Lad could further enhance the wonderful family record in the Irish Grand National, a record he had improved through Colebridge in 1974 following years of dominance by Tom Dreaper.

Top weight was the enigmatic Captain Christy. The horse had been unable to retain his Gold Cup crown at Cheltenham, pulling-up when favourite on unsuitable heavy ground behind Ten Up, but the horse had lost none of his brilliance, he simply preferred a sound surface. Between the meetings at Cheltenham and Fairyhouse, Captain Christy had responded pleasingly by winning a handicap at Naas, and Pat Taaffe's charge started second favourite for the Irish National, where he was ridden by Bobby Coonan.

With Argent a non-runner because he was due to be sold, Brown Lad's stablemate Twelve Pins withdrawn through lameness, and the decent stayer War Bonnet having strained a tendon the Saturday beforehand, the original declarations were reduced to just eight starters, the smallest field since Flyingbolt defeated five others in 1966. Rounding out the field were the Leopardstown Chase winner Highway View, the future dual-Two Mile Champion Chase winner Skymas, young Spanish Tan, the mount of Frank Berry, and outsiders Tubs VI and Jimmy Gee.

Before the race, the contest had looked a match between Brown Lad and Captain Christy, two of the finest Irish chasers of the 1970s. The difference between the two was their contrasting ground preferences. Brown Lad thrived on soft to heavy ground, while Captain Christy was the opposite, requiring good or faster ground to be at his best. When the ground on Irish National day came up soft, all indications pointed to victory for the novice, and as the race progressed, there was little to alter this prediction. Brown Lad's stablemate Lean Forward set off in front, followed by Tubs VI, Captain Christy and Brown Lad, with Spanish Tan at the back of the field.

Passing the stands after one circuit, the order remained the same, although it was evident that Captain Christy was now beginning to make mistakes.

Captain Christy was clearly uncomfortable on the surface, and it was no surprise to see the horse pulled-up with a mile to run, just as he had been at Cheltenham. After the race, Coonan explained that the horse had simply been unable to go through the soft ground.

Brown Lad had stood right off the first ditch in the race but had soon settled down into a smooth rhythm, jumping impeccably the rest of the way. Five fences out, the horse was travelling supremely, and a fence later, Brown Lad had joined Lean Forward at the head of affairs. Moving through the ground like a class act, he was able to come clear on the run to the second last fence.

Clearing the last two fences well, Brown Lad demonstrated his finishing power by coming well clear and recording a most impressive eight-length victory. In second place came the consistent Highway View, with the veteran Tubs VI (fourteenth in the 1974 Grand National at Aintree behind Red Rum) third having run well for a long way. Skymas and Lean Forward were the only others to complete the course.

It may have not been the most competitive of Irish Nationals (a rare exception in the seventies), for Captain Christy was clearly not at his best on soft ground and the majority of the remainder were distinctly average performers, but Brown Lad had won with authority and with the minimum of fuss. Jockey Tommy Carberry – winning his first Irish National – stated that if any horse had challenged Brown Lad towards the finish, his horse would have found plenty in reserve. Jim Dreaper had apparently inherited his father's gift for training Irish National winners, for this was his second in a row (with more to come). For his part, Tom Dreaper compared Brown Lad favourably to one of his Irish National winners, Royal Approach, a horse that was also a novice when he won in 1954, although Dreaper senior believed Royal Approach to have more pace that Brown Lad. Jim Dreaper had mentioned that Brown Lad's legs were not the best and that the horse did not stand a lot of work, however, Brown Lad would hold a lofty position in the ranks of steeplechasers in Ireland and England for some years to come. Brown Lad would compete in three Cheltenham Gold Cups, finishing second twice (1976 and 1978), and fifth in 1979. Ironically, the two occasions where he finished second were achieved on good to firm and good ground respectively, illustrating both the class and bravery of the horse, and although he never looked like beating the winners of those races (Royal Frolic and Midnight Court), Brown Lad's reputation was much enhanced by those performances. By the time Brown Lad finally got his favoured heavy ground for the Gold Cup, the horse was thirteen, and although he started joint favourite, he was simply run off his feet before staying-on to finish fifth.

Opposite: *Brown Lad and Tommy Carberry won in 1975, the first of the horse's three wins in the race.*

1975 IRISH GRAND NATIONAL RESULT

FATE	HORSE	AGE/WEIGHT	JOCKEY
1st	BROWN LAD	9.10.5	T. CARBERRY
2nd	HIGHWAY VIEW	10.9.12	M. MORRIS
3rd	TUBS VI	12.9.7	P. KIELY
4th	Skymas	10.10.13	S. Shields
5th	Lean Forward	9.11.2	P. McCloughlin
Fell	Jimmy Gee	7.9.7	Mr T. McCartan
Pulled-Up	Captain Christy	8.12.0	R. Coonan
Pulled-Up	Spanish Tan	7.9.8	F. Berry

31 March 1975

Going – Soft

Sponsor – Irish Distillers

Winner – £8,643

Race Distance – three miles four furlongs

Time – 8mins 35.8secs

8 Ran

Winner trained by J.T. Dreaper

Winner owned by Mrs P.E. Burrell

Brown Lad, bay gelding by Sayajirao – Caicos.

Betting – 6/4 BROWN LAD, 3/1 Captain Christy, 5/1 Highway View, 6/1 Lean Forward, 10/1 Spanish Tan, 15/1 Skymas, 50/1 Tubs VI, 100/1 Jimmy Gee.

1976 – BROWN LAD

After a somewhat disappointing turnout the year before, the field for the 1976 Irish Grand National was most competitive, with a number of class horses joined by those of promising potential. The class element was provided by the stablemates Brown Lad and Ten Up. No horse had won the Irish National in successive years since The Gift (1883 & 1884), and only four horses in total had won the race twice, but Brown Lad had run a fine race in the recent Cheltenham Gold Cup, for despite hating the fast ground, he had jumped carefully before staying-on to finish second to Royal Frolic. Brown Lad's form throughout the season had been excellent, and despite carrying top weight of 12st 2lbs, the record crowd present at Fairyhouse made the horse a worthy favourite at 7/2. Ten Up was perhaps even more of a mudlark than Brown Lad, the horse having ploughed through the most treacherous of conditions with glee when taking the 1975 Cheltenham Gold Cup. Since his finest hour, Ten Up had developed a tendency to break blood vessels, which often prompted trainer Jim Dreaper to give the horse preventative injections before his races. Such injections were prohibited in England, and as such, Ten Up could not take his place in the 1976 Gold Cup field. There were no such worries in Ireland, yet the feeling existed that Ten Up was a horse that had never quite matched the rich form of his Gold Cup year, and this was reflected in his price of 16/1 at Fairyhouse, where he was partnered by the excellent amateur and future trainer, Ted Walsh.

Like Jim Dreaper, trainer Edward O'Grady was double handed in the race, represented by a pair of progressive youngsters in Kilmakilloge and Prolan. Jockey Mouse Morris had elected to partner the novice Kilmakilloge, a rapidly improving young chaser. Kilmakilloge would be having just his fifth run over fences in the Irish National and was a hard-pulling individual, yet the horse was full of talent and had a low weight, while it had been proven time and again that novices had every chance of success in the race. The grey horse Prolan, a fine jumper and stayer, had won the Kim Muir Chase at the season's Cheltenham Festival before running a bold race in the Grand National at Aintree, where the horse was unluckily brought down at the second Becher's Brook. Like Kilmakilloge, a seven-year-old, Prolan had even less weight (9st 9lbs) to carry than his stablemate and was ridden at Fairyhouse by Tommy Kinane.

Trainer Mick O'Toole similarly ran two horses in Bit Of A Jig and Davy Lad. Bit Of A Jig had proven himself a versatile type, for as well as being a decent chaser, the horse was a very useful hurdler, recently winning the Lloyds Bank Hurdle at the Cheltenham Festival, and was a horse that appreciated quick ground. Davy Lad was another horse that appreciated softer conditions, and although somewhat of a lazy character, he was a true stayer. The horse had won the Sun Alliance Novices Hurdle at the Cheltenham Festival the season before, and despite his light weight in the Irish National, the bay had a touch of class.

Others in a mouth-watering line-up included recent Gold Cup participants Flashy Boy and Roman Bar, the promising, if sketchy-jumping, youngster Fort Fox, Highway View, twice placed in the race, and the sole English challenger, Zeta's Son. Trained by Peter Bailey, Zeta's Son had come down at the tenth fence in the Topham Trophy at Aintree's Grand National meeting, but was considered to be a horse of high potential.

Wearing first-time blinkers, Tommy Carberry had Brown Lad well placed from the outset, where big outsider April's Canter – winner of a recent moderate race at Roscommon – showed in front from Prolan and Fort Fox, and although Roman Bar fell at the tenth fence, the rest of the field remained closely bunched on the second circuit.

April's Canter continued to lead on from Prolan, Fort Fox, Flashy Boy and Zeta's Son, but the race soon began to lose many of its number. Dromore fell eight out, followed by the fancied Fort Fox a fence later. Then shortly after Fort Fox's exit, Highway View slipped-up on the flat, bringing down I'm Happy in the process. These incidents changed the race outlook dramatically, for although the unconsidered April's Canter still led, Brown Lad moved strongly into a leading position just behind, while Ten Up had come through the field and appeared ready to deliver a meaningful challenge as they approached five out.

Preceded only by April's Canter and the fine-jumping Flashy Boy, Ten Up took off at the fifth last in third place but crumpled agonisingly on landing. It transpired after the race that, once more, Ten Up had burst a blood vessel on the approach to the fence, and the unlucky horse had been denied a genuine chance of further big race glory.

The race now appeared wide open by the fourth last, with April's Canter and Flashy Boy still leading, but Brown Lad and the improving Davy Lad getting into the thick of the action, while running on from further back was Bit Of A Jig. Flashy Boy, ridden by Barry Brogan, hit the front at the third last and tried to stretch the field. But no sooner had the horse made his move than he wilted badly, seemingly hitting a wall and fading timidly. After the race, Brogan explained that he thought he would win at the third last but conceded that Flashy Boy simply did not stay.

Pouncing on the weakening Flashy Boy, Brown Lad took the race by the scruff of the neck, and as soon as the reigning champion took control by the second last, the result was a foregone conclusion. In a matter of strides, the race was over, and displaying his true class, Brown Lad came clear, jumped the final fences with grace and conviction, and to tremendous vocal encouragement, stormed up the run in to win by four lengths from the surprising April's Canter. Two-and-a-half lengths further back came Bit Of A Jig, with Flashy Boy fourth, Davy Lad fifth, Kilmakilloge sixth and Prolan seventh. Zeta's Son was pulled-up entering the home straight. Of the defeated horses, Zeta's Son went on to win the Hennessy Gold Cup at Newbury later in the season, before being tragically killed in the 1977 Grand National at Aintree, while Davy Lad enjoyed his finest hour winning the 1977 Cheltenham Gold Cup, before being forced to retire through injury when only eight-years-old.

Brown Lad had benefited enormously through the fitting of blinkers, jumping swiftly throughout and becoming just the fifth dual-winner of the Irish National. He was, without doubt, a fine racehorse with real class and seemed to be improving with age. Like Colebridge before him, Brown Lad was owned by Mrs Peter Burrell, and she became the first owner to win the race three years in a row.

Ten Up, pictured here being led in at Cheltenham by owner the Duchess of Westminster, was a faller in the 1976 Irish National.

1976 IRISH GRAND NATIONAL RESULT

FATE	HORSE	AGE/WEIGHT	JOCKEY	19 April 1976
1st	BROWN LAD	10.12.2	T. CARBERRY	Going – Good
2nd	APRIL'S CANTER	8.9.7	M. CUMMINS	Sponsor – Irish Distillers
3rd	BIT OF A JIG	8.9.9	L. O'DONNELL	Winner – £10,821
4th	Flashy Boy	8.10.8	B. Brogan	Race Distance – three miles four furlongs
5th	Davy Lad	6.10.0	Mr R.S. O'Toole	Time – 7mins 51.8secs
6th	Kilmakilloge	7.10.1	M. Morris	15 Ran
7th	Prolan	7.9.9	T. Kinane	Winner trained by J.T. Dreaper
8th	Harlent	6.9.7	E. McDonald	Winner owned by Mrs P.E. Burrell
Fell	Dromore	8.9.7	J. Brassil	Brown Lad, bay gelding by Sayajirao – Caicos.
Fell	Fort Fox	7.10.8	P. Black	
Fell	Highway View	11.9.13	S. Shields	
Fell	Roman Bar	7.9.12	G. Newman	Betting – 7/2 BROWN LAD, 4/1 Kilmakilloge, 7/1 Prolan, 15/2 Fort Fox, 8/1 Bit
Fell	Ten Up	9.11.11	Mr T.M. Walsh	Of A Jig, 10/1 I'm Happy, 12/1 Flashy Boy, 14/1 Davy Lad & Highway View,
Pulled-Up	Zeta's Son	7.9.10	R. Coonan	16/1 Ten Up, 20/1 Roman Bar & Zeta's Son, 40/1 Dromore, 100/1 April's Canter
Brought Down	I'm Happy	10.9.7	P. Kiely	& Harlent.

1977 – BILLYCAN

A big field of twenty horses for the 1977 Irish Grand National was headlined by the first two home in the recent Cheltenham Gold Cup, and was greatly enhanced by the presence of the leading staying chaser in Ireland during the season. Furthermore, the betting market was extremely tight, with these three horses – Davy Lad, Tied Cottage and Bannow Rambler – each attracting plenty of support. A most exciting renewal of the race (worth over £5,000 more to the winner than in 1976) looked assured.

Some had considered Davy Lad to be a somewhat fortunate winner of the Gold Cup at Cheltenham. Not among the first five in the betting, the horse benefited from the tragic, fatal fall of former champion hurdler Lanzarote early in the race, an incident that saw favourite Bannow Rambler brought down. Later in the race, another challenger, Summerville, broke down when travelling like the winner. But it could not be denied that Davy Lad had shown strong stamina on his favoured soft surface, meeting the last fence in stride and powering up the hill to beat Tied Cottage by six lengths. Davy Lad next went to Aintree with a featherweight in terms of a current Gold Cup champion, but was to get no further than the third fence. So it was that Davy Lad arrived at Fairyhouse relatively fresh for the Irish National. In addition, he did not even have to carry top weight, and with soft ground present, had a superb chance of joining Arkle as the only horse to win the Gold Cup and Irish National in the same season. As usual, Dessie Hughes took the ride for trainer Mick O'Toole.

Both Tied Cottage and Bannow Rambler were class Irish chasers that won many races in the late seventies, and in the case of Tied Cottage, early eighties. Trained by Dan Moore and ridden by Moore's son-in-law, Tommy Carberry, Tied Cottage had won the Sun Alliance Chase at Cheltenham in 1976 and was a bay horse that loved to front-run. The horse had run the race of his life in the Gold Cup and had only been collared at the final fence by Davy Lad, having led for most of the race. The horse had a fair racing weight in the Irish National of 10st 10lbs, and the popular horse started second favourite at 6/1. Favourite, as in the Gold Cup, was Bannow Rambler, the mount of Frank Berry. Top weight with 12st, Bannow Rambler had already won the season's Leopardstown and Thyestes Chases, and was trying to pull off a rare treble, last achieved by Kerforo.

As well as Davy Lad, a number of horses arrived at Fairyhouse seeking compensation for failing to complete in the recent Grand National at Aintree, including Castleruddery, Roman Bar and War Bonnet. Others of significance in the betting market included Shuil Donn and Billycan. Shuil Donn, trained by Pat Casserley, was a mare that had not been subjected to the rigours of Cheltenham or Aintree, instead winning at Naas the month before with great ease. Trained by Adrian Maxwell, the athletic chestnut Billycan had finished runner-up to Gay Spartan in the Sun Alliance Chase at Cheltenham, although the horse may have won but for being badly hampered by a faller at the final fence. The horse seemed to be on the rise, and was partnered at Fairyhouse by the capable Mouse Morris.

One of the biggest Easter Monday crowds in years was to witness a topsy-turvy Irish National that was, unsurprisingly, led for a long way by the tough and determined Tied Cottage. However, a huge roar of dismay erupted at the ninth fence when the favourite Bannow Rambler came to grief. After the race, Berry explained that the horse had been distracted by the vast number of people in the crowd cheering and shouting, and that the horse simply never saw the fence, crashing right through it. Another horse that was clearly not going to win was Davy Lad. Almost from the outset, the horse seemed disinterested and unwilling to respond to the urgings of his jockey. Hughes constantly tried to wake Davy Lad into a sense of urgency, but the horse was having none of it, and eventually trailed in last. Whether his fall at Aintree had left its mark was unclear, but the horse, although lazy by nature, was unrecognisable from the one that had stormed home at Cheltenham.

With a number of the big guns misfiring, the opportunity presented itself to others to stake their claim, although more grief lay in wait later on. Trainer Paddy Mullins, a three-time winner of the race, had a trio of runners representing him, but Escott had already come to grief by the time the quietly fancied Brendons Road came down, four out, when going well. Mullins' third runner, Kiltotan, was pulled-up. At the same time that Brendons Road fell, the 1976 runner-up April's Canter was pulled-up. The mare had run very well again, but there was clearly something amiss when she stopped quickly approaching the fourth last. Sadly, it transpired the horse had broken a leg.

With runners dropping like flies, the outsider Dromore screamed through to lead jumping the fourth last, with Tied Cottage, War Bonnet and Billycan all travelling purposely. Of the quartet, it was Billycan that was going the strongest, and when Morris asked the horse for his effort running to the third last, the response was instant. Picking up Dromore in a matter of strides, Billycan went for home, and after jumping three out, the race was his bar a fall. Putting daylight between himself and the chasing pack, Billycan jumped the final fences in impressive fashion, and winning the applause of the crowd, the sheepskin-noseband-wearing chestnut flew home a convincing ten-length winner. Tied Cottage may not have jumped as well as he did at Cheltenham, and was outpaced at the third last when Billycan made his move, but the horse stayed on again in the straight, holding the veteran Castleruddery for second by under a length.

Billycan had travelled well throughout the race, and despite sending Michael 'Mouse' Morris up in the saddle at the second ditch both times round, jumped well on the whole. The horse did, however, pick up an injury when rapping a near-fore, most likely at one of those ditches. It was a huge success for trainer Adrian Maxwell, who had also won a Triumph Hurdle at the Cheltenham Festival, and the victory presented the English-based Galway owner of Billycan, Vincent Kilkenny, with compensation for the horse's unlucky defeat in the SunAlliance Chase.

1977 IRISH GRAND NATIONAL RESULT

FATE	HORSE	AGE/WEIGHT	JOCKEY
1st	BILLYCAN	7.10.0	M. MORRIS
2nd	TIED COTTAGE	9.10.10	T. CARBERRY
3rd	CASTLERUDDERY	11.10.1	P. McCORMACK
4th	DROMORE	9.9.9	R.S. TOWNEND
5th	Arklow	12.9.7	E. McDonald
6th	Shuil Donn	7.10.10	Mr T.M. Walsh
7th	War Bonnet	9.10.7	S. Shields
8th	Roman Bar	9.10.7	P. Kiely
9th	Romanogan	6.9.7	G. Newman
10th	Kintai	8.9.7	T. Kinane
11th	Davy Lad	7.11.2	D.T. Hughes
Fell	Bannow Rambler	8.12.0	F. Berry
Fell	Brendons Road	9.9.9	S. Treacy
Fell	Escott	10.9.7	M. Kinane
Fell	Mr Midland	10.9.7	T.J. Ryan
Pulled-Up	April's Canter	9.9.13	S. Lynch
Pulled-Up	Golden Whin	7.9.7	M. Cummins
Pulled-Up	Harlent	7.9.7	J.P. Byrne
Pulled-Up	Kiltotan	11.9.9	J.P. Harty
Pulled-Up	Redundant Punter	7.9.7	Mr N. Madden

Billycan and jockey Mouse Morris are led in after winning.

11 April 1977
Going – Soft
Sponsor – Irish Distillers
Winner – £15,954
Race Distance – three miles four furlongs
20 Ran
Winner trained by A.J. Maxwell
Winner owned by V. Kilkenny
Billycan, chestnut gelding by Saint Denys – Boherluska.

Betting – 3/1 Bannow Rambler, 6/1 Tied Cottage, 7/1 Davy Lad & Shuil Donn, 8/1 BILLYCAN, 10/1 Brendons Road, 12/1 War Bonnet, 20/1 Romanogan, 25/1 Roman Bar, 40/1 April's Canter, Arklow, Castleruddery, Dromore, Escott, Golden Whin, Harlent, Kiltotan, Kintai, Mr Midland & Redundant Punter.

1978 – BROWN LAD

The final day of the Cheltenham Festival in March was postponed until 12 April because of snow. Five of the intended Gold Cup runners from Ireland were re-routed to Fairyhouse for the Irish Grand National of 1978, the quintet being Brown Lad, Fort Fox, Bannow Rambler, Bunker Hill and Tied Cottage. Of the five, only Brown Lad and Fort Fox actually lined-up for the Gold Cup when it was eventually run.

Having been unable to attempt to win an unprecedented third Irish Grand National in 1977 because of leg trouble, the now twelve-year-old Brown Lad had been carefully nursed back to fitness by Jim Dreaper. Always a lover of testing conditions, the horse had displayed some of his old brilliance earlier in the season when narrowly failing to give lots of weight away to fellow Irish National participant, Kintai, in the Thyestes Chase. Tommy Carberry had ridden Brown Lad to his two Irish National successes, but with that rider booked to partner Mighty's Honour on this occasion, the job went to Gerry Dowd, the Dreaper stable's top apprentice jockey. Dowd, also an excellent footballer, had ridden just eleven winners before the 1978 Irish National, and it would be his first ride in the big race. The task for Brown Lad was huge, for he was now in the veteran stage of his career and was asked to carry top weight of 12st 2lbs. Even so, the horse remained ever so popular, and started joint second favourite at 5/1 with Fort Fox, a horse that had run well in the season's King George VI Chase at Kempton Park and, more recently, the Leopardstown Chase.

As well as Fort Fox, challengers to Brown Lad were numerous. The front-running Mighty's Honour, trained by Dan Moore, started favourite, while Bannow Rambler was back, although the horse had suffered from vertebrae trouble. Bobby Coonan's mount, the useful Bunker Hill, was considered a threat if he could handle the soft going and extended distance, Thumper was an improving horse trained by Peter McCreery, while the seven-year-old Credit Card had won a three-mile handicap chase at the course during the season, and was trained and ridden by Mr John Fowler for his father.

As expected, Carberry set a terrific gallop aboard Mighty's Honour, although the horse jumped somewhat erratically at a number of fences. At the thirteenth fence, Mighty's Honour made one mistake too many, falling and bringing down Credit Card in the process. In turn, Credit Card brought down the Thyestes winner Kintai as the drama began to unfold before the large Fairyhouse crowd.

With those three horses departing the contest, the Pat Taaffe-trained lightweight Romanogan – unconsidered at 66/1 – was left in front by six lengths, followed by the smooth-travelling Sand Pit, with another six lengths back to Fort Fox. Prone to errors throughout his career, Fort Fox duly made one six fences from home, effectively ending any realistic hopes of the horse winning.

Staying out of any unnecessary trouble, Brown Lad had quietly been moved into contention by Dowd. A volcanic roar erupted from the stands as the old favourite made his presence felt for the first time at the fourth last, jumping the fence with power and moving forward menacingly to stalk the new leader Sand Pit. From here, the race developed into a battle royal between the two.

Brown Lad had begun to edge in front at the third last, but a slight mistake here knocked him back a little and allowed Sand Pit to get back on terms. Entering the straight and jumping two out together, the pair raced neck and neck to the last, a pulsating duel that brought the crowd to its feet. Brown Lad again jumped somewhat sluggishly at the last, but the horse was a real fighter. Determined and gutsy, and drawing on every ounce of his class and bravery, it was indeed Brown Lad that was able to forge ahead on the run-in, gallantly fending off the threat of Sand Pit to win by three-quarters-of-a-length. Frantouri finished a remote third with Fort Fox next, while the likes of Bannow Rambler and Bunker Hill ran poorly, never able to get competitive. The one sad note of the race was that the ten-year-old Delmoe broke a stifle and was put down.

The Kilsallaghan stable, headed first by the late, great Tom Dreaper and then by his son Jim, had now won an incredible fourteen Irish Grand Nationals. But despite this marvellous achievement, and the wonderful ride given by the relatively inexperienced Dowd, all the praise on the day was reserved for a true favourite of Irish racing, the evergreen Brown Lad. The 1978 Irish National may have been his best performance yet, for having recovered from leg trouble, the twelve-year-old had given over 2st to a useful horse in Sand Pit, and still showed incredible bravery to pull out victory. The victory meant that Brown Lad was now the first horse in history to win the Irish National three times, enshrining himself as one of the modern-day greats. Brown Lad never won a Cheltenham Gold Cup, though he certainly had the talent to do so. The horse was unfortunate that, when at his best, he failed to find his favoured going at Cheltenham. However, this failed to stop him finishing second to the very good Midnight Court in the Gold Cup a few weeks later, further enhancing the reputation of a wonderful racehorse.

1978 IRISH GRAND NATIONAL RESULT

FATE	HORSE	AGE/WEIGHT	JOCKEY	27 March 1978
1st	BROWN LAD	12.12.2	G. DOWD	Going – Soft
2nd	SAND PIT	8.10.0	P. KIELY	Sponsor – Irish Distillers
3rd	FRANTOURI	7.9.7	T.J. RYAN	Winner – £15,544
4th	FORT FOX	9.11.2	T. McGIVERN	Race Distance – three miles four furlongs
5th	Dromore	10.9.13	G. Newman	Time – 8mins 21.6secs
6th	Castleruddery	12.9.7	P. McCormack	19 Ran
7th	Artistic Prince	7.9.9	M. Cummins	Winner trained by J.T. Dreaper
8th	Romanogan	7.9.7	P.G. Murphy	Winner owned by Mrs P.E. Burrell
9th	Bannow Rambler	9.11.10	T.M. Walsh	Brown Lad, bay gelding by Sayajirao – Caicos.
10th	Spratstown	7.9.7	F. Berry	
Fell	Brendons Road	11.9.7	S. Treacy	
Fell	Miflame	8.9.7	J.P. Byrne	Betting – 4/1 Mighty's Honour, 5/1 BROWN LAD & Fort Fox, 6/1 Credit Card,
Fell	Mighty's Honour	7.10.3	T. Carberry	10/1 Thumper, 12/1 Bannow Rambler, 14/1 Bunker Hill & Sand Pit, 16/1
Pulled-Up	Bunker Hill	8.11.13	R. Coonan	Delmoe, 20/1 Frantouri & Kintai, 25/1 Brendons Road, 33/1 Dromore & Fort
Pulled-Up	Delmoe	10.10.2	Mr T. Kinane	Brady, 40/1 Castleruddery & Spratstown, 50/1 Artistic Prince, 66/1 Miflame &
Pulled-Up	Fort Brady	9.9.7	J. Cullen	Romanogan.
Pulled-Up	Thumper	7.9.9	T. Carmody	
Brought Down	Credit Card	7.10.10	Mr J. Fowler	
Brought Down	Kintai	9.9.8	T. Kinane	

1978 favourites Mighty's Honour and jockey Tommy Carberry.

1979 – TIED COTTAGE

With no fewer than twelve horses priced at 14/1 or shorter, it was clear that the 1979 Irish Grand National had an open, highly competitive feel to it. Heading the handicap was race specialist Brown Lad, but the horse was thirteen now, and had failed to make the frame on his favoured testing ground in the recent Cheltenham Gold Cup, so the stage seemed set for a new champion.

A month before the Irish National, Tied Cottage had run the race of his life in the Gold Cup at Cheltenham, driving relentlessly through the flurries of snow that fell, leading a beleaguered field a merry dance. Only the hardy chestnut Alverton put up any resistance, and when Tied Cottage came down agonisingly at the final fence, the English horse strode home unchallenged. That performance had confirmed that Tied Cottage could compete with chasing's finest, and he was quickly installed as a warm favourite for the Irish National. Riding the horse at Cheltenham had been Tommy Carberry, as he did for most of Tied Cottage's races, but the jockey was sidelined for Fairyhouse, so in his place stepped the horse's owner, the highly capable amateur, Anthony Robinson. No amateur had won the race since 1931, but this fact did not stop Tied Cottage beginning the race the 13/2 favourite.

Among the challengers were the English-trained pair of Prince Rock and Mr Batnac, and although no English raider had won since 1928, only recently had the race become economically worthwhile for overseas raiders. Certainly Prince Rock, an eleven-year-old trained by Peter Bailey, appeared to have a fine chance, having competed in many major chases in England, including the Grand National and the Hennessy (the horse would also finish in the frame in the Welsh Grand National in each of the 1979, 1980 and 1981 renewals).

Chinrullah, although possessing dubious credentials in terms of stamina, was a gifted youngster that had won the Arkle Chase at the Cheltenham Festival, while both Tarthistle and Great Dane provided strong hopes of maintained home success. Both Tarthistle and Great Dane were consistent staying chasers. The mare Tarthistle, in particular, was very popular in the betting as she looked to give trainer Edward O'Grady and jockey Tommy Ryan their first Irish National wins respectively, while the 1978 runner-up, Sand Pit, attempted to become the first horse since Overshadow in 1953 to win the Irish National, having previously run in the Grand National at Aintree but fallen.

Glorious weather at Fairyhouse attracted a huge crowd, and as at Cheltenham, it was not long before Tied Cottage had established a clear advantage, and the bay was already a long way clear by the fourth fence. At one stage, Tied Cottage was an incredible twenty-five lengths in front of the chasing pack, yet the leader was jumping sensibly, and his gallop had all nineteen of his rivals off the bit after a mile-and-a-half.

Robinson wisely gave Tied Cottage a breather passing the stands with a circuit to go, and by the thirteenth fence, the pack had closed considerably, fronted by Smiling Jim, Credit Card, Delmoss and Prince Rock. However, by six out, Tied Cottage had quickened away again, as the English challengers Prince Rock and Mr Batnac emerged as the chief dangers to the leader.

At the third last, Mr Batnac made a mistake that ruined his chance, and running towards the final two fences, Prince Rock ranged up alongside Tied Cottage as the two settled down to battle out the finish. It looked a carbon copy of the Gold Cup when Alverton had come to challenge Tied Cottage, and here, Prince Rock was driven forcefully into the race by Tommy Carmody. Marginally ahead at the last, Prince Rock looked like ending the hoodoo that had cursed English challengers since 1928, but responding gallantly to the coaxing of Robinson, Tied Cottage fought majestically to get the better of Prince Rock on the run to the line, edging in front at the death to win by a neck. Credit Card, in touch for two miles before fading, stayed on again towards the end to take third in front of Mr Batnac, while Chinrullah was beaten a long way from home and was pulled-up. Coming home safely in last place was Brown Lad, and the great horse was then gracefully retired having emphatically left his mark on the history of the Irish National.

One hundred years previously, Lee Barber had ridden Jupiter Tonans to victory in the race, becoming the first of six owner/jockeys to win the Irish National. Now Anthony Robinson had heroically become the seventh. A chemical manufacturer, Robinson had purchased Tied Cottage, with the help of Arthur Moore, for a mere 800 guineas at Doncaster Sales as a four-year-old, and now the horse had provided trainer Dan Moore with a first Irish National success. Sadly, Moore had been ill at home for some months, with his wife Joan helping out with the horses.

Having already finished second to Davy Lad in one Gold Cup, and fallen at the last when assured of at least second in Alverton's race, there was probably no horse in the history of that race that deserved a Gold Cup win more than the highly admirable Tied Cottage (although some would argue the excellent Michael/Monica Dickinson trained chaser of the 1980s, Wayward Lad, would compete for that role), and in 1980, the title finally looked his. A field of fourteen lined-up at Cheltenham, and adopting his usual front-running tactics, Tied Cottage rarely looked threatened, winning by five lengths from the young chestnut Master Smudge. Some weeks later, however, the joy turned to despair for connections, as it was discovered traces of the banned substance theobromine had been detected in Tied Cottage's post-race urine sample. Accidentally contaminated feed was the cause of the problem, and although no blame was attached to Dan Moore or Mick O'Toole (trainer of Chinrullah, fifth in that Gold Cup, and also given the same food), Tied Cottage and Chinrullah were disqualified from the Gold Cup, and Master Smudge was announced the winner. It was cruel luck, but Tied Cottage had already won over an army of fans, and racing well into his teenage years, the horse remained as popular as ever.

1979 IRISH GRAND NATIONAL RESULT

FATE	HORSE	AGE/WEIGHT	JOCKEY
1st	TIED COTTAGE	11.10.12	MR A.S. ROBINSON
2nd	PRINCE ROCK	11.10.4	T. CARMODY
3rd	CREDIT CARD	8.10.6	MR J. FOWLER
4th	MR BATNAC	9.9.7	M. CUMMINS
5th	Smiling Jim	7.9.7	G. Newman
6th	Poll's Turn	8.9.7	J.P. Byrne
7th	Great Dane	12.9.8	T. Kinane
8th	Brendons Road	12.9.7	J. Brassil
9th	Desert Bloom	8.9.7	M. Drake
10th	The Vintner	8.10.3	S. Lynch
11th	Sand Pit	9.10.2	T. McGivern
12th	Brown Lad	13.12.2	Mr T.M. Walsh
Fell	Sir Courtenay	13.9.7	M. Mulligan
Fell	Tarthistle	7.10.4	T.J. Ryan
Pulled-Up	Ballycross	9.9.7	F. Berry
Pulled-Up	Chinrullah	7.10.4	R.S. Townend
Pulled-Up	Delmoss	9.9.9	P. Kiely
Pulled-Up	Gabhran	10.10.1	J. Cullen
Pulled-Up	Some Joke	7.10.3	E.P. Wallace
Pulled-Up	Sub Rosa	8.11.4	G. Dowd

Tied Cottage launches into a fence.

16 April 1979
Going – Yielding
Sponsor – Irish Distillers
Winner – £20,040
Race Distance – three miles four furlongs
20 Ran
Winner trained by D.L. Moore
Winner owned by A.S. Robinson
Tied Cottage, bay gelding by Honour – Cottage Ray.

Betting – 13/2 TIED COTTAGE, 7/1 Chinrullah & Tarthistle, 9/1 Sub Rosa, 10/1 Brown Lad, 12/1 Ballycross, Poll's Turn, Prince Rock & The Vintner, 14/1 Credit Card, Great Dane & Sand Pit, 16/1 Delmoss, 20/1 Mr Batnac & Some Joke, 25/1 Brendons Road & Smiling Jim, 33/1 Gabhran, 100/1 Desert Bloom & Sir Courtenay.

1980 – DALETTA

The first Irish Grand National of the 1980s was one of the most open contests in years. Twenty-five horses went to post, and although the 1979 winner Tied Cottage was a late withdrawal, possibly to keep the weights down for his stablemate, Mighty's Honour, a record number of attendants at Fairyhouse were given plenty of options in selecting the winner of the big race.

With Tied Cottage an absentee, top weight on 11st 4lbs was the novice Daletta. A stylish jumper, Daletta was trained by Guy Williams, who had only taken a license out the season before and had just twelve horses in training. Daletta had improved greatly throughout the season, notably catching the eye when winning the Embassy Premier Chase at Haydock Park in February, and despite being treated harshly by the handicapper for that performance, the horse made much appeal as the sort of progressive youngster that often fared very well in the Irish National.

With prize money forever on the increase in Ireland, four English based horses made the journey to Fairyhouse in 1980, the quartet consisting of Jer, Good Prospect, Current Gold and Midday Welcome. The chestnut Jer was sired by the exceptional Epsom Derby winner of 1965, Sea Bird II, and the soft-ground specialist had proved a model of consistency during the season. Never falling-in over forty races, Jer was sent to Aintree nine days before Fairyhouse and started among the favourites for the Grand National. Agonisingly, Jer fell at the third fence there, but with a low weight and a good jockey in Phil Tuck, the horse's chance at Fairyhouse was lively, and he started 7/1 favourite. Of the other English raiders, Current Gold and Good Prospect both had their supporters. Current Gold, a good stayer trained by Gordon Richards, had finished second in the National Hunt Chase at the Cheltenham Festival, while Good Prospect had won his last three races for trainer John Edwards, including the Kim Muir at the Cheltenham Festival.

Of the home challenge, veterans Fort Fox and Mighty's Honour ran again, while youngsters such as Arthur Moore's charge Romany Count and Mick O'Toole's Leopardstown winner Kilkilwell were well supported. Kylogue Lady had enjoyed a consistent season, winning the Kerry National at Listowel, former hunter-chaser Secret Progress had progressed over a stone in the handicap, helped by a victory in the Thyestes Chase, while Tarqestral, trained by John Daly, ridden by top amateur Ted Walsh and owned by show-jumping star Eddie Macken, had won at Naas the Wednesday before to feature prominently in the betting.

On good ground, the twenty-five runners were sent keenly on their way, and it was not long before the drama started to unfold. The English raider Good Prospect proudly led at the first, but behind him, the eight-year-old Kilcoleman fell, bringing down the much-fancied Kylogue Lady in the process. Also well backed beforehand, Pillar Brae made a mistake that caused jockey Gerry Newman to lose his irons, and although the partnership were able to continue for some way after the first fence, Pillar Brae was eventually pulled-up.

As was his custom, Mighty's Honour soon took up the running and had quickly settled down into a rhythm in front, accompanied by the outsider Menlike. The pace was strong, with Mighty's Honour making a bold attempt to lead from start to finish. However there were so many horses in the field that the challengers inevitably began to stack up behind Mighty's Honour as the race progressed, and seven fences out, with Menlike already having cried enough, the trio of Eggnog, Tarqestral and Daletta began forward moves.

Eggnog, a relatively unconsidered seven-year-old, took up the running from the long-time leader, but it was Tarqestral that appeared to be travelling best under a patient ride from Walsh, and although Daletta pressed him strongly by the fourth last, Tarqestral looked every inch the winner turning into the home straight.

It was to be the second last fence that turned the race on its head. Failing to take-off at the fence, Tarqestral plunged to the ground, presenting Daletta and the resurgent Eggnog with the opportunity to fight out the finish. Also a novice, Eggnog just edged ahead at the final fence, and in receipt of 25lbs, held every chance of causing an upset. There had been some doubt beforehand as to whether Daletta had the requisite stamina to fully see out an Irish National, but the horse was the class animal in the field, and despite almost being driven into the rails by the loose-running Sand Pit (a faller during the race), he proved his worth, showing superior speed to Eggnog on the run to the line and winning by a length. Twelve lengths back in third came Secret Progress, with the David Goulding-ridden Current Gold fourth, the only female rider, Mrs Anne Ferris, fifth on Champerty, and the favourite, Jer, sixth.

In Daletta, a new star had emerged, one that was instantly nominated as a candidate for the 1981 Cheltenham Gold Cup by Williams, for which the 1980 Irish National was by far his biggest victory. Daletta was owned by Mrs Isobel Watson, a hunting friend of Williams, and the horse was ridden to victory at Fairyhouse by John Harty, brother of Eddie, the Aintree Grand National winning jockey of 1969.

1980 IRISH GRAND NATIONAL RESULT

FATE	HORSE	AGE/WEIGHT	JOCKEY
1st	DALETTA	7.11.4	J.P. HARTY
2nd	EGGNOG	7.9.7	S. TREACY
3rd	SECRET PROGRESS	11.10.11	M. CUMMINS
4th	CURRENT GOLD	9.10.2	D. GOULDING
5th	Champerty	9.9.7	Mrs A. Ferris
6th	Jer	9.10.3	P. Tuck
7th	Midday Welcome	9.9.7	Mr R. Treloggen
8th	Carlow Highway	7.9.7	P. Gill
9th	Poll's Turn	6.9.7	P. Kiely
10th	Fort Fox	11.10.9	T. McGivern
11th	Mighty's Honour	9.11.1	L. O'Donnell
12th	Persian Wanderer	7.9.7	B. Sheridan
13th	Menlike	7.9.7	M. Mulligan
14th	Sub Rosa	9.10.11	G. Dowd
Fell	Allibar	10.9.7	T. Kinane
Fell	Kilcoleman	8.10.8	S. Lynch
Fell	Sand Pit	10.9.7	P. Clarke
Fell	Tarqestral	9.10.10	Mr T.M. Walsh
Pulled-Up	Good Prospect	11.10.8	S. Morshead
Pulled-Up	Highway Patt	7.9.7	M. Morris
Pulled-Up	Hill Road	7.9.7	T.V. Finn
Pulled-Up	Kilkilwell	8.10.3	R. O'Donovan
Pulled-Up	Pillar Brae	7.9.13	G. Newman
Pulled-Up	Romany Count	8.9.8	F. Berry
Brought Down	Kylogue Lady	8.9.7	T.A. Quinn

Daletta jumps a fence en route to victory.

7 April 1980
Going – Good
Sponsor – Irish Distillers
Winner – £20,938
Race Distance – three miles four furlongs
Time – 7mins 34.7secs
25 Ran
Winner trained by G. St John Williams
Winner owned by Mrs F. Watson
Daletta, brown gelding by Majetta – Dale Way.

Betting – 7/1 Jer, 9/1 Good Prospect, Kylogue Lady & Tarqestral, 10/1 Romany Count, 11/1 DALETTA, Mighty's Honour & Pillar Brae, 12/1 Current Gold & Fort Fox, 16/1 Kilkilwell, Persian Wanderer & Sub Rosa, 20/1 Kilcoleman, Sand Pit & Secret Progress, 33/1 Champerty, Eggnog & Midday Welcome, 50/1 Allibar, Carlow Highway, Highway Patt, Hill Road, Menlike & Poll's Turn.

The crowd surround the presentation ceremony following Daletta's win in 1980.

1981 – LUSKA

A powerful pack of promising young chasers descended on Fairyhouse for the 1981 Irish Grand National for a race that was billed as the new breed against the old guard of Irish chasing, the latter group including the likes of Fort Fox, Kylogue Lady and Kilkilwell. England had a number of representatives, including the New Zealand-bred Royal Stuart and the eight-year-old Jack Madness, who was trained by Josh Gifford, a man fresh from an emotional victory at Aintree with Aldaniti. Bob Champion, who had overcome cancer to ride Aldaniti at Aintree, was out injured with a back problem, so the veteran Jeff King stepped in for the ride on Jack Madness.

In truth, the 1981 race was dominated by the up and coming prospects in Ireland, of which The Mighty Mac, Last Suspect, Bective Road, Owen's Image and Luska held firm chances. The Mighty Mac, a six-year-old novice trained by Tom Costello, was a horse considered to have a huge future. The horse had won both his starts during the season and was noted as a fluent, graceful jumper. With Niall Madden in the saddle, The Mighty Mac began the race as the 5/1 favourite. A big brown gelding, Last Suspect was out of a mare, Last Link, that had won the Irish National in 1963. Last Suspect was trained in 1981 by Jim Dreaper, already a four-time Irish National winner, and the horse appeared to have a golden chance, having won the season's Leopardstown Chase. Trained by Noel Meade and ridden by Joe Byrne, Bective Road brought a season of consistent form into the Irish National, while trainer Pat Hughes saddled Owen's Image, a good staying novice ridden by John Harty (successful aboard Daletta in 1980). Like Jim Dreaper, trainer Paddy Mullins had enjoyed much success in the Irish National, sending out novices Vulpine and Herring Gull to win in 1967 and 1968 respectively, while also training Dim Wit to win in 1972. In 1981, Mullins was represented by another novice, the seven-year-old Luska. The horse had enjoyed a solid, if unspectacular, season, but unlike most of his young rivals, Luska arrived at Fairyhouse having run poorly on his latest start, pulling up in the SunAlliance Chase at Cheltenham. Perhaps for this reason, Luska was easy to back on the day, eventually starting at 11/1 for jockey Tommy Finn.

Royal Bond, a very good novice of Cheltenham Gold Cup standard, trained by Arthur Moore, was the original top weight, but the horse was a late withdrawal, meaning Light The Wad headed the handicap on a relatively low mark of 11st 4lbs. On ground officially labelled as good, but reportedly considerably firmer, the field of twenty were sent on their way.

The two English horses, Royal Stuart and Jack Madness, were prominent for much of the race, as were outsiders Perspex Pride and Noble Star, but the sixth fence, the second ditch, was to prove a disaster for the favourite. Directly behind Grand Cru (a horse that had fallen recently at Becher's Brook in the Topham Trophy at Aintree), The Mighty Mac was left with no room to manoeuvre when that horse fell, and he was agonisingly brought down. None the worse for his accident, The Mighty Mac proved his well-being and general quality when coming out the next day and winning the Powers Gold Cup carrying 12st top weight, while as an older horse, The Mighty Mac won the Cathcart Chase at the Cheltenham Festival in 1984.

It was five fences from home where the action intensified. The English challenge had begun to deteriorate as Jack Madness faded, eventually pulling-up, while Royal Stuart later fell. Last Suspect had steadily crept into the contest, but a blunder at the fence knocked him backwards, while Bective Road had looked as dangerous as anything at that point until tiring alarmingly. But Luska had travelled well throughout, tracking Royal Stuart for much of the race before leaving that horse in his wake turning into the straight, and it was Luska and the firm-ground loving Pillar Brae – ridden by star amateur Ted Walsh – that emerged from the field to battle out the finish.

Luska had hit the front at the third last, but Walsh drove Pillar Brae through so strongly that by the final fence, the two were inseparable, touching down together. A year younger and with 16lbs less to carry, Luska had plenty in reserve, and roared on by a vociferous crowd, the final charge to the line was thrilling. But it was to be Luska's National, and at the post a length separated the winner from the brave Pillar Brae, with Last Suspect back in third and the mare Kylogue Lady making up a lot of late ground to take fourth. Of the beaten horses, Owen's Image had never got competitive, while Bective Road had seemingly held a fine chance before fading tamely. Four years later, Last Suspect ran in the Grand National at Aintree when trained by Captain Tim Forster. Considered a sulky, temperamental horse by that stage, Last Suspect's chance appeared slim, but rejuvenated by the unique Aintree fences, the horse conjured up a late run under Welsh jockey Hywel Davies to win a thriller from the well-backed Mr Snugfit.

Luska was a fully deserving winner of the Irish National, for he had travelled and jumped well throughout the race before showing real determination to fend off the firm ground specialist Pillar Brae in a brutal duel to the line. It was a fourth Irish National win for Mullins, but a first for jockey Finn and owner John Brophy – County Kilkenny farmer and a cousin of Mullins' – who had purchased Luska for 4,000 guineas at the Ballsbridge Sales when the horse was three-years-old.

1981 IRISH GRAND NATIONAL RESULT

FATE	HORSE	AGE/WEIGHT	JOCKEY
1st	LUSKA	7.9.9	T.V. FINN
2nd	PILLAR BRAE	8.10.11	MR T.M. WALSH
3rd	LAST SUSPECT	7.10.13	F. BERRY
4th	KYLOGUE LADY	9.10.4	T.A.QUINN
5th	Perspex Pride	9.9.7	Mr P.J. Healy
6th	Light The Wad	8.11.4	F. Leavy
7th	Noble Star	8.10.1	D. O'Gorman
8th	Fort Fox	12.10.10	Mr J. Fowler
9th	Glenroid	7.9.10	J. Kinane
10th	Beech King	6.9.7	T. O'Neill
11th	Owen's Image	6.10.0	J.P. Harty
12th	Kilkilwell	9.10.8	R. O'Donovan
13th	Bective Road	7.10.6	J.P. Byrne
Fell	Grand Cru	11.10.1	Mr F. Codd
Fell	Just Able	8.11.1	S. Treacy
Fell	Royal Stuart	10.10.6	R. Barry
Fell	The Mighty Mac	6.10.10	N. Madden
Pulled-Up	Brave Air	8.9.11	P. Gill
Pulled-Up	Jack Madness	8.11.1	J. King
Unseated Rider	Junes Friend	7.8.9	J. Cullen

20 April 1981
Going – Good
Sponsor – Irish Distillers
Winner – £24,185
Race Distance – three miles four furlongs
Time – 7mins 33.6secs
20 Ran
Winner trained by P. Mullins
Winner owned by J. Brophy
Luska, bay gelding by Light Brigade – Gora.

Betting – 5/1 The Mighty Mac, 6/1 Last Suspect, 7/1 Bective Road, 8/1 Kylogue Lady, 9/1 Pillar Brae, 10/1 Owen's Image, 11/1 LUSKA, 14/1 Jack Madness, Light The Wad & Royal Stuart, 20/1 Just Able, 25/1 Junes Friend, 33/1 Beech King, Brave Air, Fort Fox, Glenroid, Grand Cru, Kilkilwell, Noble Star & Perspex Pride.

Right: *Future Aintree Grand National winner Last Suspect jumps a fence before finishing third.*

Trainer Paddy Mullins and jockey Tom Finn.

Luska (black and orange colours) out-battled Pillar Brae to win.

1982 – KING SPRUCE

With prize money reaching close to £30,000, the Irish Grand National again attracted a huge field in 1982, as twenty-five runners went to post. Top weight and joint favourite was the talented, if frustrating, Arthur Moore-trained chestnut Royal Bond, a horse that had developed into the class act among Irish chasers during the season. Royal Bond had won the Leopardstown Chase in February under 12st, impressively dismantling the best chasers in Ireland in the process, and having already won at Cheltenham in January, went for the Gold Cup in March with an obvious chance. But disappointing badly on the day, Royal Bond was never in contention, trailing home eighth behind the Michael Dickinson-trained star, Silver Buck. Despite that performance, Royal Bond was held in very high regard in Ireland. With Tommy Carberry on board, he rightfully sat atop the betting market at 6/1, albeit together with the improving young handicapper Fethard Friend, a lightly-weighted bay expected to relish the drying conditions at Fairyhouse.

A number of horses arrived at Fairyhouse having fallen at the first fence in the recent Grand National at Aintree, among them the J.P. McManus-owned Deep Gale, and Royal Bond's stablemate, Mullacurry, a multiple winner during the season and partnered in the Irish National by amateur Tom Taaffe, son of the legendary Pat. Jim Dreaper again ran Last Suspect for owner Anne, Duchess of Westminster, while the hero of the previous year, Luska, again lined-up having recently finished fifth behind Scot Lane in the National Hunt Handicap Chase at the Cheltenham Festival.

Among a large band of newcomers to the race were Drumlargan and King Spruce. Drumlargan was a classy bay stayer, one good enough, in the future, to win a Whitbread Gold Cup and finish third in a Cheltenham Gold Cup. Drumlargan was trained by Edward O'Grady and had finished third to the very good Brown Chamberlin (a winner of the 1983 Hennessy at Newbury) at Cheltenham in the SunAlliance Chase before winning a handicap chase at Navan. Against Drumlargan were the good ground at Fairyhouse (he preferred softer conditions), and that the horse had a tendency to make sloppy mistakes. King Spruce was, perhaps, something of a dark horse before the race. Trained by the wheelchair-confined Michael O'Brien, King Spruce had been a brilliant novice hurdler, but had subsequently been operated on for palate trouble, and this was followed by a number of other setbacks and an enforced year of rest. In four runs during the season, King Spruce had failed to win, though he had not been disgraced at any

time, and with just 10st 2lbs to carry, he offered an intriguing alternative to the market principals.

It was to be a race where a number of the main contenders disappointed. Mullacurry was pulled-up following a poor run, as was Luska, while Royal Bond was not in contention when he fell at the final fence. Only fourteen of the twenty-five starters completed the course.

It was Drumlargan that impressed for much of the way, leading the field under Tommy Ryan, and looking likely to confirm his Cheltenham form. But at the third last, Drumlargan made one of his unfortunate errors, clouting the fence and sending him backwards as the chasing pack seized their opportunity.

With Drumlargan now under intense pressure, coming through to take control were King Spruce, Fethard Friend, Last Suspect and the Pat Hughes-trained Owen's Image (a failure in the race the year before), and by the last fence it was King Spruce and Fethard Friend that set about battling to the line.

Both horses had shown consistency throughout the season, and Fethard Friend was a young chaser on the rise, one that was clearly relishing the good ground underfoot. It was a thrilling struggle to the line, but ultimately it was King Spruce that prevailed under a strong ride from Gerry Newman, edging out Fethard Friend by two lengths. Last Suspect had again run well in the race, finishing six lengths back in third with Owen's Image fourth and Drumlargan fifth.

King Spruce was owned by American Rusty Carrier, who also acted as assistant to O'Brien. Carrier's wife Joy, a good amateur rider herself, had flown over from the United States to watch King Spruce run, having ridden in Maryland forty-eight hours previously. Indeed, when King Spruce ran at Aintree in the 1983 Grand National, it was Mrs Carrier that rode the horse, although unfortunately they came down at Becher's Brook. Winning jockey Gerry Newman was riding for the O'Brien stable for the first time in the current season, and his strength in getting King Spruce past Fethard Friend in the final hundred yards was most admirable. Gerry's father, Eddie, had won the Irish National as a jockey aboard Shagreen in 1949. Much credit too went to O'Brien for nursing the horse back to health and paving the way for King Spruce to land Ireland's most prestigious steeplechase, a win that made up for the owner's disappointment with Eggnog, a horse that had finished second in 1980.

1982 IRISH GRAND NATIONAL RESULT

FATE	HORSE	AGE/WEIGHT	JOCKEY
1st	KING SPRUCE	8.10.2	G. NEWMAN
2nd	FETHARD FRIEND	7.9.8	F. BERRY
3rd	LAST SUSPECT	8.10.6	K. MORGAN
4th	OWEN'S IMAGE	7.10.12	MR C.P. MAGNIER
5th	Drumlargan	8.10.3	T.J. Ryan
6th	Hazy Dawn	7.9.7	J.M. Byrne
7th	Deep Gale	9.10.5	N. Madden
8th	Felicity's Pet	8.9.7	P. Gill
9th	Duncreggan	9.9.7	G. McGlinchey
10th	No Hill	13.10.0	B. Sheridan
11th	Beggar's End	9.9.7	M.M. Lynch
12th	Aragorn	9.9.12	T. Carmody
13th	Old Society	8.9.13	P. Walsh
14th	Captain Freaney	10.9.7	P. Kavanagh
Fell	Barton	10.9.8	T.A. Quinn
Fell	Clash Of The Ash	9.9.7	K.F. O'Brien
Fell	Door Step	7.9.7	Mr J. Queally
Fell	Royal Bond	9.12.0	T. Carberry
Fell	Royal Dipper	7.10.12	T.M. Walsh
Pulled-Up	Kilgreaney	8.9.7	S. Treacy
Pulled-Up	Luska	8.10.8	T.V. Finn
Pulled-Up	Mullacurry	10.10.9	Mr T.J. Taaffe
Unseated Rider	Gay Return	7.10.2	J.P. Byrne
Unseated Rider	No Lemon	7.9.7	M. Dwyer
Brought Down	Light The Wad	9.10.13	T. Morgan

Joint-favourite Royal Bond, one of the finest Irish chasers of the 1980s.

12 April 1982
Going – Good
Sponsor – Jameson
Winner – £29,717
Race Distance – three miles four furlongs
Time – 7mins 33.7secs
25 Ran
Winner trained by M.J. O'Brien
Winner owned by R. Carrier
King Spruce, bay gelding by Harwell – Daemolina.

Betting – 6/1 Fethard Friend & Royal Bond, 7/1 Luska, 9/1 Drumlargan, 12/1 Clash Of The Ash & Last Suspect, 14/1 Owen's Image, 16/1 Mullacurry & Royal Dipper, 20/1 Deep Gale, Gay Return, Hazy Dawn & KING SPRUCE, 25/1 Barton, Door Step & Light The Wad, 33/1 Aragorn, Beggar's End & Old Society, 50/1 Captain Freaney, Duncreggan, Felicity's Pet, Kilgreaney, No Hill & No Lemon.

King Spruce (blue sleeves) and Fethard Friend jump the final fence.

1983 – BIT OF A SKITE

Fifty-three Irish Grand Nationals had passed since the last time an English-based horse had triumphed. But there were high hopes that the Josh Gifford-trained Royal Judgement could end the drought, despite the burden of 12st top weight. Royal Judgement, who in 1981 had finished seventh at 100/1 behind Little Owl in the Cheltenham Gold Cup, had been a model of consistency during the season, regularly making the frame in his races. His most recent run had been his most impressive yet, when at Chepstow, he beat the very good horse Political Pop by a distance. Royal Judgement was ridden by Gifford's stable jockey Richard Rowe, and started the race 4/1 favourite.

In 1983, a then record number of runners lined up for the Irish National, with twenty-seven facing the starter, among them some old favourites as well as some new names. Though his chance was remote, the evergreen Tied Cottage incredibly took part at the age of fifteen, the horse having found a new niche in the hunter-chase division, where his only run of the season had been when finishing a promising fifth to the very good Eliogarty in the Foxhunters' at Cheltenham. Others with previous experience of the Irish National included the soft-ground specialist Drumlargan, Tommy Carmody's mount, Owen's Image, and the 1982 second, but somewhat out of form, Fethard Friend.

In a wide open contest, those that had impressed in Ireland during the season included the Leopardstown Chase winner Fortune Seeker, Thyestes Chase winner Tacroy, Connor's Cross – winner of his last two races at Tralee and Limerick, Naas winner Conn Hul, a dour stayer trained locally by Patrick Griffin, and the inexperienced Paddy Mullins-trained novice Pearlstone; a horse that had run in just one chase, which he won at Leopardstown over two-and-a-half miles during the season. Another fairly unexposed type was the J.P. McManus-owned, seven-year-old, Bit Of A Skite. Trained by Edward O'Grady, Bit Of A Skite had a staying pedigree, being by the sire Menelek that produced two Aintree Grand National winners in Rag Trade and Hallo Dandy, and Bit Of A Skite had proved his affection for long distance chases when winning the four-mile National Hunt Chase at the Cheltenham Festival. Bit Of A Skite had suffered with a poisoned foot following his Cheltenham win, and O'Grady had sent the horse to Mrs Joan Moore's yard based on The Curragh, where Mrs Moore and Bit Of A Skite's lad had got the horse fit by putting him through frequent sessions in an equine pool. Lightly raced and lightly weighted, Bit Of A Skite started second favourite for the race at 7/1, where he was partnered by Tommy Ryan.

The 1983 Irish National was run in a virtual blizzard and, for a long way, a thrilling finish looked on the cards as many horses remained in contention, the majority tracking the leading group that was headed for long periods by Drumlargan. One of those that seemed poised to play a hand in the finish was the novice Pearlstone, but having taken the lead a mile from home, the horse's inexperience was exposed as he came to grief soon after.

Having sat patiently in mid-division for much of the race, Ryan began to move Bit Of A Skite forward towards the leaders four fences out, where Royal Judgement – having held every chance – began to fade. Drumlargan continued to lead, but a whole host of horses, including Fortune Seeker and Tacroy, as well as outsiders Beech King and Prince Peacock, were still in the race as the field came into the home straight.

But it was Bit Of A Skite that was travelling best, and the seven-year-old came to grab the lead from his stablemate Drumlargan running to the final fence. What had looked like turning into a thrilling, multi-horse finish just moments before, quickly turned into a ruthless destruction, as Bit Of A Skite switched into another gear, leaving his rivals toiling as he flew the last fence with devastating conviction. Belittling the problems that had plagued him since Cheltenham, Bit Of A Skite was untroubled on the run to the line, comfortably beating Beech King by six lengths in a performance of surprising authority. Prince Peacock was a further five lengths away in third, and like Beech King, returned at a starting price of 25/1. Stand, trained by Jim Dreaper, ran on resolutely in the closing stages to take fourth from Tacroy, who impressed trainer Francis Flood enough to earn a tilt at the imminent Grand National at Aintree, in which he was ultimately pulled-up. Of the others, Royal Judgement's bid had petered out meekly having looked most promising at one stage, and he eventually came home in ninth, one place behind Drumlargan. As for old Tied Cottage, he had shown plenty of enthusiasm early on, only to tire later, and was eventually pulled-up.

After his easy victory, Bit Of A Skite pulled-up lame, yet this could not dampen the joy of trainer O'Grady, who followed in the footsteps of his father, Willie, who had trained Hamstar to win in 1948 as well as Icy Calm in 1951. O'Grady was quick to praise the efforts of Mrs Moore for her part in the horse's success, for having made a big impression at Cheltenham, Bit Of A Skite – described as a very good horse by winning jockey Ryan – had now confirmed his promise with victory in the Irish Grand National.

Owner J.P. McManus receives the trophy with trainer Edward O'Grady to the left and jockey Tommy Ryan behind.

Bit Of A Skite (green and yellow) jumps a fence in the 1983 race.

Royal Judgement, the favourite, jumps a fence.

1983 IRISH GRAND NATIONAL RESULT

FATE	HORSE	AGE/WEIGHT	JOCKEY
1st	BIT OF A SKITE	7.9.7	T.J. RYAN
2nd	BEECH KING	9.9.12	M. SLEATOR
3rd	PRINCE PEACOCK	8.9.7	G. McGLINCHEY
4th	STAND	9.9.12	K .MORGAN
5th	Tacroy	9.11.6	F. Berry
6th	Fortune Seeker	8.9.7	P. Clarke
7th	Connors Cross	8.9.7	A.J. O'Brien
8th	Drumlargan	9.11.3	Mr F. Codd
9th	Royal Judgement	10.12.0	R. Rowe
10th	Fethard Friend	8.11.0	A. Powell
11th	Aragorn	10.9.12	G. Newman
12th	Caherdaniel	8.9.7	P. Kavanagh
13th	Black Orchid	7.9.7	R.J. King
14th	Tabasco Time	14.9.7	P. Leech
Fell	Conn Hul	9.9.7	P. Connell
Fell	Felicity's Pet	9.9.11	P. Kiely
Fell	High Diver	10.10.0	J.K. Kinane
Fell	Hondike	9.9.7	T.V. Finn
Fell	Owen's Image	8.10.13	T. Carmody
Fell	Paulines Fancy	10.9.7	Mr D. Hassett
Fell	Pearlstone	7.9.12	A. Mullins
Fell	Ramrajya	10.9.10	M.M. Lynch
Fell	Silent Member	8.9.10	M.J. Byrne
Pulled-Up	Carrigeensharragh	7.9.7	Mr P.J. Healy
Pulled-Up	Door Step	7.9.7	J.P. Byrne
Pulled-Up	Jameys Fancy	8.9.7	R. Baltour
Pulled-Up	Tied Cottage	15.10.2	T.J. Taaffe

4 April 1983

Going – Soft

Sponsor – Jameson

Winner – £28,462

Race Distance – three miles four furlongs

Time – 8mins 0secs

27 Ran

Winner trained by E.J. O'Grady

Winner owned by J.P. McManus

Bit Of A Skite, bay gelding by Menelek – Mrs Brady.

Betting – 4/1 Royal Judgement, 7/1 BIT OF A SKITE, 8/1 Conn Hul, 10/1 Stand, 12/1 Owen's Image & Pearlstone, 16/1 Felicity's Pet, 20/1 Connors Cross, Door Step, Paulines Fancy, Ramrajya, Silent Member & Tacroy, 25/1 Aragorn, Beech King, Black Orchid, Caherdaniel, Carrigeensharragh, Drumlargan, Fethard Friend, Fortune Seeker, High Diver, Hondike, Jameys Fancy, Prince Peacock, Tabasco Time & Tied Cottage.

1984 – BENTOM BOY

The record field size for an Irish Grand National was set in the 1984 race as twenty-nine runners went to post. In what appeared a renewal where most of the horses held some semblance of a chance, it was, at first glance, something of a surprise that the favourite, Macks Friendly, started as short as 3/1. However, when studying the credentials of the favourite, the price appeared justified.

A seven-year-old grey novice trained by four-time Irish National winner Paddy Mullins and ridden by his son Tony, Macks Friendly had progressed into a very decent chaser as the season had drawn on. The horse had won six of his last seven races, and his adaptability was apparent, the horse having won chases between two and four miles on a variety of grounds including good and heavy. Macks Friendly's latest run had perhaps been his most impressive, taking the race indicative of a progressive, young staying chaser, the four-mile National Hunt Chase at the Cheltenham Festival. Macks Friendly had all the correct attributes of an Irish National winner, as well as having a low weight, and the horse started one of the hottest favourites in years.

Some of the most recognisable names in National Hunt racing featured in the 1984 Irish National, including much-loved individuals such as Drumlargan, Royal Bond and The Ellier, while their was also a debut in the race for the popular chestnut Greasepaint. Trained by Dermot Weld, Greasepaint had run with the utmost courage in both the 1983 and 1984 Aintree Grand Nationals, proving a natural over the big fences. In 1983, the horse appeared to be cutting down the Jenny Pitman-trained Corbiere at the death only to be denied by the narrowest of margins by the time the winning post arrived. The 1984 race had similarly produced more heartache for the admirable Greasepaint, beaten only by Gordon Richards' Hallo Dandy in another close call. Owned by Michael Smurfit, Greasepaint's chance at Fairyhouse was obvious if reproducing his Aintree form, but the worry was that the horse – never a prolific winner despite his brilliant efforts in the Grand National – may not have recovered from his recent exertions, and Tommy Carmody's mount took second place in the betting at 6/1.

Outside of Macks Friendly and Greasepaint, there were many other viable contenders to be found at far longer odds, among them Eliogarty, Mister Donovan and Carrigeensharragh. One of the leading Irish hunter-chasers of the early eighties, Eliogarty had been a late gamble for the recent Grand National, in which the dark chestnut ran well for a long way before a mistake at the second Valentines Brook led to an eventual finishing position of fifteenth. A former Cheltenham Foxhunters' winner, Eliogarty was ridden in the Irish National by the very good female amateur, Caroline Beasley. As well as saddling the smart Drumlargan, trainer Edward O'Grady also sent out the good eight-year-old Mister Donovan. The horse had been well fancied recently at Cheltenham, but could only finish seventh behind Broomy Bank in the Kim Muir Chase. A victory at Newbury eleven days later helped to reignite the belief that Mister Donovan could run very well at Fairyhouse, and with Jonjo O'Neill aboard – fresh from winning the Champion Hurdle at Cheltenham aboard the great mare Dawn Run – Mister Donovan received much support. With the ground drying out considerably, one horse well

backed before the start was the improving grey mare, Carrigeensharragh. The mare had beaten two good yardsticks in Irish racing, Monanore and Lantern Lodge (also a runner at Fairyhouse) over three miles at Naas in February, and the horse was most consistent. Having been pulled-up on each of his last two starts, the nine-year-old Bentom Boy was virtually ignored in the betting. The most striking aspect of his challenge was that the horse was ridden by one of three female riders taking part, Mrs Anne Ferris, the daughter of trainer Willie Rooney, who had finished second aboard Barney's Link in the 1952 race. This fact aside, Bentom Boy took his place among the sixteen listed at 33/1, with little to suggest he could improve on his recent form.

For much of the way, it was one of the many outsiders, Braes O'Tully that made the running, with Dawson Prince in close attendance. The favourite, Macks Friendly, too was prominent, and despite being slightly slow to get away from some of his fences, the horse gave Tony Mullins a great ride round the inside. Not so fortunate were Royal Bond, an early faller, and the nine-year-old Royal Appointment, the latter's saddle slipping, carrying the horse wide after the winning post first time round and leading to the horse being pulled-up.

By the time the leaders had turned into the home straight for the final time, the tempo had increased greatly. Eliogarty, who had run well, had already made a mistake to ruin his chances at the fourth last, and Macks Friendly, having always been in the leading group, was the next to fade, simply unable to stick with the leaders as the extra pace was injected into the contest.

The leading group consisted of – rather surprisingly – Lantern Lodge, Bentom Boy, Sicilian Answer and Dawson Prince, none of which had been strongly considered beforehand. Lantern Lodge was the first to bite the dust, the horse coming down when in the lead at the second last, a fall that sent his jockey Martin Lynch to hospital with a broken hand. Having made rapid progress from three out, Bentom Boy was now left in the lead, and seizing her opportunity, Mrs Ferris kicked for home on the bay.

With just one fence to jump, it was left to Sicilian Answer to chase the leader, but Bentom Boy was now in full flow, and safely negotiating the last, the horse ran on strongly for a shock win by twelve lengths. Sicilian Answer followed him home, with Dawson Prince third, five lengths adrift. Dawson Prince was a stablemate of the winner, and completing a memorable family occasion, the horse was ridden by Mrs Rosemary Stewart, the younger sister of Anne Ferris. In fourth came the Peter McCreery-trained Daring Run, the horse pulling-up lame after the race but returning perfectly sound. Macks Friendly, having failed to quicken in the straight, returned unharmed in seventh, with the likes of Eliogarty and Drumlargan completing further back. Greasepaint, possibly over the top after his brave Aintree run, was never in contention and was pulled-up, as was Mister Donovan, apparently unable to handle the quick ground.

It was a wonderful family occasion, with a real sense of accomplishment for the winning connections. Rooney, seventy-one-years-old, had ridden over 400 point-to-point winners in his time, but this was by far his biggest success as a

Winning jockey Mrs Ann Ferris enjoys the presentation.

trainer. The stewards held an enquiry into Bentom Boy's dramatic improvement in form, but accepted Rooney's explanation that the horse had been unable to handle the sticky ground at Naas in his previous race. The win marked another notable achievement in the career of Mrs Ferris, she had been the first woman to win a chase against male opposition when she won the 1976 Ulster National on Mourneview. On Bentom Boy, the rider had always been well placed and, taking advantage of the fall of the unlucky Lantern Lodge, had come home a most deserving winner to add further romance to the history of the Irish Grand National.

Bentom Boy jumps a fence en route to a surprise victory.

Aintree Grand National runner-up Greasepaint goes to post.

1984 IRISH GRAND NATIONAL RESULT

FATE	HORSE	AGE/WEIGHT	JOCKEY
1st	BENTOM BOY	9.9.9	MRS A. FERRIS
2nd	SICILIAN ANSWER	7.10.7	J.P. BYRNE
3rd	DAWSON PRINCE	8.9.9	MRS R. STEWART
4th	DARING RUN	9.10.0	T. MORGAN
5th	Braes O'Tully	9.9.7	J.K. Kinane
6th	Carrigeensharragh	8.10.0	Mr P.J. Healy
7th	Macks Friendly	7.9.10	A. Mullins
8th	Beech King	10.9.9	P. Kiely
9th	Tom Miller	7.9.8	B. Sheridan
10th	Eliogarty	9.11.2	Miss C. Beasley
11th	Drumlargan	10.12.0	Mr F. Codd
12th	Grafton Fashions	6.9.7	P. Clarke
13th	Felicity's Pet	10.9.11	P. Gill
14th	Smartside	9.9.7	R. O'Donovan
15th	Richardstown	8.10.1	Mr T.S. Costello
16th	Fortune Seeker	9.9.8	P. Leech
Fell	Clonthturtin	10.9.7	T.V. Finn
Fell	Lantern Lodge	7.9.8	M.M. Lynch
Fell	Master Elliot	7.9.7	T.J. Ryan
Fell	Royal Bond	11.11.13	T.J. Taaffe
Fell	Silent Member	9.10.4	H. Rogers
Fell	The Ellier	8.9.10	M.J. Byrne
Pulled-Up	Greasepaint	9.10.13	T. Carmody
Pulled-Up	Mister Donovan	8.10.12	J.J. O'Neill
Pulled-Up	Royal Appointment	9.9.10	A. Powell
Pulled-Up	Yer Man	9.9.7	J.J. Maher
Unseated Rider	Doubtful Venture	8.9.11	P. Kavanagh
Unseated Rider	Gala Song	8.9.7	J. Goodwin
Refused	Master Vincents	8.9.11	K. Morgan

23 April 1984
Going – Good
Sponsor – Jameson
Winner – £28,578
Race Distance – three miles four furlongs
Time – 7mins 31.8secs
29 Ran
Winner trained by W.E. Rooney
Winner owned by T. Dorrian
Bentom Boy, bay gelding by Mon Capitaine – Fineskin.

Betting – 3/1 Macks Friendly, 6/1 Greasepaint, 12/1 Mister Donovan, 14/1 Carrigeensharragh, Daring Run & Drumlargan, 16/1 Eliogarty, Royal Bond & Tom Miller, 20/1 Doubtful Venture, Lantern Lodge, Richardstown & Sicilian Answer, 33/1 Beech King, BENTOM BOY, Braes O'Tully, Clonthturtin, Dawson Prince, Felicity's Pet, Fortune Seeker, Gala Song, Grafton Fashions, Master Elliot, Master Vincents, Royal Appointment, Silent Member, Smartside, The Ellier & Yer Man.

1985 – RHYME 'N' REASON

Antarctic Bay, the impressive winner of the SunAlliance Chase at the recent Cheltenham Festival, had been ante-post favourite for the 1985 Irish Grand National. But when the horse, trained by Pat Hughes, failed to sparkle in a preparatory gallop just days before the contest, Antarctic Bay was withdrawn, robbing the race of its star attraction. Though twenty-three runners went to post in 1985, the overall quality of the race was a little disappointing, although there were some obvious exceptions, with the likes of Rhyme 'N' Reason, Ballinacurra Lad, Rainbow Warrior, Excursion, The Ellier, Cranlome and Monanore all worthy contenders.

Two years previously, Royal Judgement had arrived at Fairyhouse, hotly fancied to end the long drought endured by British-based runners in the Irish National, only to finish down the field. However, in Rhyme 'N' Reason, there was every reason to believe that the horse could become the first since Don Sancho in 1928 to triumph for Britain. A high quality six-year-old novice, Rhyme 'N' Reason had unseated behind Antarctic Bay at Cheltenham, but had responded admirably by winning a three-mile novice chase at Aintree's Grand National meeting. Indeed, from five runs during the season, the horse had won three times and finished second once. Rhyme 'N' Reason was trained by David Murray-Smith and ridden by Graham Bradley, a jockey that had won the 1983 Cheltenham Gold Cup on Bregawn, as well as the season's Welsh Grand National on Righthand Man. Murray-Smith and Bradley were having their first attempts at the race in their respective roles, and the trainer had been encouraged to run after noting the success that other six-year-olds had enjoyed in the race, most recently Garoupe and Tartan Ace in the 1970s. There was a feeling that Rhyme 'N' Reason could potentially be very good, and as such, the horse started 6/1 favourite.

Both Ballinacurra Lad and Rainbow Warrior had run in the recent Cheltenham Gold Cup without success, the former finishing eleventh and the latter pulling-up, but the pair were two of the classier runners in the big field. Ballinacurra Lad was trained by John Crowley and had fallen heavily at Leopardstown in February, an incident that clearly unnerved the horse. However, bouncing back to form, the horse won at Limerick nine days before the Irish National and carried top weight of 12st at Fairyhouse. Trained by Michael Cunningham, Rainbow Warrior had been considered good enough to contest the recent Gold Cup, and although he had disappointed there, the horse had winning form during the season. He was well backed at Fairyhouse, despite a heavy weight burden and the suspicion he may lack the necessary stamina to win an Irish National.

Of the others, Cranlome and Monanore were both fancied to run well off low weights. Cranlome had enjoyed a fruitful season for trainer Kevin Woods, while Monanore was expected to relish the soft ground and long distance of the Irish National, the popular chestnut displaying his well-being with a facile success a Gowran Park a few weeks before the race. Excursion was very well backed in the preceding days having carved a rich sequence of results into his season, including an impressive three-mile chase win at Down Royal in March, while The Ellier was a popular Irish chaser trained by Arthur Moore and sired by Menelek, the stallion responsible for Bit Of A Skite, winner of the Irish National in 1983.

Once on their way, the lightly weighted outsider Black Orchid set the pace, and although Excursion made a bad blunder at the third fence, it would be a fairly run race with no hard luck stories and only one faller, the hat-trick seeking youngster Cerimau.

Black Orchid's lead lasted the entire first circuit, but soon after, Rainbow Warrior and Kolme took over, the latter ridden by 7lb claimer Conor O'Dwyer. Hot on their heels, having always been in the leading ten, was Rhyme 'N' Reason, the favourite merely cruising, never once coming off the bridle.

At the third last, Bradley made his move, asking Rhyme 'N' Reason to quicken. The response from the horse was instant and decisive, and the favourite quickly put daylight between himself and the chasing pack. Bradley took the horse wide over the final two fences, the last of which was a plain, upright fence. It was at the last where Rhyme 'N' Reason made his only mistake, brushing the top with his knees and causing one or two anxious moments. But landing safely, the partnership remained intact, and displaying excellent stamina, Rhyme 'N' Reason galloped home strongly to win by a most convincing twelve lengths. In second place came Seskin Bridge, staying on under Martin Lynch, with Kolme taking third, two-and-a-half lengths back for O'Dwyer, a future Cheltenham Gold Cup and Champion Hurdle-winning jockey. Future Prosperity was fourth for trainer Arthur Moore, whose other runner, The Ellier, came home sixth, ahead of other fancied runners Cranlome (eighth), Monanore (ninth), Ballinacurra Lad (tenth), Excursion (eleventh) and Rainbow Warrior, who faded to finish twelfth having been prominent on the second circuit.

Rhyme 'N' Reason was originally trained by his breeder, Jeremy Maxwell, in Northern Ireland, and then won three times over hurdles for Michael Dickinson

Rhyme 'N' Reason ploughs through a fence in 1985.

his class and courage by fighting back to overthrow the Arthur Stephenson-trained Durham Edition and win the race (Monanore was third), at last fulfilling the rich promise of his novice season that saw the horse win Ireland's biggest prize.

1985 IRISH GRAND NATIONAL RESULT

FATE	HORSE	AGE/WEIGHT	JOCKEY
1st	RHYME 'N' REASON	6.10.6	G. BRADLEY
2nd	SESKIN BRIDGE	7.10.12	M.M. LYNCH
3rd	KOLME	8.9.10	C. O'DWYER
4th	FUTURE PROSPERITY	8.9.7	A. POWELL
5th	Doubtful Venture	9.10.3	P. Kavanagh
6th	The Ellier	9.10.6	T.J. Taaffe
7th	Fortune Seeker	10.9.7	P. Clarke
8th	Cranlome	7.9.7	P. Gill
9th	Monanore	8.9.9	M.J. Byrne
10th	Ballinacurra Lad	10.12.0	H. Rogers
11th	Excursion	9.11.0	Mrs R. Stewart
12th	Rainbow Warrior	8.11.7	K. Morgan
13th	Daltmore	7.10.3	P. Leech
14th	Prince Peacock	10.9.7	N. Byrne
15th	Ginger For Sport	10.9.7	M. Flynn
Fell	Cerimau	7.9.7	P. Kiely
Pulled-Up	Black Orchid	9.9.8	J.P. Byrne
Pulled-Up	High Diver	12.10.7	T.J. Ryan
Pulled-Up	Larry's Latest	8.10.1	M. Cummins
Pulled-Up	Pillar Brae	12.10.8	T. McGivern
Pulled-Up	Regal Pleasure	7.9.7	R. O'Donovan
Pulled-Up	Tubbertelly	8.10.2	K.F. O'Brien
Unseated Rider	Dudie	7.10.5	A. Mullins

8 April 1985
Going – Yielding to Soft
Sponsor – Jameson
Winner – £27,522
Race Distance – three miles four furlongs
Time – 8mins 10.8secs
23 Ran
Winner trained by D. Murray-Smith
Winner owned by Miss J. Reed
Rhyme 'N' Reason, bay gelding by Kemal – Smooth Lady.

Betting – 6/1 RHYME 'N' REASON, 7/1 Excursion, 9/1 Monanore, 10/1 Cranlome & The Ellier, 12/1 Future Prosperity, 14/1 Cerimau & Rainbow Warrior, 16/1 Larry's Latest, 20/1 Ballinacurra Lad, Black Orchid & Doubtful Venture, 25/1 Pillar Brae & Seskin Bridge, 33/1 Daltmore, Dudie, Fortune Seeker, Ginger For Sport, High Diver, Kolme, Prince Peacock, Regal Pleasure & Tubbertelly.

Above: *Monanore, a hardy and consistent Irish chaser during the 1980s, goes to post for the 1985 Irish National.*

Left: *Rhyme 'N' Reason in the parade.*

before transferring to the yard of Murray-Smith, a former assistant to Vincent O'Brien. Rhyme 'N' Reason was an excellent winner of the Irish National, successfully ending the long drought of British-trained horses. A bright career at the very top looked certain for the horse, but it never materialised, at least not for a while. Plagued by jumping problems over the next few seasons, the horse was eventually switched to the stables of David Elsworth, and the horse enjoyed a swift and welcome change of fortune. In the 1987/88 season, Rhyme 'N' Reason won four chases and was going tremendously well in the Gold Cup at Cheltenham before falling late on. Undeterred, Elsworth sent the horse to Aintree for the 1988 Grand National, and despite a terrible mistake at Becher's first time (the horse was down on his knees and reduced to a standstill), Rhyme 'N' Reason showed

1986 – INSURE

Favourite for the 1986 Irish Grand National was the Monica Dickinson-trained Righthand Man, one of three representatives from Britain hoping to continue the success Rhyme 'N' Reason had enjoyed the year before. A top-class bay chaser, Righthand Man had enjoyed his best season the year before, winning the Welsh Grand National and finishing second to Forgive 'N' Forget in the Cheltenham Gold Cup. Righthand Man had, most recently, finished fifth in a wonderful Gold Cup won by the Paddy Mullins-trained mare Dawn Run, and the horse, despite carrying a big weight, was hotly fancied, starting at 3/1 for jockey Graham Bradley, the previous year's hero.

The other two British runners also held live chances. Top weight with 12st, the white-faced front-runner Run And Skip had finished second in the season's Hennessy Gold Cup at Newbury before winning the Welsh Grand National on heavy ground, conditions strikingly similar to that at Fairyhouse in 1986. Trained by the quietly spoken John Spearing, Run And Skip was ridden by one of England's leading jockeys, Steve Smith-Eccles. Maori Venture was a chestnut trained by Andy Turnell, who was having his first runner in Ireland. A ten-year-old, Maori Venture was a horse of real ability, although his efforts were often spoiled by careless jumping. Maori Venture was owned by the elderly Mr Jim Joel, and the horse had boosted his chances of victory in the Irish National by winning at Lingfield on his latest start.

Both the Jim Dreaper-trained Hard Case – a winner at Leopardstown in February – and the Peter McCreery-trained Seskin Bridge, runner-up in 1985, had their supporters, but with heavy ground ensuring a real slog of a race, a number of the lightly-weighted horses saw their chances improve. Of this group, none were more intriguing than the six-year-old chestnut Omerta, a horse that had run in just two lifetime chases, the latest when impressing mightily winning the four-mile National Hunt Chase at the Cheltenham Festival. Trained by Homer Scott and ridden by the hugely talented amateur, Lorcan Wyer, Omerta had yet to make a mistake in his two chases, and despite his inexperience, a steady wave of money saw Omerta's price reduced from 12/1 earlier in the week to a starting price of 4/1. Both the experienced bay The Ellier and Bold Agent, winner of his last two races, were other lightweights given consideration. Also towards the bottom of the handicap was the eight-year-old Insure, a bay trained by Pat Hughes that had warmed up for the Irish National by winning a three-mile hurdle race at Limerick, and was thought to be appreciative of a marathon trip in testing conditions.

It may well have been the heaviest ground of any Irish National in the modern era, and right from the start, the pace was steady, with Run And Skip always in the front rank on the first circuit, as was his custom. Fortunately, there were few fallers, although Androy went at the eighth, and by the time the second circuit got under way, many in the field were already beginning to suffer as the gruelling conditions took their toll.

The key moment in the race arrived at the seventh-last fence. Run And Skip still held the lead, but only narrowly from Righthand Man, with Insure tracking these close behind. It was here that Righthand Man made a mistake that knocked him backwards, while Tommy Carmody's mount, Mister Donovan, came down. Having been travelling smoothly at this stage, Hard Case was left with nowhere

to go when Mister Donovan fell, and was brought down. This incident left Hard Case's jockey, Ken Morgan, most frustrated, for he later revealed that Hard Case had been making ground at every fence and was just beginning his challenge when he was put out of the race. From that moment, Insure took the race by the scruff of the neck, pushed on by twenty-one-year-old jockey Mickey Flynn, and the partnership opened up a gap to the chasing pack, of which Omerta was now starting to show boldly.

A huge roar erupted from the crowd as Omerta began to close on Insure three fences from home, while further back, the three British challengers – Run And Skip, Righthand Man and Maori Venture – were pulled-up. Omerta appeared to be mounting a winning challenge, looking for all the world as though he would be able to pick off Insure as he pleased.

But when Wyer went for his whip a fence later, the outlook changed again, as Insure found fresh reserves and surged on once more. The closing stages of the race were turned into a procession through the mud as, relishing the conditions, Insure ploughed home to win comfortably by ten lengths from the beaten but not disgraced Omerta. Bold Agent came in third, a further eight lengths away, followed by The Ellier and Daltmore. So taxing had the contest been that only five horses completed the course, all carrying under 10st. One of those that failed to finish was Maori Venture. The season after, however, Maori Venture would be belittling his apparent suspect jumping and winning the Grand National at Aintree, a race in which The Ellier finished seventh and Insure twenty-second.

Hard Case goes to post in 1986.

Insure jumps a fence in grand style.

Pat Hughes was overjoyed following the race. The trainer had been sure Omerta would catch his horse running to the second last, but stated that Insure was a horse that needed long distances in testing conditions and was also a far better horse around Fairyhouse, where his previous form had been good. Flynn was having only his second ride in the race, having finished fifteenth on Ginger For Sport the year before. The jockey had ridden fifty winners on the flat for trainer Kevin Prendergast, but had found life much more difficult when turning his attentions to jumping. It may only have been his seventh National Hunt winner, but Insure's victory in the 1986 Irish Grand National was a race that Mickey Flynn would never forget.

1986 IRISH GRAND NATIONAL RESULT

FATE	HORSE	AGE/WEIGHT	JOCKEY
1st	INSURE	8.9.11	M. FLYNN
2nd	OMERTA	6.9.9	MR L. WYER
3rd	BOLD AGENT	10.9.7	J.P. BYRNE
4th	The Ellier	10.9.13	T.J. Taaffe
5th	Daltmore	8.9.7	A. Mullins
Fell	Androy	7.9.7	Mrs A. Ferris
Fell	Mister Donovan	10.10.4	T. Carmody
Pulled-Up	Daring Run	11.9.9	T. Morgan
Pulled-Up	Lucisis	7.10.4	F. Berry
Pulled-Up	Maori Venture	10.10.13	S.C. Knight
Pulled-Up	Marcolo	9.9.7	Mr J. Queally
Pulled-Up	Righthand Man	9.11.9	G. Bradley
Pulled-Up	Run And Skip	8.12.0	S. Smith-Eccles
Pulled-Up	Seskin Bridge	8.10.7	N. Madden
Brought Down	Hard Case	8.10.13	K. Morgan

31 March 1986
Going – Heavy
Sponsor – Jameson
Winner – £34,320
Race Distance – three miles four furlongs
Time – 8mins 20.4secs
15 Ran
Winner trained by P. Hughes
Winner owned by P. Hughes
Insure, bay gelding by Dusky Boy – Shady Tree.

Betting – 3/1 Righthand Man, 4/1 Omerta, 5/1 Run And Skip, 8/1 Hard Case, 10/1 Mister Donovan, 14/1 Lucisis & The Ellier, 16/1 Androy, Bold Agent, INSURE, Maori Venture & Marcolo, 20/1 Daring Run & Seskin Bridge, 33/1 Daltmore.

Trainer Pat Hughes and jockey Mickey Flynn with Insure.

1987 – BRITTANY BOY

Better ground in 1987 attracted another huge field for the Irish Grand National, with twenty-six lining up as opposed to fifteen the year before. Sponsorship money had also been dramatically increased. With whisky company Jameson now in their sixth year of sponsorship, prize money to the winner now stood at over £60,000, almost double what Insure's connections had received for winning in 1986. It was noticeable that the British-based challengers were becoming more frequent too, and in 1987, five made the journey to Fairyhouse, with each of Bucko, Gainsay, Catch Phrase, Castle Warden and Church Warden holding decent prospects.

Form horses in a hotly competitive renewal were the John Fowler-trained Bankers Benefit and the Jenny Pitman-trained Gainsay. Despite the drying ground being slightly detrimental to his chances, Bankers Benefit was in tremendous form, winning five of his previous six races, including a three-and-a-half-mile handicap chase at Punchestown in February, where he beat a number of his Irish National rivals, including Tommy Carberry's talented runner, Over The Last, Monanore, Sound Judgement, and the promising youngster trained by Mouse Morris, Lastofthebrownies. Bankers Benefit had long been ante-post favourite for the race, and even without his favoured soft ground, the horse started 4/1 favourite for jockey Anthony Powell, having his fourth ride in the race. The little brown gelding Gainsay was similarly in great form. An eight-year-old owned by Hot Chocolate singer Errol Brown, Gainsay had won the National Hunt Handicap Chase at the Cheltenham Festival by twenty lengths, and had followed up that performance by winning at the Aintree Festival. Gainsay was ridden by Mrs Pitman's son, Mark, having his first ride in the race, although there were worries that the ground may be too quick for the horse, carrying a big weight of 11st 11lbs.

Of the other contenders, Josh Gifford's runner, Catch Phrase, had won well at Newbury recently, Attitude Adjuster (a stablemate of Lastofthebrownies) was a tough chestnut hunter-chaser that had run well recently at Aintree in the Grand National, finishing eighth behind Maori Venture, while John Edwards saddled the consistent Castle Warden, a fresh horse that had bypassed both Cheltenham and Aintree to run at Fairyhouse. Of the other Irish contenders, one horse with class form to his name was Brittany Boy. A most consistent novice chaser trained by Kelvin Hitchmough, Brittany Boy had finished an excellent third to two of the best novices in England for many years, Kildimo and Playschool, in the SunAlliance Chase at Cheltenham on his latest start. Brittany Boy was ridden at Fairyhouse by Tom Taaffe, whose father Pat had ridden the winner of the Irish National no fewer than six times.

The crowd roared their approval as the big field – including top weight Lucisis and 1984 winner Bentom Boy – were sent on their way, and it was Gainsay that cut out the running, with Brittany Boy and Bankers Benefit in close attendance. In behind, Bucko took up a good position on the first circuit, while Tom Morgan took the fancied Castle Warden around the inside, later explaining that this was because the horse was jumping to his right.

There was a scary incident eight fences from home when the outsider Sandy Hussar partially parted company with jockey Paul Kinane. The jockey was dragged along on the ground for some while and had his hand trodden on. Fortunately,

Kinane escaped without any serious damage, and was well enough to drive himself to Navan hospital after the race for treatment.

Four fences from home, Gainsay began to tire. The horse had run a splendid race but was heavily weighted, eventually fading into ninth. As Gainsay began to retreat, both Brittany Boy and Bankers Benefit swept past the long-time leader, both still full of running, setting up a duel between the pair over the final three fences.

Gainsay's front-running exploits had set the race up perfectly for the duo, both of whom had stayed out of any unnecessary trouble by taking up positions in the front rank throughout. However, it was Brittany Boy that appeared to be travelling the stronger, and by the last, the horse had taken the measure of his rival. Though Brittany Boy idled somewhat when hitting the front, Taaffe merely had to keep the bay up to his work, and ultimately, the partnership came home most impressively by six lengths. Bankers Benefit had jumped to his left during the race and was a horse that preferred softer ground, but he had run a fine race, and only one horse had proved superior. Four lengths back came Bold Agent, third for the second consecutive year, with Castle Warden – the best of the British runners – staying-on for fourth. Of the others, Bucko and Catch Phrase had both travelled poorly on the second circuit, finishing down the field together with another fancied runner, Over The Last.

It had been a fine performance by Brittany Boy, and he had looked a class act on the day. Hitchmough immediately nominated the 1988 Cheltenham Gold Cup as the long-term target for a horse that had already proved he could handle the

The presentation to winning connections – trainer Kelvin Hitchmough and jockey Tom Taaffe.

The blinkered Attitude Adjuster, eighth in the Aintree Grand National two weeks previously, jumps a fence in the Fairyhouse showpiece.

Brittany Boy was an excellent winner of the 1987 Irish National.

The favourite Bankers Benefit goes to post.

The well-fancied Bucko (noseband) disappointed in the race itself.

undulations of Cheltenham. It was by far the biggest success in Hitchmough's career, and was a fine accomplishment for a trainer that had first taken out a license four years ago, basing himself at Monkston, just outside of Cork. The 1987 Irish National was only the trainer's twelfth winner. Twenty-three-year-old Taaffe had now successfully followed in his father's footsteps, and if Brittany Boy's win was the highlight of his career as a jockey, further success awaited Taaffe when he eventually turned his hand to training, sending out Kicking King to win the Cheltenham Gold Cup in 2005. As for Brittany Boy, hopes that he would win a Gold Cup of his own were dashed, for the horse's career was plagued by injury. In the 1987 Irish Grand National, however, he was clearly the best horse on the day, memorably landing the richest ever race run in Ireland.

1987 IRISH GRAND NATIONAL RESULT

FATE	HORSE	AGE/WEIGHT	JOCKEY
1st	BRITTANY BOY	8.10.10	T.J. TAAFFE
2nd	BANKERS BENEFIT	7.11.0	A. POWELL
3rd	BOLD AGENT	11.11.4	P. GILL
4th	CASTLE WARDEN	10.11.5	T. MORGAN
5th	Randoss	8.9.10	M.M. Lynch
6th	Sound Judgement	8.10.7	K. Morgan
7th	Oonagh's Jolly	8.10.5	P. Leech
8th	Kolme	10.10.9	C. O'Dwyer
9th	Gainsay	8.11.11	M. Pitman
10th	Bentom Boy	12.10.9	Mrs A. Ferris
11th	Bartres	8.10.11	R. O'Donovan
12th	Boro Quarter	8.11.10	P. Kavanagh
13th	Gallaher	11.11.1	Mr A.J. Martin
14th	Bucko	10.10.13	M. Dwyer
15th	Attitude Adjuster	7.11.1	N. Madden
16th	Catch Phrase	9.11.7	R. Rowe
17th	Over The Last	7.11.3	Mr J. Queally
18th	Church Warden	8.11.0	P. Croucher
19th	Monanore	10.11.0	Mr M.F. Barrett
20th	Caherdaniel	12.9.7	S. Reilly
21st	Lady Mearlane	7.9.7	T. O'Neill
22nd	Lucisis	8.12.0	F. Berry
Fell	Sandy Hussar	8.9.7	P.P. Kinane
Pulled-Up	Daring Run	11.10.12	B. Sheridan
Pulled-Up	Lastofthebrownies	7.10.2	K.F. O'Brien
Pulled-Up	Sicilian Answer	10.10.8	J. Byrne

20 April 1987
Going – Good to Yielding
Sponsor – Jameson
Winner – £62,700
Race Distance – three miles four furlongs
Time – 7mins 35.4secs
26 Ran
Winner trained by K. Hitchmough
Winner owned by J. Glynn
Brittany Boy, bay gelding by The Parson – Digynia.

Betting – 4/1 Bankers Benefit, 7/1 Bucko, 8/1 Over The Last, 12/1 Gainsay, 14/1 BRITTANY BOY, Castle Warden & Catch Phrase, 16/1 Gallaher, Lastofthebrownies & Sound Judgement, 20/1 Attitude Adjuster & Church Warden, 25/1 Bartres & Kolme, 33/1 Bentom Boy, Bold Agent, Boro Quarter, Caherdaniel, Daring Run, Lady Mearlane, Lucisis, Monanore, Oonagh's Jolly, Randoss, Sandy Hussar & Sicilian Answer.

1988 – PERRIS VALLEY

The 1988 Irish Grand National did not have the appearance of a strong renewal, with a number of the leading candidates untested in such long distance handicaps. Both Abbey Glen and Master Aristocrat VI were viewed as potential stars of the future, although both had a lot to prove if they were going to be good enough to win an Irish National.

Despite only being a six-year-old, the novice Abbey Glen was a horse with tremendous upside. Trained by Pat Hughes, Abbey Glen had been running over distances far shorter than that of the Irish National, but had progressed nicely during the season, winning numerous races and displaying fine jumping ability every time he ran. It had been his performance at the recent Cheltenham Festival that really took the eye, the horse finishing second behind Danish Flight in the Arkle Trophy. Behind Abbey Glen that day in third place was Barnbrook Again, a horse that subsequently won the next two Queen Mother Champion Chase runnings. There was no doubting that Abbey Glen was an exciting horse, but the fact he would be carrying 11st 7lbs over three-and-a-half-miles, given his stamina doubts, was a worry for those that backed him.

Some very good hunter-chasers had run in the Irish Grand National in recent editions, with the likes of Eliogarty and Attitude Adjuster running well without winning. However, there was a feeling that the seven-year-old Master Aristocrat VI could be a real star for trainer Frank Lehane. Registered with his dam's pedigree 'unknown', the horse was barred from running in Britain under Jockey Club rules, but Master Aristocrat VI had turned into a hunter-chaser of rich promise in Ireland. During the season, the horse had recorded wins in three-mile hunter-chases at Gowran Park, Wexford and Fairyhouse, the lattermost performance coming just eleven days before the big race. Despite being 4lbs out of the handicap, Master Aristocrat VI had plenty of support in the betting market, starting the 7/1 third favourite.

Favourite, however, was the John Edwards-trained Castle Warden, fourth in the 1987 race. A winner of two of his last three races, including one over an extended three miles at Sandown most recently, Castle Warden arrived at Fairyhouse in good form and was much fancied to improve on his performance of the year before, for he acted on any going and was well weighted. Also in the horses' favour was the booking of 1985 winning jockey Graham Bradley, replacing broken rib victim Tom Morgan.

Arthur Moore's pair of Thinking Cap and the grey Sergeant Sprite attracted support, while Cranlome ran again for Mouse Morris having missed the cut in the recent Grand National at Aintree won by Rhyme 'N' Reason. Jockey Tom Taaffe held a decent chance of winning a second consecutive Irish National aboard the recent Fairyhouse winner, Have A Barney, while Dermot Weld ran the seven-year-old Perris Valley. Owned, like a previous Weld runner, Greasepaint, by Michael Smurfit, Perris Valley had disappointed in that same Fairyhouse race won by Have A Barney. Perris Valley's performance at Fairyhouse seemed puzzling, since the horse had been in good form prior to that, winning numerous races during the season, albeit mostly at far shorter distances. The horse had been well backed ante-post for the Irish National, but on the day was allowed to start at 12/1 for twenty-seven-year-old jockey Brendan Sheridan.

The feature of the 1988 race was the run of Master Aristocrat VI. Looking every inch a top-class performer, the hunter-chaser took the field along at a strong pace on quick ground for much of the way, tracked by 100/1 outsider Noble Music – trained by Paul Blockley in Britain (the trainer's first Irish National runner) – and the favourite Castle Warden.

Everything seemed to be going well for Master Aristocrat VI as he boldly attempted to make all the running, but misjudging the fifth fence from home, the horse hit the deck and was out of the race. The favourite Castle Warden had been well placed up until the fence before Master Aristocrat's departure, but a mistake six out knocked him back and he eventually faded to finish ninth, although Bradley later stated the horse was beaten before his mistake.

All this had left the John Stirling-trained Captain Batnac in front, but there was a fantastic finish lying in wait. Sheridan had followed Weld's instructions to ride a patient race aboard Perris Valley – the trainer unsure as to whether the horse had the necessary stamina required to win – and the plan had been to pick off horses courtesy of a late run. But when Perris Valley remained fifteen lengths off the pace at the time of Master Aristocrat's fall, victory seemed unlikely, and Perris Valley was still four lengths behind Captain Batnac at the last.

However, making up tremendous ground coming up the stands-side rails, Perris Valley thrilled the crowd with a devastating late burst, and in a gripping duel, got up in the last few strides to deny Captain Batnac and jockey Conor O'Dwyer by three-quarters-of-a-length. Captain Batnac had run a most courageous race, and may well have emerged victorious but for a bad error three out. Six lengths back in third came Feltrim Hill Lad, with Have A Barney fourth.

At the Cheltenham Festival in March, leading Flat racing trainers Michael Stoute and Guy Harwood had saddled winners. Now Weld, predominantly a flat trainer, had won the Irish National with Perris Valley. Weld had the odd jumper in his yard, and had come mightily close to winning the Grand National at Aintree in 1984 with Greasepaint, but this was his biggest success in the jumping sphere, as it was for winning jockey Sheridan, who demonstrated fine strength and determination

Castle Warden (red and white) soars over a fence in 1988.

to rally Perris Valley close to home. Weld co-owned Perris Valley with Smurfit, the latter (chairman of the Irish Racing Board) having named the horse after a Californian landmark. Perris Valley had been purchased by Smurfit as an unbroken three-year-old and the owner originally planned to sell the horse three weeks prior to Fairyhouse, only for the deal to fall through. Now Weld and Smurfit could celebrate victory in Ireland's premier chase, and plot a raid on the 1989 Aintree Grand National, for which Perris Valley ultimately ran in without success.

Jockey Brendan Sheridan with Perris Valley.

1988 IRISH GRAND NATIONAL RESULT

FATE	HORSE	AGE/WEIGHT	JOCKEY
1st	PERRIS VALLEY	7.10.0	B. SHERIDAN
2nd	CAPTAIN BATNAC	10.10.10	C. O'DWYER
3rd	FELTRIM HILL LAD	7.10.1	M.M. LYNCH
4th	HAVE A BARNEY	7.10.10	T.J. TAAFFE
5th	Cranlome	10.10.0	T.J. Ryan
6th	Ceolbridge Baby	7.10.10	M. Fitzsimons
7th	Super Furrow	8.12.0	M.M. Treacy
8th	Sergeant Sprite	8.10.0	P. Gill
9th	Castle Warden	11.10.8	G. Bradley
10th	Noble Music	8.10.0	R. Crank
11th	Rockfersistan	8.10.0	C.F. Swan
12th	Abbey Glen	6.11.7	F. Berry
13th	Thinking Cap	7.10.0	P.L. Malone
14th	Fair Is Fair	10.10.0	P. Leech
15th	No Hastle VI	8.10.0	A. Powell
16th	Master Elliot VI	11.10.0	F. Woods
Fell	Master Aristocrat VI	7.10.0	L.P. Cussack
Pulled-Up	Sound Judgement	9.10.10	K. Morgan

16 April 1988
Going – Good
Sponsor – Jameson
Winner – £49,729
Race Distance – three miles four furlongs
Time – 7mins 33.60secs
18 Ran
Winner trained by D.K. Weld
Winner owned by Sir Michael W.J. Smurfit
Perris Valley, bay gelding by Le Bavard – Margerval

Above: *Perris Valley (blue) jumps a fence in the 1988 race.*

Below: *Master Aristocrat VI takes a fence in glorious style but was later to fall.*

Betting – 9/2 Castle Warden, 6/1 Have A Barney, 7/1 Master Aristocrat VI, 8/1 Abbey Glen, 12/1 PERRIS VALLEY, Sergeant Sprite, Sound Judgement & Thinking Cap, 14/1 Cranlome, Feltrim Hill Lad & Rockfersistan, 16/1 Fair Is Fair & Super Furrow, 20/1 Captain Batnac, 50/1 Ceolbridge Bay & No Hastle VI, 100/1 Master Elliot VI & Noble Music.

1989 – MAID OF MONEY

In 1989, with the ground riding on the soft side of good, twenty-two horses went to post for the Irish Grand National. With the National Hunt world still on a high following the majestic win of the immensely popular grey horse, Desert Orchid, in the Cheltenham Gold Cup, expectation was high for a race to match the excitement of Perris Valley's triumph the year before. Although the 1988 winner was an absentee due to a pending engagement at Aintree for the Grand National, the likes of Captain Batnac, Feltrim Hill Lad, Have A Barney and Master Aristocrat VI returned to Fairyhouse to renew their rivalries.

Joint favourites at 7/1 were the 1987 runner-up, Bankers Benefit, and the former star hurdler, Barney Burnett. Now a nine-year-old, Bankers Benefit was the number one hope from the John Fowler stable, and the horse had won impressively last time out at Navan over two-and-three-quarter-miles. Trained by Ruby Walsh, Barney Burnett had been the best novice hurdler in Ireland three years previously, before embarking on a chasing career that had got off to a somewhat rocky start. But, with experience, Barney Burnett had improved greatly, and the horse had really run well on his most recent outings, including winning the Leopardstown Chase in February. A chestnut nine-year-old, Barney Burnett was ridden at Fairyhouse by Brendan Sheridan, successful aboard Perris Valley in 1988.

With Padge Gill's mount Super Furrow carrying 12st top weight, and the veteran Ballinacurra Lad the oldest horse in the race at fourteen, others that attracted interest were Lost The Bit, Cool Ground and Maid Of Money. Lost The Bit was the representative of Brittany Boy's trainer, Kelvin Hitchmough, and was a horse expected to relish the conditions and distance, while the seven-year-old chestnut, Cool Ground, was a tough, consistent stayer that had won the Kim Muir Chase at the Cheltenham Festival and gave young jockey Anthony Tory a first ride in the Irish National. A resilient, sound-jumping seven-year-old mare, Maid Of Money was thought to be the second-string from the yard of John Fowler. A most consistent horse by the sire Crash Course (that would get the 1996 Aintree Grand National winner Rough Quest), Maid Of Money had uncharacteristically fallen last time out at Leopardstown, but had previously run up a fine sequence of results, winning three of her previous four races. A sure stayer that appreciated soft conditions, Maid Of Money was ridden by Anthony Powell, who came second two years before on Bankers Benefit.

It was to be one of the most clear-cut Irish National results in recent years. Candy Well VI, an outsider ridden by John Kavanagh, had led the field for much of the way, with the chestnut Cool Ground travelling strongly together with Maid Of Money. But jumping the final ditch, six fences from home, the mare was travelling by far the strongest, and when Cool Ground started to fade four out, Maid Of Money was the only horse still on the bridle.

The unfortunate Lost The Bit fell two fences from home, coming down heavily and, sadly, fatally injuring his back. In the same incident, Cool Ground swerved to avoid the faller and unseated Tory. But by then, Powell, who had wanted to hold his horse up for as long as possible, had set sail for home on Maid Of Money, the horse pulling her way irresistibly to the front.

A slight mistake two fences from home did little to stop the mare in her tracks, and powering resolutely all the way to the line, Maid Of Money ran out a most convincing ten-length winner. Having been unable to stay with the mare once she had stormed clear, Candy Well VI came in second, with Have A Barney another ten lengths away in third. The two joint favourites had been no match for the mare on the day, but they returned home safely, virtually neck and neck, with Barney Burnett just edging out Bankers Benefit for fourth. Although he had unseated Tory, Cool Ground had run well and would enjoy plenty of future success, winning the Welsh Grand National in 1990 before causing a huge surprise by taking the Cheltenham Gold Cup in 1992.

But there was no doubting the star of the show was Maid Of Money, presenting Fowler and Powell with the biggest wins of their respective careers. Fowler, who had admitted to thinking Bankers Benefit was the more likely winner from his stable, had sent out that horse to finish second in 1987, while in 1979, he had ridden Credit Card (the dam of Bankers Benefit) into third place, and had previously ridden Kilburn into fourth in the 1969 race. The twenty-eight-year-old Powell was the son of race starter, Paddy, while the jockey's grandfather, also called Paddy, had won the Irish National in 1927 on Jerpoint. Only a novice, Maid Of Money's jumping had been exceptional in the Irish National. Records showed her effort was the finest weight-carrying performance by a mare since the race became a handicap eighty years previously and she also became the first of her sex to win since Sweet Dreams in 1969. Clearly a very good horse, Maid Of Money was allowed to take her chance in the following season's Gold Cup at Cheltenham, and although she did not win, she ran with credit to finish sixth.

1989 IRISH GRAND NATIONAL RESULT

FATE	HORSE	AGE/WEIGHT	JOCKEY
1st	MAID OF MONEY	7.11.6	A. POWELL
2nd	CANDY WELL VI	7.10.4	J.R. KAVANAGH
3rd	HAVE A BARNEY	8.11.8	T.J. TAAFFE
4th	BARNEY BURNETT	9.11.0	B. SHERIDAN
5th	Bankers Benefit	9.10.12	N. Madden
6th	Navallus VI	10.10.0	P. Kavanagh
7th	Ceolbridge Baby	8.10.0	D. O'Gorman
8th	Super Furrow	9.12.0	P. Gill
9th	Master Aristocrat VI	8.10.10	L.P. Cusack
10th	Feltrim Hill Lad	8.11.2	M.M. Lynch
Fell	Derry Gowan	7.10.0	J.F. Titley
Fell	Lost The Bit	8.10.0	P. Leech
Pulled-Up	Afford A King	9.10.4	C. O'Dwyer
Pulled-Up	Ballinacurra Lad	14.10.2	Mr P.J. Healy
Pulled-Up	Bean Alainn	7.10.0	C.F. Swan
Pulled-Up	Boreen Prince	12.10.8	Mr J. Queally
Pulled-Up	Captain Batnac	11.10.3	K.B. Walsh
Pulled-Up	Kalamalka	7.10.2	T. Kinane
Pulled-Up	Lady Mearlane	9.10.0	T. Old O'Neill
Pulled-Up	L'Ane Rouge	8.10.7	M. Flynn
Pulled-Up	Vulgan's Pass	8.10.0	K.F. O'Brien
Unseated Rider	Cool Ground	7.10.0	Mr A. Tory

Maid Of Money jumps a fence during a fine victory.

27 March 1989
Going – Good to Soft
Sponsor – Jameson
Winner – £46,000
Race Distance – three miles four furlongs
Time – 8mins 0.1secs
22 Ran
Winner trained by J.R.H. Fowler
Winner owned by Mrs H.A. McCormick
Maid Of Money, bay mare by Crash Course – Hansel Money.

Betting – 7/1 Bankers Benefit & Barney Burnett, 8/1 Cool Ground, 10/1 Feltrim Hill Lad, Have A Barney, Lost The Bit & MAID OF MONEY, 12/1 Afford A King, 16/1 Master Aristocrat VI, 25/1 Candy Well VI, Captain Batnac & Kalamalka, 33/1 Ballinacurra Lad, Bean Alainn, L'Ane Rouge, Navallus VI & Super Furrow, 40/1 Boreen Prince & Lady Mearlane, 50/1 Ceolbridge Baby, Derry Gowan & Vulgan's Pass.

Candy Well VI puts in a strong leap but cannot match the winner, Maid Of Money.

Opposite: Jockey Tony Powell and trainer John Fowler revel in their success.

1990 – DESERT ORCHID

The twentieth century witnessed a plethora of popular steeplechasers, each an individual, and each holding certain characteristics that made them wonderful racehorses, as well as names of authority with a high standing in the sport. The likes of Easter Hero, Golden Miller, Prince Regent, Cottage Rake, Mill House, Arkle, Flyingbolt, L'Escargot, Red Rum, Dawn Run and Aldaniti all created huge interest in racing, while in more modern times, horses such as One Man, Edredon Bleu, Florida Pearl, Moscow Flyer and Best Mate have attracted huge fan-bases in Britain and Ireland. As brilliant as all those horses have been, it would be hard to imagine a more popular, well-known and distinctive racehorse than the great grey of the late 1980s and early 1990s, the unforgettable Desert Orchid.

Desert Orchid was trained by David Elsworth in Hampshire, and the near-white horse had been a high-class hurdler (finishing third in the 1984 Champion Hurdle at Cheltenham) before commencing a remarkable career as a chaser. Desert Orchid was a phenomenal steeplechaser to watch, being a bold front-runner that attacked his fences with vigour and splendid enthusiasm. He was a well-built, powerful horse with a fine turn of foot, and was at his best between two-and-a-half and three miles, especially on quick, right-handed tracks such as Kempton, Wincanton and Sandown. Indeed, it was at Kempton Park where Desert Orchid really shone, winning a record four King George VI Chases at the course (1986, 1988, 1989 and 1990) and was second in the 1987 race there. The horse had also won a Whitbread Gold Cup at Sandown, and the fact that he regularly raced and won at far shorter distances demonstrated his adaptability and versatility, as well as a genuine love for racing. It was, however, in the 1989 Cheltenham Gold Cup where Desert Orchid forever stole the public's heart. A horse that appreciated good ground, or faster, treacherous weather, had left the ground at Cheltenham on Gold Cup day heavy, and there was even talk of the horse being withdrawn on the morning of the race. However, race he did, and the sight of a mud-drenched, weary, but doggedly determined Desert Orchid out-battling the soft ground-loving Yahoo up that famous finishing hill is an image that remains one of the most famous in racing.

Before that Gold Cup, Desert Orchid had always had his stamina questioned, but that performance proved he was a horse of both iron will and sheer class. In the 1989/90 season, the horse as popular as was possible, Desert Orchid again won the King George, as well as three other races, and started hot favourite to win the Gold Cup again, even though he was now eleven. Not disgraced, the horse was beaten into third by Norton's Coin and Toby Tobias, younger rivals that proved too good on the day. But 'Dessie' remained the public darling, and the decision was taken to let the horse run at Fairyhouse in the 1990 Irish Grand National, where the course was expected to suit him, being a right-handed track. Top weight with 12st, Desert Orchid would be giving each of his thirteen rivals on the day 2st (apart from Have A Barney carrying 10st 2lbs), but with drying winds making the chance of the horse lasting the race distance more probable, the grey was made even-money favourite. Partnering Desert Orchid at Fairyhouse was the brilliant Richard Dunwoody, a jockey that had already won a Gold Cup and Aintree Grand National prior to 1990,

and would also win three Jockey's Championships in Britain in his time. It was Dunwoody's first ride in the Irish Grand National.

In truth, it was a poor bunch that faced Dessie in 1990. The new star of Irish chasing, Carvill's Hill, was withdrawn by trainer Jim Dreaper because of the ground, as were four others, including the 1989 Gold Cup runner-up Yahoo. Former Irish National favourites Barney Burnett and Bankers Benefit ran again, although neither was in the form of the year before, while Homer Scott's runner, The Committee, had been second in the SunAlliance Chase at Cheltenham and was expected to relish the trip at Fairyhouse. The two expected to give Dessie most to think about, however, were Bold Flyer and Have A Barney. Like Desert Orchid, Bold Flyer was a natural front-runner, although the horse was more recognised for running over shorter distances. Trained by Jim Dreaper, Bold Flyer had finished second on his latest start and was a lightly raced horse, partnered in the Irish National by the good amateur rider, Miss Sarah Collen. The fact that Have A Barney was as low as 7/1 in the betting was something of a surprise considering his recent form, which had included two falls. However, the Arthur Moore-trained horse had finished third in 1989, and the hope was that he could reproduce that course form once more for jockey Tom Taaffe.

The enormous Easter Monday crowd, despite being bombed by hail and snow while the horses were in the paddock, mobbed and cheered Desert Orchid as he made his way out on to the course, showing their full appreciation of a wonderful racehorse. Once the race was underway, Bold Flyer, as expected, jumped off into the lead, but showing no respect for his young rival, Desert Orchid swept by him at the second fence and assumed control.

Barney Burnett (7) goes to post under Brendan Sheridan.

Desert Orchid and Richard Dunwoody pre-race.

no doubting Desert Orchid was one of the finest winners of the Irish National in the race's history, and as a fitting tribute, the horse was given a resounding 'three cheers' in the winner's enclosure, followed by a fourth just for good measure.

1990 IRISH GRAND NATIONAL RESULT

FATE	HORSE	AGE/WEIGHT	JOCKEY
1st	DESERT ORCHID	11.12.0	R. DUNWOODY
2nd	BARNEY BURNETT	10.10.0	B. SHERIDAN
3rd	HAVE A BARNEY	9.10.2	T.J. TAAFFE
4th	Cloney Grange	11.10.0	D.H. O'Connor
5th	Riska's River	8.10.0	F.J. Flood
6th	The Committee	7.10.0	C. O'Dwyer
7th	Feltrim Hill Lad	9.10.0	M.M. Lynch
8th	Cushinstown	7.10.0	A.J. O'Brien
Fell	Another Plano	9.10.0	C.F. Swan
Fell	Caddy	9.10.0	T.J. Ryan
Fell	Us And Joe	7.10.0	M. Flynn
Pulled-Up	Bankers Benefit	10.10.0	A. Powell
Pulled-Up	Belsir	8.10.0	T. Carmody
Pulled-Up	Bold Flyer	7.10.0	Miss S. Collen

16 April 1990
Going – Good
Sponsor – Jameson
Winner – £53,592
Race Distance – three miles four furlongs
Time – 7mins 30.09secs
14 Ran
Winner trained by D.R.C. Elsworth
Winner owned by R. Burridge
Desert Orchid, grey gelding by Grey Mirage – Flower Child.

Betting – Evens DESERT ORCHID, 6/1 Bold Flyer, 7/1 Have A Barney, 14/1 Us And Joe, 16/1 Barney Burnett & The Committee, 20/1 Another Plano & Belsir, 25/1 Riska's River, 33/1 Caddy & Feltrim Hill Lad, 40/1 Bankers Benefit & Cushinstown, 100/1 Cloney Grange.

The whole race centred on the front-running tactics of the grey, and despite Bold Flyer consistently snapping at the favourite's heels, Desert Orchid jumped with his useful panache, though there were at least eight horses still in contention by the time the field arrived at the sixth last, with the Conor O'Dwyer-ridden seven-year-old The Committee most prominent.

But with Bold Flyer unable to maintain his challenge, Dunwoody soon asked Desert Orchid to increase the tempo, and by the third last, the last of the grey's challengers, The Committee, had been shrugged off defiantly. The crowd were on their feet with excitement as the grey superstar prepared to take the final fences. A slight mistake three out was followed by a leap of gigantic proportions at the second last, and although the horse was clearly getting tired, the race was his bar a fall at the last. At the final fence, Desert Orchid brought gasps from all in attendance as he clattered the obstacle. A lesser horse may well have come down, but twisting his way cleverly out of trouble, Desert Orchid's strength held him upright, together with Dunwoody sitting calmly in the saddle. With disaster averted, the grey sauntered up the run-in to a tremendous reception, winning the race by twelve lengths. Brendan Sheridan guided Barney Burnett into second, with Have A Barney and the rank outsider Cloney Grange the next to finish. Bold Flyer was pulled-up on the second circuit by Miss Collen.

It had been a mightily brave performance by Desert Orchid, Dunwoody confirming the horse the best he had ever ridden. The jockey thought the horse's hard race at Cheltenham had understandably taken a lot out of the grey, but the horse's class and courage had won him the Irish National in convincing style, and he became the second British-trained winner in six years. Although he was eleven at the time of his Fairyhouse success, this was far from the last fine moment for Dessie. He still had his fourth King George win to come later in the year, and would also finish third again in the Gold Cup in 1991 behind Garrison Savannah. There was

Dunwoody being interviewed following Dessie's great win.

1991 – OMERTA

One of the feel-good stories of the 1990/91 National Hunt season had been the performance of leading British trainer Martin Pipe in rescuing former Irish National runner-up Omerta from the racing scrapheap, and producing the horse, fit and well, on the racecourse. Omerta had looked a star in the making when finishing second to Insure in the 1986 Irish Grand National, when trained by Homer Scott. But suffering terribly from injury in the interim period, Omerta had barely seen a racecourse until March 1991, where having been restored to fighting fitness, Omerta won the Kim Muir Chase at the Cheltenham Festival. Omerta had won in runaway style at Cheltenham, able to settle into a smooth, fluent jumping rhythm, and the chestnut with the distinctive white face was subsequently made favourite for the 1991 Irish Grand National, for which he would be the record-breaking trainer's first ever runner. One of the other intriguing elements of Omerta's revival had been the presence of nineteen-year-old claiming jockey Adrian Maguire. Cool, capable and bullishly strong, Maguire was a star on the rise, and would soon become one of the finest jockeys in the sport, especially effective in a finish. It was of testament to Omerta's owners, Jim and Dermot McMorrow, that they kept faith with the amateur rather than opting for a seasoned professional.

Opposition to Omerta was strong and plentiful, with both Cahervillahow and Cool Ground expected to give the favourite much to worry about. Trained, together with the useful chestnut novice Rawhide, by Mouse Morris, Cahervillahow had been the leading staying novice in Ireland the season before. A classy brown seven-year-old, Cahervillahow had been sent to Newbury at the beginning of the season to contest the Hennessy Cognac Gold Cup, where he had finished third behind Arctic Call and Master Bob. Although an administrative mistake had prevented the horse from running in the Cheltenham Gold Cup, Cahervillahow ran instead in the National Hunt Handicap Chase at the Festival, losing ground at the start before rallying late to be denied by only the imminent Aintree Grand National winner, Seagram. Cool Ground, a previous Irish National runner, had run in the Gold Cup. Formerly trained by Richard Mitchell but now with Reg Akehurst, the leggy chestnut had won the season's Welsh Grand National before finishing fourth at Cheltenham. As a result, Cool Ground carried top weight of 12st at Fairyhouse, where he was partnered by Englishman Jimmy Frost.

Other British challengers included the Gordon Richards-trained grey Four Trix, third in the Midlands National at Uttoxeter in March, and the Kim Bailey-trained Man O' Magic, a good, consistent chaser between two and three miles, but unproven at the Irish National trip. Of the home team, Paddy Mullins saddled the useful duo Us And Joe and The Gooser, while the likes of Have A Barney and Cloney Grange ran in the race again.

It was the outsider, Capincur Boy, that led them to the first fence, where Final Tub was an early casualty, and the leader held his place until halfway, with Four Trix, Cool Ground, Cahervillahow and Omerta well positioned.

Despite being a little bit hesitant over the initial fences, Omerta settled well for Maguire, and the horse was soon settled into the admirable jumping rhythm he had found at Cheltenham. At the start of the second circuit, Maguire sent Omerta up to dispute the lead, and by the fourteenth fence, the horse had carved open a clear lead. In behind Omerta, Four Trix had weakened rapidly, struggling to maintain a position on the yielding ground, and was soon pulled-up, while the challengers began lining-up as the second circuit progressed, among them Cool Ground, Rawhide, The Gooser, Mirage Day, Man O' Magic, Cahervillahow and Mr Hoy, with the lattermost going well until coming down at the fifteenth.

An exciting finish looked in store, although Omerta was beginning to draw clear, and the crowd roared their approval as the favourite came into the finishing straight with a healthy advantage, further back Man O' Magic and later Rawhide fell by the wayside. As he had turned for home, Maguire had glanced over his shoulder and seen most of his rivals in trouble, including Cool Ground, the top weight appearing one-paced. But one horse mounting a serious late challenge was Cahervillahow, and the Charlie Swan-ridden horse was closing all the time on the favourite.

It was developing into a fascinating spectacle, and Maguire later admitted that he knew Omerta had to jump the final two fences with the maximum precision to fend off the threat of Cahervillahow. Omerta duly flew the last two, but Cahervillahow was classy and resilient, and the two were soon involved in an all-out battle to the line. In one of the most exciting finishes ever to an Irish National, Maguire galvanised Omerta for one last extra effort, and thrilling the vast crowd, held on to beat Cahervillahow by a short head. Cool Ground, winner of the Cheltenham Gold Cup the year after, was a distance away in third, followed in by the stablemates The Gooser and Us And Joe. Giving the winner nearly 2st, Cahervillahow won many supporters with his brave run, and emerged as the class horse of the contest. The runner-up would most likely have been a major factor in the 1992 Gold Cup but for injury, and he was not a lucky horse throughout his career, although an ultra-consistent one. Cahervillahow twice finished in the places in the Hennessy at Newbury, was disqualified after winning the Whitbread Gold Cup at Sandown later in the season, and also finished runner-up in the void Grand National at Aintree in 1993.

Omerta, however, had proved a fairytale winner, with Pipe deservedly reaping much praise for his efforts in recuperating the horse. Maguire was the toast of the hour, and although he never did win the Jockey's Championship in Britain that his ability deserved, he was one of the toughest and most determined riders of the 1990s, winning the Gold Cup on Cool Ground in 1992 in a finish every bit as stirring as Omerta's Irish National win. Omerta was quickly installed among the favourites for the imminent Grand National at Aintree, but Pipe withdrew him from that contest, instead contesting the Scottish National at Ayr three weeks later, where Omerta finished second to Killone Abbey, before finishing fifth in the Whitbread. Omerta's final racecourse appearance came at Aintree in 1992, when he was pulled-up in the Grand National.

1991 IRISH GRAND NATIONAL RESULT

FATE	HORSE	AGE/WEIGHT	JOCKEY
1st	OMERTA	11.10.9	MR A. MAGUIRE
2nd	CAHERVILLAHOW	7.11.12	C.F. SWAN
3rd	COOL GROUND	9.12.0	J. FROST
4th	THE GOOSER	8.10.4	C. O'DWYER
5th	Us And Joe	8.11.8	M. Flynn
6th	Astral River	8.10.8	D.P. Murphy
7th	Mirage Day	8.10.0	N. Williamson
8th	Fatal Hesitation	8.9.8	Mr R. Kehoe
9th	Roc De Prince	8.11.8	B. Sheridan
10th	Welcome Pin	10.10.6	T. Carmody
Fell	Final Tub	8.10.6	K. Morgan
Fell	Kindly King	7.10.0	A.J. O'Brien
Fell	Man O' Magic	10.11.8	M. Perrett
Fell	Mr Hoy	8.10.0	F. Woods
Fell	Rawhide	7.10.0	K.F. O'Brien
Fell	Writer's Quay	8.10.0	A. Powell
Pulled-Up	Capincur Boy	9.10.0	J.F. Titley
Pulled-Up	Cloney Grange	12.10.7	D.H. O'Connor
Pulled-Up	Four Trix	10.10.13	N. Doughty
Pulled-Up	Have A Barney	10.11.7	T.J. Taaffe
Pulled-Up	Mountain Prince	12.10.0	D.P. Geoghegan
Pulled-Up	What A Fox	9.10.0	J.P. Banahan

1 April 1991
Going – Good to Yielding
Sponsor – Jameson
Winner – £51,111
Race Distance – three miles five furlongs
Time – 7mins 52.60secs
22 Ran
Winner trained by M.C. Pipe
Winner owned by Mrs E. McMorrow
Omerta, chestnut gelding by Quayside – Cherry Princess.

Betting – 6/1 OMERTA, 7/1 Cool Ground, 8/1 Cahervillahow, 10/1 Final Tub
& Rawhide, 11/1 Four Trix, 14/1 Man O' Magic, Mr Hoy & Us And Joe, 16/1
Welcome Pin, 20/1 Cloney Grange, Have A Barney, Roc De Prince, What A Fox
& Writer's Quay, 25/1 Mirage Day & The Gooser, 28/1 Astral River, 50/1 Kindly
King, 66/1 Capincur Boy, 100/1 Fatal Hesitation & Mountain Prince.

Omerta (8) puts in a magnificent leap.

Above: *Omerta holds off Cahervillahow
(pink hearts) in a thrilling finish.*

Right: *Adrian Maguire shows off his trophy.*

1992 – VANTON

The defection of the Martin Pipe-trained, dual Welsh Grand National winner Bonanza Boy from the 1992 Irish Grand National meant that carrying top weight would be the seven-year-old novice Captain Dibble. Trained in England by Nigel Twiston-Davies, Captain Dibble had, nine days earlier, won the Scottish Grand National at Ayr by eight lengths, continuing what had been a highly successful and consistent season for the horse. He had also finished fifth in a very good renewal of the SunAlliance Chase at Cheltenham, finishing behind the likes of Miinnehoma, Bradbury Star and Run For Free. Captain Dibble was sired by Crash Course, the same sire as Maid Of Money and future Aintree Grand National hero Rough Quest, yet not since Herring Gull had a novice won the Irish National with such a hefty weight (Captain Dibble carried 11st 11lbs). But with the British Champion Jockey Peter Scudamore on board, confidence in the horse was plentiful, and Captain Dibble started as the 4/1 favourite.

Besides Captain Dibble, other British runners included Over The Road, Ace Of Spies and Boraceva. The chestnut Over The Road had finished fourth and eighth in the last two runnings of the Grand National at Aintree and was cleared to take his chance at Fairyhouse by trainer John Upson, having wrenched a joint when pulling-up at exercise earlier in the week. Like Over The Road, an eleven-year-old, Ace Of Spies was trained by Mrs Gill Jones and was partnered in the Irish National by 1991 winning jockey Adrian Maguire, sufficiently recovered from breaking his collar-bone on the second day of the Grand National meeting at Aintree. Boraceva was trained by Toby Balding, who had recently won the Cheltenham Gold Cup with former Irish National runner Cool Ground, and the nine-year-old had finished second to Captain Dibble in the Scottish National to earn his place in the Fairyhouse line-up.

Of the home team, most fancied were Ebony Jane, Rawhide, Open The Gate, Bishops Staff and Vanton. Trainer Fergie Sutherland was extremely confident over the chances of Ebony Jane, a tough, sound-jumping brown mare that was on a four-timer, while, despite coming unstuck at the first fence at Aintree recently in the Grand National, the Mouse Morris-trained Rawhide had run very well for a long way in the 1991 Irish National. Open the Gate was a very consistent grey seven-year-old ridden by Charlie Swan, while the Mick O'Toole-trained Bishops Staff, a course winner and also the winner of the season's National Trial at Punchestown, carried the same colours as Party Politics, the very impressive winner of the recent Grand National at Aintree. Vanton was trained by Michael O'Brien, a trainer whose previous two representatives in the race had been Eggnog and King Spruce, second in 1980 and the winner in 1982 respectively. Vanton had won three times during the season, and despite also suffering a number of falls, the eight-year-old held second place in the betting at 13/2.

It was the Jim Dreaper-trained River Tarquin, together with Ebony Jane, that disputed the lead on the first circuit, with the likes of Vanton, Sooner-Still, War Melody and Boraceva all prominent. The yielding ground meant the pace was steady, but a large number of horses stayed in contention until well into the second circuit.

For some way, it was clear that the two horses travelling the best were Vanton and Over The Road. Both had been tucked in just behind the leaders, well placed by their respective jockeys, Jason Titley and Robbie Supple. Vanton was going so well five fences from home, that Titley sent him on, dashing by the long-time leaders River Tarquin and Ebony Jane, and setting sail for home. With the likes of Ace Of Spies, Over The Gate and War Melody having fallen, and with both Captain Dibble and Boraceva making mistakes and being pulled-up, it was Over The Road that was the one to chase after Vanton.

Vanton had carved open a useful lead, but a mistake three out allowed Over The Road the chance to get back at him. The stage was set for a real battle in the straight, but despite his mistake, Vanton kept on finding more. Strongly driven by Titley, having cleared the final fence, Vanton ground out the final yards to the line in bullish fashion, holding the game Over The Road by four lengths by the time the winning post was reached. Twenty lengths back in third came River Tarquin, with New Mill House, Rossi Novae, Ebony Jane and Rawhide the next to complete. Captain Dibble had never been a factor. The horse had raced mainly in midfield throughout the contest but when asked by Scudamore to challenge seven out, the horse came under pressure quickly and was pulled-up before the fourth last. After the race, Captain Dibble was found to be lame and the vet reported the horse to be 'clinically abnormal', however, within twenty-four hours, Captain Dibble was fine. Sadly, the same was not true of the brave runner-up, Over The Road. It emerged the horse had fractured a cannon bone at the second last fence, and only through sheer determination and courage had the horse completed. Over The Road remained in Ireland for some days as vets tried valiantly to save the horse. Alas, the efforts were to no avail and sadly Over The Road had to be put down.

The Irish National was the culmination of a fine season for the twenty-one-year-old rising star Titley, a season that had seen the jockey win important races such as the Ladbroke Hurdle, Thyestes Chase and Coral Hurdle Final. While it is fair to say his career never really progressed as had been initially expected, Titley did enjoy one glorious moment in 1995, when he won the Grand National at Aintree aboard Jenny Pitman's runner Royal Athlete. A second Irish National win proved the training skills of Michael O'Brien. The trainer had been confined to a wheelchair ever since a riding fall ended his career. The Naas-based trainer had planned to run Vanton (a horse that never won again after Fairyhouse, despite racing until 1996) in the Irish National for some time, and the win was ultimately very impressive.

1992 IRISH GRAND NATIONAL RESULT

FATE	HORSE	AGE/WEIGHT	JOCKEY
1st	VANTON	8.10.11	J.F. TITLEY
2nd	OVER THE ROAD	11.11.5	R. SUPPLE
3rd	RIVER TARQUIN	8.11.4	K. MORGAN
4th	NEW MILL HOUSE	9.11.7	T.J. TAAFFE
5th	Rossi Novae	9.10.10	A.J. O'Brien
6th	Ebony Jane	7.11.3	A. Powell
7th	Rawhide	8.11.8	K.F. O'Brien
8th	Sooner-Still	8.10.10	N. Williamson
Fell	Ace Of Spies	11.11.1	A. Maguire
Fell	Candy Well VI	10.11.5	L.P. Cusack
Fell	Grand Habit	8.10.12	J. Magee
Fell	Lacken Beau	8.11.1	P. McWilliams
Fell	Open The Gate	7.10.12	C.F. Swan
Fell	War Melody	9.10.0	H. Rogers
Pulled-Up	Bishops Staff	7.10.0	C. O'Dwyer
Pulled-Up	Boraceva	9.11.4	Richard Guest
Pulled-Up	Captain Dibble	7.11.11	P. Scudamore
Pulled-Up	Cloney Grange	13.10.8	D.H. O'Connor
Pulled-Up	Cloughtaney	11.10.11	Niall Byrne
Pulled-Up	Final Tub	9.12.0	G.M. O'Neill
Pulled-Up	Forgestown	10.10.7	J. Old Jones
Pulled-Up	Writer's Quay	9.10.9	J.P. Banahan
Brought Down	Treat Me Good	9.10.0	J. Pearse

20 April 1992
Going – Yielding
Sponsor – Jameson
Winner – £54,392
Race Distance – three miles five furlongs
Time – 7mins 56.4secs
23 Ran
Winner trained by M.J.P. O'Brien
Winner owned by N. McCabe
Vanton, chestnut gelding by Orchestra – Subiacco.

Betting – 4/1 Captain Dibble, 13/2 VANTON, 10/1 Open The Gate, 11/1 Rawhide, 12/1 Ebony Jane & Lacken Beau, 14/1 Bishops Staff, 16/1 Boraceva, Over The Road & Writer's Quay, 20/1 Ace Of Spies, New Mill House & Rossi Novae, 25/1 Final Tub, Grand Habit, River Tarquin & Sooner-Still, 33/1 Treat Me Good, 40/1 Cloney Grange, Cloughtaney & Forgestown, 100/1 Candy Well VI & War Melody.

Top: *English raider Over The Road (white) flies a fence.*

Middle: *The strong chestnut Vanton puts in a stylish jump en route to victory.*

Right: *Trainer Michael O'Brien with the winning trophy.*

1993 – EBONY JANE

The 1993 Grand National at Aintree had been a total fiasco. The race was marred by two false starts, and after the second of these, nearly every runner in the field, amidst a sea of confusion, had continued racing. Seven horses, led home by the Jenny Pitman-trained Esha Ness, completed the entire two circuits, only for the race to be declared void. It had been an absolute disaster, making a mockery of racing and branding the sport unprofessional. At Fairyhouse nine days later, the 1993 Irish Grand National attracted a very big field of twenty-seven, five of which (Zeta's Lad, The Gooser, Royal Athlete, Laura's Beau and The Committee) had run in the shambles at Aintree and were seeking compensation. Zeta's Lad and Royal Athlete were representing Britain, and were joined in the field by three compatriots, the high-class trio of Rushing Wild, Sibton Abbey and Cool Ground, making the 1993 one of the strongest, in terms of both quality and quantity, for some time.

Favourite, and rightly so, was the John Upson-trained chestnut Zeta's Lad. Having struggled through a series of injuries the season before, Zeta's Lad was perhaps the most improved chaser in training during the 1992/93 season, running up a sequence of five consecutive victories, improving each time and showing fine jumping ability, staying prowess and a dogged determination not to be beaten in his races. He had got the better of Ebony Jane in the Thyestes Chase at Gowran Park and then won the Racing Post Chase at Kempton, a victory that convinced Upson to aim the horse at the Aintree showpiece. Having jumped safely for a circuit at Aintree, the horse, along with many others recognising the sorry state of affairs, was pulled-up. After the race, Upson was perhaps the most furious of all the trainers involved, indicating that the situation 'wouldn't have happened in a point-to-point field in Ireland'. Obviously, these comments offended some, yet Upson insisted no offence was intended. The media blew the situation out of proportion, with the trainer receiving a number of abusive telephone calls. But all those at Fairyhouse welcomed the trainer and Zeta's Lad on their arrival at Fairyhouse, and thankfully, the situation soon subsided. Having sent the ill-fated Over The Road over to finish a brave second the year before, Upson saw Zeta's Lad begin the race the 11/2 favourite.

Cases could be made for each of the British representatives. Royal Athlete, an injury-plagued horse, had run the race of his life to finish third behind Jodami and Rushing Wild in the Cheltenham Gold Cup, and despite falling on the first circuit at Aintree, both trainer Jenny Pitman and jockey Mark Pitman indicated their confidence in the horse's chance. Sibton Abbey, trained by Ferdy Murphy, had won the Hennessy at Newbury earlier in the season and finished an honourable fifth in the Cheltenham Gold Cup, but had now risen considerably in the handicap, while Cool Ground, the Gold Cup hero of 1992, had regressed somewhat during the season, but remained a dangerous opponent to the younger brigade. However, Zeta's Lad aside, the real gem from Britain was the beautiful, dark-bay ex-hunter from Martin Pipe's yard, Rushing Wild. The horse had won the 1992 Foxhunters' at Cheltenham and had gone from strength to strength during the season, running with rich promise each time in his front-running style, with his season reaching its high point with a narrow defeat by Jodami in the Gold Cup. His efforts had not gone unnoticed though, and the horse carried 12st top weight at Fairyhouse, but with Richard Dunwoody in the saddle, the horse was a hot fancy, and started 6/1.

The home team challenge was similarly strong and deep. Both The Committee and Laura's Beau had jumped round the course in the void National and were fancied to continue their good form, while, despite falling in the same race, Paddy Mullins' hope, The Gooser, remained one of the better outsiders. Recent Leopardstown winner For William was fancied for trainer Michael Hourigan, but it was the Thyestes Chase runner-up, Ebony Jane, that found most support. A tough, little brown mare, now trained by Francis Flood, Ebony Jane was a very gutsy horse, always prepared to give her all. Only eight, she was from the excellent sire Roselier, and was ridden by the darling of Irish racing, Charlie Swan, who had enjoyed a fantastic season, including taking the top jockey honours at the Cheltenham Festival.

It was to be a race of much incident, and started with River Tarquin jumping out into a lead before Rushing Wild took over at the third fence. At the fifth, much of the British challenge fell by the wayside. Huge groans could be heard amongst the crowd when Royal Athlete came down in mid-division, and independently, Cool Ground also fell, together with the Irish outsider Lamh Eile. Cool Ground's departure had ramifications later in the race, for when running loose, the horse interfered with Captain Brandy, carrying that horse out, and in the same process, forcing Ferromyn to unship his rider.

Rushing Wild was still tanking along merrily in the lead, albeit at a conservative pace, as the second circuit began, closely followed by the likes of Ebony Jane, Zeta's Lad, Joe White, Dagwood and River Tarquin. But on the approach to the top bend, tragedy struck. Pulled-up sharply by Dunwoody, something had gone seriously wrong with Rushing Wild. Later at the racecourse stables, it was revealed that the horse had suffered a broken pelvis and was haemorrhaging because the jagged edges of the bone had cut into an artery. Despite valiant attempts to save him, Rushing Wild was put down. It was a cruel twist and a sad end for a horse that was rapidly turning into one of the best steeplechasers in Britain and Ireland. Dunwoody later suggested he thought Rushing Wild would have eventually won a Gold Cup. Sadly, we will never know.

Ebony Jane had been third at the time of Rushing Wild's demise, but the horse was left prominent behind new leader Joe White as the race entered its final stages. Outsider Allezmoss was making progress, while Zeta's Lad was in the picture too as favourite backers rose to their feet expectantly. But it was Ebony Jane that hit the front at the third last and began to come clear as Joe White weakened quickly and both Zeta's Lad and Allezmoss soon came under pressure.

Jumping the last, Ebony Jane looked set for an easy win, but having been held up, the unconsidered Rust Never Sleeps had made tremendous progress from the sixteenth onwards. Really flying the last two fences under an inspirational ride from Tony O'Brien, Rust Never Sleeps came with a devastating late attack on the leader. However, Swan was able to keep Ebony Jane up to her work, and although the mare was clearly tiring in the closing stages, she had enough left to thwart the brave challenge of Rust Never Sleeps at the line, and held on for a length success. Zeta's Lad, carrying a big weight of 11st 5lbs, had battled bravely in the closing stages, but could not quicken when Ebony Jane had gone for home, yet still finished with credit in third ahead of Allezmoss. Zeta's Lad had been the only one of the heralded British

Left: *The brilliant but tragic Rushing Wild (black and yellow) takes off during the 1993 race.*

Above left: *Charlie Swan with Ebony Jane.*

Above right: *Charlie Swan salutes a narrow victory on Ebony Jane over Rust Never Sleeps.*

challenge to complete, with Sibton Abbey never a factor, pulled-up by Steve Smith-Eccles before five out.

Ebony Jane, owned by County Cork businessman James Lynch, had proved a most worthy winner of the Irish National, and despite being a small horse, had benefited from a relatively light weight of 10st 7lbs. She would prove a worthy stayer in big races, finishing a very good fourth behind Miinnehoma in the following season's Grand National at Aintree. It was a first Irish National win for Swan, one of the very best jockeys of the 1990s, and second as a trainer for seven-time Champion Irish amateur jockey Flood, following Garoupe's success in 1970.

1993 IRISH GRAND NATIONAL RESULT

FATE	HORSE	AGE/WEIGHT	JOCKEY
1st	EBONY JANE	8.10.7	C.F. SWAN
2nd	RUST NEVER SLEEPS	9.10.6	A.J. O'BRIEN
3rd	ZETA'S LAD	10.11.5	R. SUPPLE
4th	ALLEZMOSS	7.10.0	F. WOODS
5th	For William	7.10.0	K.F. O'Brien
6th	Crawford Says	8.10.0	P. McWilliams
7th	Joe White	7.10.0	P. Carberry
8th	Mass Appeal	8.10.1	B. Sheridan
9th	The Committee	10.10.9	J. Shortt
10th	Ounavarra Creek	8.10.0	H. Rogers
11th	Dagwood	8.10.0	D.T. Evans
12th	Laura's Beau	9.10.8	C. O'Dwyer
13th	Bishops Hall	7.10.3	J.F. Titley
Fell	Cool Ground	11.11.12	A. Maguire
Fell	Gerties Pride	9.10.0	C. O'Brien
Fell	Inch Lady	8.10.0	T. Horgan
Fell	Kindly King	9.10.0	J. Magee
Fell	Lamh Eile	10.10.0	T.J. Mitchell
Fell	Royal Athlete	10.10.13	M. Pitman
Pulled-Up	Haki Saki	7.10.3	G.M. O'Neill
Pulled-Up	River Tarquin	9.11.0	K. Morgan
Pulled-Up	Rushing Wild	8.12.0	R. Dunwoody
Pulled-Up	Sibton Abbey	8.11.13	S. Smith-Eccles
Pulled-Up	The Gooser	10.10.4	S.H. O'Donovan
Unseated Rider	Rossi Novae	10.10.0	M. Duffy
Carried Out	Captain Brandy	8.10.0	F.J. Flood
Carried Out	Ferromyn	8.10.0	Mr S.R. Murphy

12 April 1993
Going – Yielding
Sponsor – Jameson
Winner – £62,580
Race Distance – three miles five furlongs
Time – 7mins 59.8secs
27 Ran
Winner trained by F. Flood
Winner owned by James Lynch
Ebony Jane, brown mare by Roselier – Advantage.

Betting – 11/2 Zeta's Lad, 6/1 EBONY JANE & Rushing Wild, 13/2 Royal Athlete, 12/1 Cool Ground, For William & Sibton Abbey, 14/1 Laura's Beau, 16/1 River Tarquin, 20/1 Allezmoss, Bishops Hall, Captain Brandy, Haki Saki & The Committee, 25/1 Ferromyn & Mass Appeal, 33/1 Joe White & The Gooser, 50/1 Crawford Says, 66/1 Dagwood, Inch Lady, Ounavarra Creek & Rust Never Sleeps, 100/1 Kindly King, Lamh Eile & Rossi Novae, 150/1 Gerties Pride.

1994 – SON OF WAR

Favourite for the 1994 Irish Grand National was the talented but fragile ten-year-old, High Peak. Trained by Edward O'Grady, High Peak was a big, heavy horse that had not run at all the season before because he had broken down on both front legs. Indeed, O'Grady admitted that the horse required a serious amount of individual attention and regarded it as an achievement just to get High Peak back on the racecourse. But get High Peak back he had, and the horse had been very impressive when winning the Leopardstown Chase in January. Like O'Grady's previous Irish National winner, Bit Of A Skite, High Peak was owned by J.P. McManus, and with the trainer reporting the horse to be in grand shape, High Peak started the race the 9/4 favourite, his chance boosted by an enticing weight of 10st 7lbs.

With a British challenge consisting of only the Sue Smith-trained mare Baltic Brown and the winner of the Midlands Grand National at Uttoxeter, Glenbrook D'Or, the Irish horses were the focus of the betting interest. With the Cheltenham Gold Cup fourth, Flashing Steel, being withdrawn by trainer John Mulhern because of soft ground, the task of carrying top weight fell to the Michael Hourigan-trained chestnut, Deep Bramble. A seven-year-old by Deep Run, Deep Bramble was a progressive staying chaser that had finished eighth in the Cheltenham Gold Cup behind the French horse The Fellow, a race that the 1993 Irish National heroine, Ebony Jane, had also run in, although the mare had unseated Charlie Swan in that contest. Deep Bramble was a hot fancy in the market at 8/1, while Ebony Jane, partnered by Liam Cusack after Swan opted to ride High Peak, was a 10/1 chance.

It certainly appeared an open renewal of the Irish National, with trainers Mouse Morris and Austin Leahy confident over the chances of their respective entrants, Belvederian and Callmecha, while Peter McCreery saddled the seven-year-old grey, Son Of War. A good novice chaser the season before, Son Of War had run five times during the season, winning once at Fairyhouse in late November, and his form throughout the season had the grey closely matched to the likes of Callmecha and High Peak, finishing third behind the latter in the Leopardstown Chase in January. Opined to be a strong stayer, Son Of War was ridden, as he normally was, by Frank Woods, whose father Paddy had won the race on both Last Link in 1963 and Splash in 1965.

Fairyhouse was subjected to snowstorms during the day, including a severe one shortly before the off that left conditions testing, but by the time of the start, the excitement amongst the vast crowd was as high as ever. It was Nuaffe, trained by Pat Fahy and ridden by Sean O'Donovan, that was to set the pace for the 1994 Irish National. He took the field along intently, closely marshalled by Son Of War, Ebony Jane and Baltic Brown, with High Peak lodged into a mid-division position.

It soon became obvious that Nuaffe was attempting to run the legs off his rivals, as he set a strong pace, and despite some awful fencing, the leader had many in the field in trouble quicker than expected. Among those unable to live with the gallop were Deep Bramble and Glenbrook D'Or, but it was the run of the favourite, High Peak, that was giving most cause for concern. The horse was never able to improve from a position in the middle of the pack, and when he became increasingly detached, he was eventually pulled-up by Swan four out. The

jockey later reported that High Peak had run 'dead', leaving O'Grady perplexed. Frustratingly, High Peak was found to be post-race normal.

With many of his rivals long since beaten off, Nuaffe continued his merry dance towards the latter stages. Belvederian, ridden by English jockey Jamie Osborne, had briefly looked like mounting a challenge, making strong progress into fourth place until falling six fences out, while Baltic Brown had moved into second until weakening from the fourth last. With Nuaffe shooting clear after three out, it was left to Son Of War and the stablemates, Ebony Jane and Captain Brandy, to give chase.

Son Of War had made a mistake at the third last that seemed sure to ruin his chance of winning. But the horse was a resilient stayer, and strongly ridden by Woods, rallied to throw down a challenge to Nuaffe. For his part, Nuaffe understandably began to tire by the final fence, and with the grey finishing powerfully, a rousing finish was on. With Son Of War finishing the stronger, Woods was able to drive his horse past the tiring Nuaffe, and staying on stoutly. Son Of War won the Irish National by four-and-a-half lengths. Nuaffe was a gallant second, the horse was far from a graceful jumper, but he had run with heart and had only found one horse better on the day. Ebony Jane was nine lengths back in third, with Captain Brandy following her home.

An intriguing Irish National had been won by Son Of War, expertly guided home by Woods, who would, in 1996, achieve his greatest success outside of Ireland by riding the Arthur Moore-trained Klairon Davis to victory in the Queen Mother Champion Chase at Cheltenham. Thirty-one-year-old trainer Peter McCreery,

The favourite High Peak goes to post prior to a disappointing run in the 1994 race.

The hardy grey Son Of War jumps a fence in splendid fashion.

Son Of War leaves 1993 winner Ebony Jane trailing in his wake to win the Irish National.

based at Clane, County Kildare, had taken over his stable when his father, also named Peter, had died from a massive heart attack in 1988. His father had sent out Seskin Bridge to be second in the 1985 race, and for the younger McCreery, the initial years of training had proved difficult, but the victory of Son Of War had been a tremendous boost to the stable, whose string had risen to around twenty-five. After the race, McCreery immediately targeted Son Of War at future Aintree Grand Nationals, given the horse's strong ability to stay longer trips. The grey ran in the Aintree race in 1996, running well until unseating his rider at the second Canal Turn. Despite his misfortune at Aintree, Son Of War enjoyed a long racing career that carried on until the horse was thirteen.

1994 IRISH GRAND NATIONAL RESULT

FATE	HORSE	AGE/WEIGHT	JOCKEY
1st	SON OF WAR	7.10.10	F. WOODS
2nd	NUAFFE	9.10.0	S.H.O. DONOVAN
3rd	EBONY JANE	9.11.1	L.P. CUSACK
4th	CAPTAIN BRANDY	9.10.0	F.J. FLOOD
5th	Commercial Artist	8.10.12	C.N. Bowens
6th	Baltic Brown	9.10.0	Richard Guest
7th	Callmecha	9.10.0	T. Hogan
8th	Jassu	8.10.0	C. O'Brien
9th	Mass Appeal	9.10.0	B. Sheridan
Fell	Belvederian	7.10.8	J. Osborne
Pulled-Up	All The Aces	7.10.0	C. O'Dwyer
Pulled-Up	Buckboard Bounce	8.11.3	J. Shortt
Pulled-Up	Deep Bramble	7.11.13	M. Dwyer
Pulled-Up	Glenbrook D'Or	10.10.0	B. Clifford
Pulled-Up	High Peak	10.10.7	C.F. Swan
Pulled-Up	Merapi	8.10.0	A. Powell
Pulled-Up	River Tarquin	10.10.8	K.F. O'Brien
Pulled-Up	Rust Never Sleeps	10.10.12	P. Carberry

4 April 1994
Going – Soft
Sponsor – Jameson
Winner – £55,428
Race Distance – three miles five furlongs
Time – 8mins 10.3secs
18 Ran
Winner trained by Peter McCreery
Winner owned by Mrs V. O'Brien
Son Of War, grey gelding by Pragmatic – Run Wardasha.

Betting – 9/4 High Peak, 6/1 Belvederian, 8/1 Deep Bramble, 10/1 Ebony Jane & Jassu, 12/1 Callmecha, Glenbrook D'Or & SON OF WAR, 14/1 All The Aces, 16/1 Nuaffe, 20/1 Buckboard Bounce, Commercial Artist, River Tarquin & Rust Never Sleeps, 25/1 Baltic Brown & Captain Brandy, 50/1 Mass Appeal & Merapi.

1995 – FLASHING STEEL

With the 1993 Cheltenham Gold Cup winner Jodami a late withdrawal, the weights rose significantly for the 1995 Irish Grand National. The new top weight was the powerful bay gelding, Flashing Steel, a son of the useful former hurdler Broadsword. Flashing Steel was a class act on his day, and had been good enough to finish fourth in the 1994 Gold Cup before falling in the same race in 1995. A strong, well built ten-year-old, Flashing Steel was trained by John Mulhern, and from four runs during the season (his latest being his fall at Cheltenham), the horse had won once though, significantly, this was at Fairyhouse over three-miles-one-furlong in January. With top British jockey Jamie Osborne booked to ride, Flashing Steel started at 9/1 as he attempted to become the first since Desert Orchid to carry 12st to victory in the Irish National.

Favourite for the race was Mr Boston, trained in England by Mary Reveley. The bay ten-year-old was a most consistent chaser in his prime, and from five runs during the season, Mr Boston had never been out of the first three places. It was his latest start, a three-mile chase win at Sandown in March, that propelled Mr Boston to favouritism for the Irish National, with Mrs Reveley bypassing a crack at the Grand National at Aintree (in which Mr Boston had fallen in the 1994 race) to run the horse at Fairyhouse. With one of Britain's leading northern-based jockeys, Peter Niven, in the saddle, Mr Boston started at 11/2.

Irish National old hands Ebony Jane, Nuaffe, Belvederian, Rust Never Sleeps and Captain Brandy were back to renew acquaintances, while among the interesting newcomers to the race were Antonin, Feathered Gale, Sullane River and Belmont King. Trained by Sue Bramall, the seven-year-old chestnut Antonin was something of a lazy individual, although he possessed a fair amount of talent. Antonin had most recently finished a good second in the National Hunt Handicap Chase at Cheltenham behind future Aintree National winner Rough Quest, although the horse had run in snatches there, and consequently, was fitted with first-time blinkers at Fairyhouse. As well as the nine-year-old Scribbler, Arthur Moore saddled the talented Feathered Gale, a good-ground lover that had won the Galway Plate the previous July, while the young bay mare Sullane River, from the yard of David McGrath, had won the re-routed Leopardstown Chase at Fairyhouse in January – beating Belmont King, Antonin and Scribbler in the process – before running an excellent second in the Cathcart Chase at Cheltenham. One of the most intriguing runners was Belmont King, a rapidly improving seven-year-old trained by Wexford permit-holder Simon Lambert. The trainer had been due to sell the horse sixteen months beforehand, but had failed to find a buyer and instead took out a permit to train. Since then, Belmont King had shown great potential, winning at Fairyhouse, never falling or finishing out of the first two places. In addition, Belmont King had a marked liking for the good ground present at Fairyhouse in 1995.

It was to be an incident packed Irish National, with the stiff Fairyhouse fences taking their toll on the field. With Flashing Steel and Royal Mountbrowne disputing the lead over the first, Jassu was the first to fall, bringing down The Committee – who had also gone at the first in the Aintree Grand National – in the process. After the race, Jassu's jockey, Charlie Swan, was furious, stating that Jassu had

jumped the fence well only for someone on the outside to bump him and knock his horse over. The early spills did not end there, Belmont King took his first ever fall at the second before Sullane River fell when in mid-division at the fifth.

With no more casualties for a while, it was 20/1 shot Royal Mountbrowne that continued to lead, hunted up by a chasing pack consisting of Belvederian, Nuaffe, Mr Boston, Flashing Steel and Captain Brandy, with Antonin and Rust Never Sleeps held up but travelling smoothly just behind.

The favourite Mr Boston was in the process of running a big race, and was prominently placed by the fifth last as Niven sent him forward to dispute the lead with Royal Mountbrowne and Belvederian. But a fence later, Belvederian made a bad mistake, and in doing so, badly hampered both Mr Boston and outsider Loshian. The partnership of Trevor Hogan and Loshian remained intact, but so badly had Mr Boston been hampered that Niven was unseated, frustratingly ending the favourite's involvement in the race.

By three out, both Royal Mountbrowne and Belvederian were sending out distress signals and weakening rapidly, and it was to be Rust Never Sleeps that came from off the pace to take command, no sooner had he grabbed the lead, than he quickly went clear of his rivals. Picking off the tiring horses from behind was Flashing Steel, and with every other runner now beaten, it was left to the top weight to challenge the leader.

Rust Never Sleeps had, two years previously, come from well off the pace to throw down a late challenge to the eventual winner Ebony Jane, but on this occasion, it was he that held the advantage, although he was a horse that was notorious for idling in front. Under an inspired, forceful ride from Osborne, Flashing Steel began to cut into Rust Never Sleeps' lead, having jumped the last, and in a pulsating finish that had the crowd roaring the two home, Flashing Steel's extra class prevailed, for although giving Rust Never Sleeps 2st, the top weight managed to get

Rust Never Sleeps finishes second again, this time denied by top weight Flashing Steel in 1995.

Left: *Winning trainer John Mulhern.*

Right: *Jockey Jamie Osborne with his trophy.*

up on the line to win by half-a-length. Rust Never Sleeps, again totally unconsidered beforehand, had run a blinder. Trained by Donal Hassett, the horse deserved to win an Irish Grand National, but alas, he never would. It was a terrible shame when the horse suffered a fatal shoulder injury at Aintree in the 1996 Grand National when well fancied for that race. Some way back in third came Feathered Gale, with Belvederian fourth having ruined his round with late jumping errors.

Flashing Steel had not been without his critics during the season, with many believing the ten-year-old to be past his best. But on his day, Flashing Steel was a classy performer, and Osborne later stated that the horse had travelled and jumped better than at any time during the season. The 1995 Irish National was the fifth time Flashing Steel had won at Fairyhouse, with much credit going to Mulhern for turning out the horse in such sparkling form, to become the first to carry 12st to victory since Desert Orchid, and only the second since Brown Lad in 1978. Flashing Steel was owned by Charles Haughey, a man that had helped to secure the survival of Fairyhouse racecourse when it had met with financial problems a number of years before, and Mulhern – for whom this was the biggest win of his training career – was the owner's son-in-law.

Rust Never Sleeps leads Flashing Steel over the final fence.

1995 IRISH GRAND NATIONAL RESULT

FATE	HORSE	AGE/WEIGHT	JOCKEY	17 April 1995
1st	FLASHING STEEL	10.12.0	J. OSBORNE	Going – Good
2nd	RUST NEVER SLEEPS	11.10.0	T.J. O'SULLIVAN	Sponsor – Jameson
3rd	FEATHERED GALE	8.10.0	F. WOODS	Winner – £62,079
4th	BELVEDERIAN	8.10.12	C. O'DWYER	Race Distance – three miles five furlongs
5th	Force Seven	8.10.13	Mr T.J. Murphy	Time – 7mins 41.8secs
6th	Royal Mountbrowne	7.10.0	N.T. Egan	18 Ran
7th	Antonin	7.11.11	J. Burke	Winner trained by J.E. Mulhern
8th	Ebony Jane	10.10.10	B. Sheridan	Winner owned by C.J. Haughey
9th	Nuaffe	10.11.7	J. Shortt	Flashing Steel, bay gelding by Broadsword – Kingsfold Flash.
10th	Captain Brandy	10.10.0	A. Powell	
11th	Loshian	6.10.0	T. Hogan	
12th	Bishops Hall	9.10.10	P.A. Roche	Betting – 11/2 Mr Boston, 8/1 Belvederian & Sullane River, 9/1 FLASHING
Fell	Belmont King	7.10.10	T.P. Treacy	STEEL, 10/1 Belmont King & Feathered Gale, 11/1 Antonin & Scribbler, 14/1
Fell	Jassu	9.11.1	C.F. Swan	Force Seven & Jassu, 16/1 Ebony Jane & Nuaffe, 20/1 Royal Mountbrowne, 25/1
Fell	Sullane River	7.10.10	M. Dwyer	Loshian, 33/1 Bishops Hall, Captain Brandy & The Committee, 50/1 Rust Never
Pulled-Up	Scribbler	9.10.2	K.F. O'Brien	Sleeps.
Unseated Rider	Mr Boston	10.10.10	P. Niven	
Brought Down	The Committee	12.10.0	T.J. Mitchell	

1996 – FEATHERED GALE

With the inclusion of British raiders Jodami and Cool Dawn in the field, the 1996 Irish Grand National had a classy feel to it. Although he had endured a frustrating season, Jodami remained a class act, and at eleven-years-of-age, retained plenty of ability. The horse had looked a very good winner of the Cheltenham Gold Cup in 1993 when he beat Rushing Wild, and was a close second in the race to The Fellow a year later. Jodami, trained in Yorkshire by Peter Beaumont, had proved his worth in Ireland as well, winning the valuable Irish Hennessy Cognac Gold Cup at Leopardstown no fewer than three times. Beaumont reported that Jodami – a strapping, dark bay chaser by the good sire Crash Course – to be in very good health prior to the Irish National, and despite carrying a big weight of 11st 12lbs, the horse started the 5/1 favourite.

The other important British challenge came from Cool Dawn, a hunter-chaser trained in Dorset by Robert Alner. Cool Dawn had finished an excellent second to the outstanding Irish hunter, Elegant Lord, in the Foxhunters' at the Cheltenham Festival, where he was ridden, as usual, by his amateur owner, Dido Harding. The owner had ridden Cool Dawn for three seasons (winning seven races), but realised it would have been foolish to have her first ever ride against professionals in such a race, therefore, the ride on Cool Dawn went to Conor O'Dwyer. Cool Dawn was a progressive horse and became the subject of a huge gamble before the race. From a price of 20/1, floods of money arrived for the brown gelding by Over The River, Cool Dawn eventually starting at 15/2.

While the drying ground, officially good, was considered too quick for two other British raiders, Suny Bay and Tartan Tyrant (both withdrawn), conditions were deemed perfect for Arthur Moore's runner, the 1995 third Feathered Gale. A brown gelding by Strong Gale, the horse had run his first race since November 1995 recently when finishing second to fellow Irish National runner Another Excuse at Uttoxeter in the Midlands National, although the muddy conditions were totally against Feathered Gale. Moore, knowing that his horse would be far better on a sound surface, was quietly optimistic of a big run from Feathered Gale, and with 1994 winning jockey Frank Woods booked to ride, the horse started at 8/1.

Flashing Steel returned to defend his crown with 12st top weight, while the 1994 hero Son Of War was also back having unseated his rider at the second Canal Turn in the recent Grand National at Aintree. Go Go Gallant, a stablemate of the brilliant winner of the Cheltenham Gold Cup, Imperial Call, represented Fergie Sutherland, the veteran Fissure Seal was well supported for trainer Harry De Bromhead, despite not having won for nearly three years, while Leopardstown winner Lord Singapore had been running well all season and was the mount of Richard Dunwoody. One interesting contender was Norman Conqueror, owned by Her Majesty Queen Elizabeth The Queen Mother, who was having her first runner in Ireland for twenty-five years. Despite being a stone wrong at the weights, Norman Conqueror had won his last three races for trainer Tim Thomson-Jones.

It was to be Cool Dawn that set the pace, merrily bowling along in front and taking his fences well by and large. Also prominent in the early stages were Go Go Gallant, Flashing Steel, Norman Conqueror, Son Of War and Carrigeen Kerria, but Son Of War dropped out quickly from the sixth fence and Carrigeen Kerria came down at the seventh.

As Cool Dawn continued to lead on the second circuit, the action flowed thick and fast. Jodami cruised up to join the leaders at halfway, with Feathered Gale, having been niggled along by Woods on the first circuit, also beginning to get into the argument. But Lord Singapore, having made one bad mistake at the tenth, crashed out of contention for good at the thirteenth.

There were still plenty of horses in contention as the race neared its conclusion. By the fourth last, Cool Dawn was still disputing the lead, with Go Go Gallant, Feathered Gale and Minella Lad all in the leading group. But it was Jodami, running a fine race under jockey Mark Dwyer, that appeared to be travelling the best, coming right back to his best form. Minella Lad had survived one terrible blunder at the fourteenth and although he was a close fourth at the time, the horse was tiring when he fell four out, leaving four horses to battle out the finish.

Jodami grabbed the lead from Cool Dawn before the second last, and seemed likely to record a memorable win, as both Go Go Gallant and Feathered Gale came under pressure. In fact, of the four leaders, Feathered Gale had appeared to be going the worst, and had been somewhat outpaced as Jodami made his move after three out. But first recovering and then finding extra for Woods, Feathered

Trainer Arthur Moore, jockey Fran Woods and the trilby-wearing Feathered Gale.

second victory in the race for the underrated Woods, who had similarly emulated his father, Paddy, by twice riding the winner of the race. As was his custom for big race winners, Moore placed his trilby on Feathered Gale's head as winning connections posed for photographs post-race. Although he never reached the winner's enclosure for such an important race again, Feathered Gale ran in many more top contests, including the Whitbread Gold Cup at Sandown a few weeks later (where the horse finished fifth behind fellow Irish raider Life Of A Lord), the 1996 Hennessy Cognac Gold Cup at Newbury (sixth), and the Grand National at Aintree in 1997 (pulled-up).

Above: *Feathered Gale leads Jodami over the final fence.*

Left: *Former Cheltenham Gold Cup winner Jodami in the parade.*

1996 IRISH GRAND NATIONAL RESULT

FATE	HORSE	AGE/WEIGHT	JOCKEY
1st	FEATHERED GALE	9.10.0	F. WOODS
2nd	JODAMI	11.11.12	M. DWYER
3rd	COOL DAWN	8.10.0	C. O'DWYER
4th	GO GO GALLANT	7.10.0	C.F. SWAN
5th	Another Excuse	8.10.0	B. Powell
6th	Son Of War	9.11.4	P. Carberry
7th	Johneen	10.10.0	P. McWilliams
8th	King Of The Gales	9.11.0	C. O'Brien
Fell	Lord Singapore	8.10.0	R. Dunwoody
Fell	Minella Lad	10.10.0	T. Hogan
Pulled-Up	Carrigeen Kerria	8.10.0	D.J. Casey
Pulled-Up	Fissure Seal	10.10.4	J. Shortt
Pulled-Up	Flashing Steel	11.12.0	K.F. O'Brien
Pulled-Up	Norman Conqueror	11.10.0	T.P. Treacy
Pulled-Up	Second Schedual	11.10.8	J.P. Broderick
Unseated Rider	Captain Brandy	11.10.0	F.J. Flood
Unseated Rider	Friends Of Gerald	10.10.0	P.A. Roche

8 April 1996
Going – Good
Sponsor – Jameson
Winner – £64,639
Race Distance – three miles five furlongs
Time – 7mins 25.4secs
17 Ran
Winner trained by A.L.T. Moore
Winner owned by M. O'Connor
Feathered Gale, brown gelding by Strong Gale – Farm Approach.

Betting – 5/1 Jodami, 7/1 Fissure Seal, Go Go Gallant & Lord Singapore, 15/2 Cool Dawn, 8/1 FEATHERED GALE & Son Of War, 12/1 Another Excuse & Flashing Steel, 14/1 Minella Lad, 20/1 King Of The Gales, 25/1 Norman Conqueror, 33/1 Carrigeen Kerria, Friends Of Gerald & Second Schedual, 50/1 Captain Brandy & Johneen.

Gale reeled in Cool Dawn, and then set his sights on Jodami as they approached the last.

Clearly appreciating the good ground, Feathered Gale was able to find plenty in reserve after taking the final fence, and though he had run an admirable race, Jodami – giving nearly 2st away – had no answer to his rival's renewed challenge. Drawing clear on the run-in, the margin was eight lengths at the line as Feathered Gale won the Irish National of 1996. Jodami's effort had been gallant, looking the winner for some time, while six lengths away in third came Cool Dawn. Clearly impressed by Cool Dawn's run was jockey Conor O'Dwyer, who stated his belief that the horse was far more than just a hunter-chaser. So it proved, running a similarly bold, front-running race, Cool Dawn won the Cheltenham Gold Cup in 1998 for Alner when ridden by jockey Andrew Thornton. Go Go Gallant was a long way back in fourth as the front three displayed their class, while of the eight finishers, Son Of War made up a lot of late ground to finish sixth. Amongst the race casualties had been Second Schedual, pulled-up before the ninth fence having broken a blood vessel, and Norman Conqueror, the horse pulled-up between the final two fences having cracked a bone in his knee.

In winning, trainer Arthur Moore achieved a lifetime's ambition, and joined his father Dan in both riding and training winners of the Irish National, while it was the

1997 – MUDAHIM

The largest British challenge in the history of the Irish Grand National graced the 1997 renewal. Eight horses, Giventime, Sister Stephanie, Percy Smollett, Aardwolf, Church Law, St Mellion Fairway, Mudahim and The Grey Monk, made their way to Fairyhouse for what promised to be a most interesting and exciting renewal of the race.

It was The Grey Monk that attracted most of the attention before the race, and rightly so. The horse had won eight of the ten chases he had run in, including six novices chases the season before, and wins at Ayr and Haydock in the current campaign. Trained by Gordon Richards, The Grey Monk was a big, imposing grey son of Roselier, and was a horse that jumped, stayed and had class. A beautiful traveller in his races, The Grey Monk had been made favourite for the Hennessy at Newbury earlier in the season, but despite jumping immaculately, had been beaten by a very good horse called Coome Hill, trained by Walter Dennis in Cornwall. There was no doubting the horse's credentials, yet there were two worries for his supporters. Firstly, The Grey Monk was a far better horse on softer surfaces, and with the drying ground at Fairyhouse officially good, even Richards admitted to being slightly concerned. Secondly, The Grey Monk was allocated top weight of 12st, meaning he was giving virtually every other horse in the race close to 2st. Although certainly a high-class horse, it was questionable whether The Grey Monk could emulate Desert Orchid by winning in such circumstances. Despite this, the horse started favourite at 9/2 for jockey Tony Dobbin.

Of the other British challengers, trainer David Nicholson saddled his first ever Irish Grand National runners in St Mellion Fairway and Percy Smollett, the latter a winner of six races on right-handed tracks in the previous two seasons, and a runner-up in the Racing Post Chase at Kempton the season before. One of the oldest horses in the race at eleven was Mudahim, a former high-class staying hurdler. The horse had been rejuvenated since moving to the yard of Jenny Pitman, and his performances during the season had included beating subsequent Cheltenham Festival winner, King Lucifer, at Kempton on good ground in February, and a decent sixth in the National Hunt Handicap Chase at Cheltenham. A bay gelding by Shareef Dancer, Mudahim was ridden at Fairyhouse by Jason Titley, who had formerly ridden Royal Athlete to win a Grand National for Mrs Pitman at Aintree in 1995, but who was suffering through a hard season having missed two months with a split kidney.

Heading the home challenge was Papillon, a strong six-year-old bay trained twenty-five miles from Fairyhouse by Ted Walsh. That he was a very good jumper, enjoyed good ground and was partnered by the excellent Charlie Swan was in Papillon's favour, although no horse of his age had won the race for twelve years. Lord Singapore and Fissure Seal both ran again, while Arthur Moore saddled the novice Amble Speedy, a good young stayer on the upgrade and the choice of stable jockey Frank Woods.

It was to be an incident-packed race, with much drama. Sister Stephanie caused the first rumblings by refusing to start, while Corymandel was the first to show. Aardwolf, trained by Charlie Brooks, fell at the second, and as the first circuit progressed, more falls clouded the race. At consecutive fences in the home straight first time round, the Noel Meade-trained pair of Coq Hardi Affair and The Latvian

Lark took falls. Tragically, both horses suffered broken shoulders and would later be put down, leaving Meade understandably devastated.

Having been behind early on, both Mudahim and Amble Speedy began to make rapid progress on the second circuit, while The Grey Monk also began an ominous forward move under Dobbin. With the third and second last fences omitted because the two Meade horses remained stricken, Mudahim went for home, swiftly brushing aside the long-time leader Corymandel. The Grey Monk was now under pressure and hard ridden by Dobbin. The horse had travelled well as usual but could find no extra when the leaders went for home, and Dobbin later reported that The Grey Monk had hated the good ground.

Having been guided round with expertise by race specialist Woods, Amble Speedy came to join Mudahim at the last, going by far the better of the two, but an awful mistake again gave the advantage to Mrs Pitman's horse as the drama continued. However, there was more to come. Amble Speedy, encouraged mightily by Woods, managed to claw back Mudahim and get to the front, only to drift alarmingly to the left as the line loomed, separating the two horses by some breadth as they raced for the post. Despite this, it looked from every angle as though Amble Speedy was edging ahead on Mudahim, and following a rousing finish, Woods' horse appeared to have won the day as they flashed past the line. All camera shots suggested Amble Speedy had won, Woods was convinced he had won, as were the crowd, but there remained some doubt and the verdict went to the judge. Matters were not helped when the riderless Aardwolf, running in the opposite direction, came from nowhere to cause a most frightening episode as the leaders neared the winning line, although, fortunately, no major damage was done to any other runner. Jason Titley was halfway back to the weighing room, having

An early fence in the dramatic 1997 contest.

Left: *Jenny Pitman and Mudahim.*

Despite all television angles indicating a win for Amble Speedy, the photo proves that Mudahim (far side) had won by a nose.

1997 IRISH GRAND NATIONAL RESULT

FATE	HORSE	AGE/WEIGHT	JOCKEY
1st	MUDAHIM	11.10.3	J.F. TITLEY
2nd	AMBLE SPEEDY	7.10.0	F. WOODS
3rd	THE GREY MONK	9.12.0	A. DOBBIN
4th	PAPILLON	6.10.4	C.F. SWAN
5th	St Mellion Fairway	8.10.3	A. Thornton
6th	Lord Singapore	9.10.10	D.J. Casey
7th	Heist	8.10.0	K.F. O'Brien
8th	Fissure Seal	11.10.3	T.P. Treacy
9th	Corymandel	8.10.0	T.P. Rudd
10th	Church Law	10.10.0	R. Bellamy
11th	Flashy Lad	6.10.0	J.P. Broderick
Fell	Aardwolf	6.10.1	G. Bradley
Fell	Coq Hardi Affair	9.10.1	Mr B.M. Cash
Fell	Teal Bridge	12.10.0	T.J. Mitchell
Fell	The Latvian Lark	9.10.0	C. O'Dwyer
Pulled-Up	Consharon	9.10.3	T. Hogan
Pulled-Up	Giventime	9.10.0	L. Harvey
Pulled-Up	Percy Smollett	9.11.5	R. Dunwoody
Pulled-Up	Trench Hill Lass	8.10.0	L.P. Cusack
Left	Sister Stephanie	8.10.0	D. Bridgwater

31 March 1997
Going – Good
Sponsor – Jameson
Winner – £62,079
Race Distance – three miles five furlongs
Time – 7mins 28.6secs
20 Ran
Winner trained by Mrs J. Pitman
Winner owned by In Touch Racing Club
Mudahim, bay gelding by Shareef Dancer – Mariska.

Betting – 9/2 The Grey Monk, 6/1 Papillon, 13/2 MUDAHIM, 10/1 Giventime & Sister Stephanie, 14/1 Amble Speedy, Lord Singapore, Percy Smollett & The Latvian Lark, 16/1 Aardwolf, 20/1 Coq Hardi Affair, Fissure Seal, Heist, St Mellion Fairway & Teal Bridge, 33/1 Consharon, Corymandel & Flashy Lad, 50/1 Church Law & Trench Hill Lass.

already apologised to Mrs Pitman for getting beaten, when the announcement was made that it had been Mudahim and not Amble Speedy that had won, shocking all those in attendance. Picked up by one of the 100 members of the In Touch Racing Club that owned Mudahim, Titley was promptly carried back to the winner's enclosure to celebrate what had, at first glance, seemed an unlikely success. The Grey Monk finished eleven lengths behind the front two in third, with Papillon staying on for fourth, despite being hampered by the hazardous Aardwolf after the last. Only six at the time of the 1997 Irish National, Papillon would develop into a fine chaser, with his finest moment arriving at Aintree in 2000 when he won the Grand National for Ted Walsh and his jockey son Ruby.

Mudahim's victory meant that Jenny Pitman had now trained winners of the Irish, Scottish, English and Welsh Nationals, and her victory was the first by a woman in the Fairyhouse showpiece. Mrs Pitman had advised the owners of Mudahim to run at Fairyhouse in preference to the Aintree version, and her advice had paid off with a thrilling victory, providing Titley with a much-needed boost in the process. It was to prove Mudahim's finest hour, for he was never able to display such form again, running four more times without success, including when unseating his jockey at Aintree in the 1999 Grand National.

1998 - BOBBYJO

On the face of it, the 1998 Irish Grand National had a below average feel to it in terms of quality, but time would prove that, in fact, it was one of the stronger renewals of the 1990s, with many of the principals recording big victories afterwards. A quartet of British challengers, headed by the Kim Bailey-trained Druid's Brook, ventured to Fairyhouse for Ireland's richest jumps prize, while the top of the handicap was dominated by some of the most famous Irish staying chasers of the late nineties.

Top weight was the Ted Walsh-trained Papillon, fourth in the race twelve months before and a horse of undoubted talent but questionable character. A strong, bay seven-year-old, Papillon had been a good novice the season before and was considered a fine jumper, although one that was inclined to lose concentration if making a mistake. Papillon had run four times during the current season and had impressed when winning a race at Cheltenham in January. But it was his last performance – a disappointing eighth in the Kim Muir at the Cheltenham Festival – coupled with his weight of 12st, which put punters off somewhat. Starting at 20/1, Papillon was ridden by the trainer's son, the talented youngster Ruby Walsh.

Besides Papillon, other Irish horses that had run in the race before included the out-of-form 1994 winner, Son Of War, and the 1995 fourth, Go Go Gallant, while newcomers included Miss Orchestra, Wylde Hyde, Eton Gale, Tell The Nipper, Bob Treacy and Bobbyjo. The dour stayer Miss Orchestra was a seven-year-old mare, trained by Jessica Harrington, which had won the season's Midlands National at Uttoxeter. Miss Orchestra was a horse thought to thrive on marathon chases, especially in the mud, and was a first ride in the race for eighteen-year-old Barry Geraghty, who had been attached to the Noel Meade stable from the age of sixteen. Wylde Hyde had run, without joy, in the 1996 and 1997 Grand Nationals at Aintree, but had missed the 1998 renewal having missed work with a stone bruise to his foot. Trained by Arthur Moore and owned by J.P. McManus, Wylde Hyde was subsequently re-routed to Fairyhouse, although he shouldered a big weight of 11st 13lbs and had not won a race since the 1996 Thyestes Chase. Eton Gale had impressed during the season as a staying novice, winning twice at Navan, and the Strong Gale gelding, trained by Meade, had run very well at Cheltenham in the Royal & SunAlliance Chase before his rider had lost an iron. Tell the Nipper, trained by Michael Hourigan, had won the Grand National Trial Chase at Fairyhouse earlier in the season before finishing fourth at Cheltenham in the National Hunt Handicap Chase. Race favourite was the vastly improved ex-hunter, Bob Treacy, a nine-year-old trained by Michael Hickey. Bob Treacy had won his last three races, but had subsequently risen 22lbs in the handicap since the first of those wins. Bobbyjo had long been considered an Irish National-winning type by his trainer, Tommy Carberry, and the race had become the horse's target ever since winning the Porterstown Chase at Fairyhouse in November. An eight-year-old ridden by the trainer's very talented son, Paul, Bobbyjo had been campaigned primarily over hurdles in his preparation for the Irish National, and started the race well fancied at 8/1, having been 18/1 in the morning.

In the history of the Irish Grand National, five British-trained horses had won the race, including Desert Orchid, Omerta and Mudahim in the 1990s, and the challenge

this time focused on Druid's Brook and Call It A Day. Druid's Brook, a lightly raced nine-year-old bay, had run just four times in two seasons for Bailey, with soft ground considered essential for the horse. Druid's Brook was considered a good jumper and sure stayer, if a little on the slow side, and was ridden by Andrew Thornton, a jockey enjoying a fine season that had included winning the Gold Cup on former Irish National third, Cool Dawn. David Nicholson was represented by Call It A Day, the mount of eight-times Irish Champion, Charlie Swan. Call It A Day was a consistent chaser that had run in many of the important staying chases in England during the season, although he had been knocked over at the first fence in the Midlands National.

With ground declared as yielding, the twenty-two runners were sent on their way, with Una's Choice, Son Of War, Heist and Druid's Brook well to the fore at the first fence. At the opening obstacle, Astings and Roundwood both fell, causing a mini pile-up behind, as both Nelson's Tipple and Tryfirion were brought down.

Leaving behind the early carnage, Druid's Brook had pulled his way to the front by the fourth fence, but the well fancied English challenger hit the deck having brushed through the fence, and his fall badly affected Papillon, who had been tracking the leaders when Druid's Brook came down, and was sent backwards through the field.

Heist, also trained by Meade, was left in the lead courtesy of Druid's Brook's departure, and the outsider continued to run a big race, still holding command by the time they reached the fifth last, with Bob Treacy improving steadily as the race progressed, followed by the now recovered Papillon, Eton Gale, Call It A Day and Bobbyjo. But the fifth last was to prove significant. Pressing Heist for the lead, both Bob Treacy and Heist clipped the top of the big black fence and fell independently, causing gasps of shock from the crowd.

Bobbyjo and Paul Carberry went on to win the Aintree Grand National the year after their Fairyhouse success.

Bobbyjo is flanked by Paul Carberry and owner Robert Burke following his win.

The top weight Papillon was left in front followed by the novice Eton Gale – running a fine race under Jason Titley – and then the rapidly improving Bobbyjo. Titley thrust Eton Gale forward to lead at the third last, but the horse was now coming to the end of his tether, and a fence later, he had been engulfed by the resurgent Papillon and Bobbyjo, and these two then settled down to fight out the remainder of what was becoming a thrilling contest.

Coming clear of the pack, Bobbyjo and Papillon engaged in a rousing finale. Bobbyjo ranged upsides Papillon by the last, and once the two horses flew the final fence, both were then flat out in a pulsating, epic battle to the line. In receipt of 11lbs from the top weight, it was to be Bobbyjo that got his head in front, and despite being pressed all the way to the line, held on to win by half-a-length. Papillon earned much respect in defeat, with Ted Walsh delighted with his jumping, stating that when the horse was on song, he was very good. Nine lengths away in third was Call It A Day, one paced towards the finish, with the Henrietta Knight-trained veteran, Full Of Oats, fourth, followed in by Tell The Nipper and Eton Gale. Miss Orchestra had tracked the leaders on the second circuit but the lack of real soft ground prevented her from playing a hand in the finish, while Wylde Hyde had never threatened to get competitive.

It was a fantastic family success for the Carberrys, with Tommy based just a mile from the course at Ratoath. The race also confirmed what a rising talent Paul Carberry was, for he was indeed a natural in the saddle, and Bobbyjo's Irish National win cemented the jockey's place as a rider to watch in future years. Paul Carberry later revealed it was an extra special win, being that his father trained the horse. Bobbyjo was owned by Robert Burke (the recipient of a IR£50,000 bonus after Bobbyjo had won both the Porterstown Chase and Irish National), who had placed horses with Tommy Carberry since 1983 and whose brother, Eugene, reared Bobbyjo on his farm in Galway.

The first three home in the Irish National of 1998 emerged as fine individuals. Call It A Day rounded off a consistent season by winning the Whitbread Gold Cup at Sandown a few weeks later, while for Bobbyjo and Papillon, rich success lay in wait. The following season, Bobbyjo landed a huge gamble when winning the Grand National at Aintree, while a year later, a similar scenario saw another father/son combination, Ted and Ruby Walsh, land the Aintree prize with Papillon.

1998 IRISH GRAND NATIONAL RESULT

FATE	HORSE	AGE/WEIGHT	JOCKEY
1st	BOBBYJO	8.11.3	P. CARBERRY
2nd	PAPILLON	7.12.0	R. WALSH
3rd	CALL IT A DAY	8.11.12	C.F. SWAN
4th	FULL OF OATS	12.10.0	T.J. MITCHELL
5th	Tell The Nipper	7.10.12	G. Bradley
6th	Eton Gale	9.10.13	J.F. Titley
7th	Una's Choice	10.10.7	F.J. Flood
8th	Miss Orchestra	7.10.7	B.J. Geraghty
9th	Wylde Hide	11.11.13	C. O'Dwyer
10th	Son Of War	11.11.6	B.M. Cash
11th	Hermes Harvest	10.10.12	S. Durack
Fell	Astings	10.10.9	D.J. Casey
Fell	Bob Treacy	9.11.5	T.P. Treacy
Fell	Druid's Brook	9.10.8	A. Thornton
Fell	Heist	9.11.2	K.P. Gaule
Fell	Ontheroadagain	10.10.7	T.P. Rudd
Fell	Roundwood	9.10.1	G. Cotter
Pulled-Up	Dun Belle	9.11.12	S.H. O'Donovan
Pulled-Up	Go Go Gallant	9.11.2	K.F. O'Brien
Pulled-Up	Padashpan	9.10.10	B. Fenton
Brought Down	Nelson's Tipple	8.10.0	J.M. Maguire
Brought Down	Tryfirion	9.10.8	K. Whelan

13 April 1998
Going – Yielding
Sponsor – Jameson
Winner – £68,130
Race Distance – three miles five furlongs
Time – 8mins 1.5secs
22 Ran
Winner trained by T. Carberry
Winner owned by Robert Burke
Bobbyjo, bay gelding by Bustineto – Markup.

Betting – 7/1 Bob Treacy, 8/1 BOBBYJO, Eton Gale & Miss Orchestra, 9/1 Druid's Brook & Tell The Nipper, 12/1 Call It A Day & Ontheroadagain, 16/1 Tryfirion, Una's Choice & Wylde Hide, 20/1 Dun Belle, Go Go Gallant, Heist, Hermes Harvest, Papillon & Roundwood, 25/1 Nelson's Tipple, 33/1 Padashpan, 40/1 Astings, 50/1 Full Of Oats, 66/1 Son Of War.

1999 – GLEBE LAD

Rather unusually, the Irish Grand National of 1999 featured five co-favourites, although Papillon aside, none of the quintet concerned possessed real quality in what was one of the poorer renewals of the race in recent times. With only Bob Treacy anywhere near him in the weights, Papillon again shouldered top weight of 12st for trainer Ted Walsh and jockey Ruby Walsh. Although he proved he stayed the trip in the previous year's race, Papillon was a versatile performer capable of running well at far shorter distance. However, he had been outclassed in the recent Queen Mother Champion Chase at Cheltenham, where he finished eighth. Even so, Papillon was the best horse in the field, and with four others, started atop the market at 8/1.

Completing the list of co-favourites were Celtic Giant, Manus The Man, The Quads and Glebe Lad. Celtic Giant was trained in Britain by leading northern handler Len Lungo, and the big chestnut had recently run the race of his life to win the Kim Muir Chase at the Cheltenham Festival. Celtic Giant was a son of Celtic Cone, the same sire that had produced the 1998 Aintree Grand National winner Earth Summit, so the horse possessed plenty of stamina, however, he also possessed a fibrillating heart, which meant he was very unpredictable, as well as being susceptible to soft ground. Celtic Giant had improved greatly throughout the season, winning at Musselburgh before triumphing unchallenged at Cheltenham, though Lungo admitted it was very much a case of 'race by race' with his horse. Manus The Man was a rare Irish National runner for fifty-six-year-old trainer Michael Cunningham, whose previous best horses had been Cheltenham Champion Hurdle winner For Auction and Aintree National runner-up Greasepaint. The last time Cunningham had a runner in the Irish National was when the non-stayer Rainbow Warrior finished down the field in 1985. Manus The Man was an ex-point-to-pointer that had run just three times under rules, although he had displayed great potential by winning twice. Manus The Man, partnered by Jason Titley, was a good jumper, despite his inexperience, and was lightly weighted, while Cunningham was confident the horse would get the trip. The Quads, one of three horses representing Arthur Moore, was one of the bottom weights, while Michael O'Brien was hopeful of sending out his third Irish National winner in the shape of Glebe Lad. A useful novice the season before, Glebe Lad had been in contention when falling five out in the season's Thyestes Chase before finishing third on his last run over fences at Leopardstown. After that Leopardstown race, Glebe Lad ran on the flat at The Curragh, where he was kicked in the shoulder beforehand, an injury that later became infected, requiring treatment by laser and antibiotics. However, O'Brien suggested the horse had now recovered and was confident he would run a big race at Fairyhouse.

With Newbury's Mandarin Chase winner, Rightsaidfred, in the field together with former smart hurdler Feathered Leader and British hopefuls Druid's Brook and Full Of Oats, the eighteen-strong field were sent on their way. Celtic Giant had not appeared keen to line-up at the start and hung left throughout his journey. Sadly, it was not to be a going day for the big chestnut, and he ran no sort of race, eventually being pulled-up before the second last.

The leading group on the first circuit consisted of Risk Of Thunder, Druid's Brook, Papillon and Rightsaidfred, while among those held-up further back were Glebe Lad, Feathered Leader and Manus The Man. The field lost Roundwood at the tenth and outsiders Tarthooth and Ultra Flutter were both pulled-up before the thirteenth, but with the exception of Celtic Giant, all the chief contenders remained in the hunt deep into the second circuit.

Having tracked the leaders on the second circuit, Glebe Lad, ridden by twenty-seven-year-old Tom Rudd, began to make a move at the fourth last, and came through so strongly on the inside that the horse had reached the front a fence later. However, there were still many horses left in the argument, including Manus The Man, Oneofourown, Risk of Thunder and Rightsaidfred, and although the lattermost came down when tiring three out, the race was on in earnest by the second last.

However, of all those still involved, none were travelling better than Feathered Leader, who had come smoothly through the field, and although only fourth two out, Conor O'Dwyer soon had the Arthur Moore horse primed to attack by the final fence. With Manus The Man and Risk Of Thunder unable to quicken once away from the last, Feathered Leader joined Glebe Lad in the lead and the two set sail for the winning post. Feathered Leader had approached the last with real intent, but as he tried to thrust past Glebe Lad, he became one-paced. Rallying bravely under pressure, it was Glebe Lad that stayed-on the better, and finishing with a real zest, ultimately pulled clear of Feathered Leader to win by three lengths. Feathered Leader, only seven, delighted Moore with his performance, and the

The big chestnut Celtic Giant goes to post in 1999.

Feathered Leader (blue, red cap) comes to challenge Glebe Lad (green cap) at the final fence, with Manus The Man also in contention in third.

Jockey Tom Rudd, Glebe Lad and the winning connections.

trainer confirmed the horse to have plenty of class. Manus The Man had similarly run a great race finishing three lengths away in third, with Risk Of Thunder fourth. Despite being third four fences out, Papillon weakened rapidly and came home in his own time in tenth and was later reported to be lame.

O'Brien, confined to a wheelchair since a riding accident ended that side of his career, had targeted the Irish National with Glebe Lad ever since the horse had run with promise in the season's Thyestes Chase. The win gave the Naas-based trainer his third victory following those of King Spruce and Vanton, while the winner got a tremendous, resolute ride from Rudd, for whom the victory was by far the biggest of his career.

1999 IRISH GRAND NATIONAL RESULT

FATE	HORSE	AGE/WEIGHT	JOCKEY
1st	GLEBE LAD	7.10.0	T.P. RUDD
2nd	FEATHERED LEADER	7.10.4	C. O'DWYER
3rd	MANUS THE MAN	8.10.6	J.F. TITLEY
4th	RISK OF THUNDER	10.10.0	D.J. CASEY
5th	Oneofourown	8.10.0	K.P. Gaule
6th	The Quads	7.10.0	P. Carberry
7th	Full Of Oats	13.10.2	B. Powell
8th	Pauls Run	10.10.0	L.P. Cusack
9th	Druid's Brook	10.10.5	R. Wakley
10th	Papillon	8.12.0	R. Walsh

Fell	Rightsaidfred	11.10.12	G. Bradley
Fell	Roundwood	10.10.1	K.A. Kelly
Pulled-Up	Bob Treacy	10.11.10	N. Williamson
Pulled-Up	Celtic Giant	9.10.9	R. Supple
Pulled-Up	Rocketts Castle	9.10.0	B.J. Geraghty
Pulled-Up	Tarthooth	8.10.0	T.P. Treacy
Pulled-Up	The Real Article	10.10.0	J.R. Barry
Pulled-Up	Ultra Flutter	12.10.0	P.G. Hourigan

5 April 1999
Going – Yielding
Sponsor – Jameson
Winner – £69,955
Race Distance – three miles five furlongs
Time – 7mins 53.9secs
18 Ran
Winner trained by M.J.P. O'Brien
Winner owned by T.B. Conroy
Glebe Lad, bay gelding by Le Bavard – Mugs Away.

Betting – 8/1 Celtic Giant, GLEBE LAD, Manus The Man, Papillon & The Quads, 9/1 Bob Treacy, 10/1 Roundwood, 12/1 Feathered Leader, 14/1 Rightsaidfred & Risk Of Thunder, 16/1 Full Of Oats, 20/1 Druid's Brook, 25/1 Rocketts Castle & Tarthooth, 40/1 Ultra Flutter, 50/1 Pauls Run, 66/1 Oneofourown & The Real Article.

2000 – COMMANCHE COURT

The 2000 Irish Grand National saw the name of Powers Gold Label sponsor the race for the first time, and this new dawn brought with it a tremendously competitive renewal of the race, with the big field of twenty-four swelled by no fewer than eight runners from Britain. In addition, the Irish challenge threw forward some intriguing novice chasers, as well as some older horses of sterling reputation.

Joint favourites for the race were the British-trained pair of Edmond and Ackzo. Joined in the race by stablemate Lancastrian Jet, Edmond was trained by Henry Daly, who had taken control of his stable from his previous boss, Captain Tim Forster, who had sadly died earlier in the season. Edmond was a real lover of mud, and had become something of a Chepstow specialist, winning a number of races there before landing the Welsh Grand National at the track earlier in the season. Ackzo was a seven-year-old novice trained by Ferdy Murphy and ridden by Adrian Maguire, who had stormed on to the National Hunt scene when winning the Irish National aboard Omerta in 1991. Ackzo was a thorough stayer that had improved steadily having run five times during the season. It was his most recent performance, a win in the Midlands National at Uttoxeter, that marked Ackzo down as a stayer of note, and with the Murphy stable in tremendous form having recently taken the Scottish National with Paris Pike, Ackzo was a strong fancy at Fairyhouse.

The home team was strong and deep. Tony Martin's bay Hollybank Buck had won both the Leopardstown Chase and the Eider Chase the season before, and had run well for a long way before finishing tenth behind Papillon in the recent Aintree Grand National. Arthur Moore ran Feathered Leader, fifth in the Mildmay of Flete at Cheltenham recently and looking to go one better than his second place in 1999. The 1998 hero Bobbyjo returned to the race having also finished behind Papillon at Aintree, and carried top weight of 12st, while both Noel Meade's young mare, Rose Of Picardy, and Jim Dreaper's charge, Saxophone, were fancied, despite having had just four and six runs over fences respectively. Two other seven-year-olds given definite chances were Foxchapel King and Commanche Court. Trained by Mouse Morris, the big bay Foxchapel King had won the Troytown Chase earlier in the season and was reported to be in fine form. Foxchapel King was a horse that had taken a while to adjust to chasing, but seemed to be improving with every race, and arrived at Fairyhouse a fresh horse having only raced twice since Christmas. The chestnut Commanche Court was a former winner of the Triumph Hurdle at Cheltenham and was trained by Ted Walsh and ridden by his son, Ruby. The Triumph Hurdle has been notorious for the lack of successful future chasers that it has produced, but despite still being a maiden, Commanche Court had undoubted class, although whether he would get the trip in the Irish National was of huge debate, the horse having run in the two-mile Arkle Chase at Cheltenham. He may not have won a chase yet, but Commanche Court had been running over far shorter distances in Ireland during the season, and the horses that had defeated him were of high quality, among them the likes of Native Upmanship, Frozen Groom and Go Roger Go.

With the British challenge boosted by the likes of Red Marauder and Jocks Cross, the crowd roared their approval as the race got under way on ground reported to be somewhat livelier than the official description of good to yielding. It was the stablemates, Edmond and Lancastrian Jet, that took the field along in the early stages, tracked most prominently by Foxchapel King, Northern Sound, Roundwood, Jocks Cross, Pauls Run, Sweep Gently and Saxophone, the lattermost racing towards the outside. There were no casualties until Sue Smith's runner Sweep Gently fell at the sixth fence, bringing down the outsider Pauls Run in the process.

One of the joint-favourites, Ackzo, had appeared to be squeezed for room at the first two fences, and thereafter never seemed to be travelling with any great relish. As the race progressed, it was obvious that he, together with the disappointing Bobbyjo, Red Marauder and Hollybank Buck, were among the more heralded horses that would not be playing a hand in the finish. In the case of Ackzo, the horse was eventually pulled-up on the second circuit, with Murphy later admitting that the hustle and bustle of such a big race may have been too much for the horse at the current stage of his career.

With six fences to jump, both Edmond and Lancastrian Jet had lost their places at the head of the field while Jocks Cross had earlier unseated Brian Crowley, and it was the outsider Roundwood that temporarily took control. Commanche Court, Feathered Leader, Northern Sound and Golden Drum (trained in Britain by Ian Williams), had all progressed through into challenging positions, but it was young Foxchapel King that had looked most dangerous, swinging through into second place, and taking the lead for himself by the fourth last.

The finish of the race was to be conclusive, although as Foxchapel King came clear in the straight, it seemed as though the race was his for the taking. But travelling ever so strongly in behind was Commanche Court, ridden by Walsh to get the trip, yet clearly with plenty in reserve. The horse was already getting the better of Foxchapel King when the latter made a bad mistake at the second last, and having been left in the lead, it was now Commanche Court's race to lose.

Jumping the final fence as well as he had jumped the previous twenty-two, Commanche Court powered home to win by a most convincing ten lengths, despite the fact that all the horses in touching distance of the lead in the latter stages had considerably less weight to carry than the 11st 4lbs on the back of the winner. This fact proved Commanche Court's class. Foxchapel King came home in second and had run his best race yet. There were more nice races to come from the runner-up, and he would win a good handicap at Cheltenham later in his career before running well in the 2002 Cheltenham Gold Cup itself. Two veterans filled the minor places, with Irish Light gaining the advantage over the hunter chaser Gillan Cove, the latter a recent acquisition for the Joe Byrne stable. The British horses had disappointed, only Golden Drum and Red Marauder completed, with Edmond, having found the ground too quick, pulled-up before the third last. Of those beaten, some went on to achieve great things. Jocks Cross would win the Welsh National the following season, while Red Marauder won a remarkable Grand National at Aintree in 2001, a race run in treacherous conditions and featuring mayhem at the Canal Turn.

Commanche Court had won the Irish National, providing an historical moment for overjoyed trainer Ted Walsh. Based at Kill, County Kildare, Walsh became the first trainer to win both the English National and Irish National in the same year, and

Above left: *Commanche Court goes to post under Ruby Walsh.*

Above middle: *Trainer Ted Walsh (far right) and his jockey son Ruby won the Irish National with Commanche Court two weeks after winning the Aintree Grand National with Papillon.*

Above right: *Commanche Court leads Foxchapel King at the final fence.*

the trainer revealed he could not believe how strongly his horse was going in the latter stages before shooting clear to win easily. Ruby Walsh had emulated Tommy Carberry, who had won both races in 1975 (Aintree with L'Escargot and Fairyhouse with Brown Lad), and the brilliant jockey would achieve the double again five years later. Commanche Court had won the Irish National in the manner of a very good horse, proving he had real stamina and class. Largely unconsidered for the 2002 Gold Cup, the horse ran perhaps his best ever race, jumping brilliantly and staying on well, and was only denied glory by one of the great modern day chasers, Best Mate.

Pulled-Up	Edmond	8.11.10	R. Johnson
Pulled-Up	Hollybank Buck	10.10.12	F.J. Flood
Pulled-Up	Lancastrian Jet	9.10.13	J.F. Titley
Pulled-Up	Native Estates	6.10.13	D.J. Casey
Pulled-Up	Native Status	10.10.0	P.A. Carberry
Pulled-Up	Roses Of Picardy	7.10.1	B.J. Geraghty
Pulled-Up	Saxophone	7.11.2	T.P. Treacy
Unseated Rider	Jocks Cross	9.11.2	B.J. Crowley
Brought Down	Pauls Run	11.10.0	K. Whelan

2000 IRISH GRAND NATIONAL RESULT

FATE	HORSE	AGE/WEIGHT	JOCKEY
1st	COMMANCHE COURT	7.11.4	R .WALSH
2nd	FOXCHAPEL KING	7.10.13	J.R. BARRY
3rd	IRISH LIGHT	12.10.0	K.P. GAULE
4th	GILLAN COVE	11.10.2	T.J. MITCHELL
5th	Northern Sound	7.10.0	G. Cotter
6th	Feathered Leader	8.10.7	C. O'Dwyer
7th	Golden Drum	10.10.3	Mr R. Widger
8th	Ardnataggle	8.10.0	S. Fitzgerald
9th	Avanti Express	10.10.0	N. Williamson
10th	Red Marauder	10.11.12	Richard Guest
11th	Roundwood	11.10.0	K.A. Kelly
Fell	Sweep Gently	8.10.0	S. Durack
Pulled-Up	Ackzo	7.11.2	A. Maguire
Pulled-Up	Blue Irish	9.10.10	P. Moloney
Pulled-Up	Bobbyjo	10.12.0	P. Carberry

24 April 2000
Going – Good to Yielding
Sponsor – Powers Gold Label
Winner – £62,680
Race Distance – three miles five furlongs
Time – 7mins 58.3secs
24 Ran
Winner trained by T.M. Walsh
Winner owned by D.F. Desmond
Commanche Court, chestnut horse by Commanche Run – Sorceress.

Betting – 8/1 Ackzo & Edmond, 9/1 Feathered Leader, Foxchapel King & Saxophone, 14/1 COMMANCHE COURT, Northern Sound & Roses Of Picardy, 16/1 Golden Drum & Red Marauder, 20/1 Avanti Express, Bobbyjo, Hollybank Buck & Native Estates, 25/1 Jocks Cross, Lancastrian Jet & Sweep Gently, 33/1 Gillan Cove, Irish Light & Native Status, 66/1 Blue Irish & Roundwood, 100/1 Pauls Run, 200/1 Ardnataggle.

2001 – DAVIDS LAD

The Irish Grand National had to be postponed in 2001 because of the foot-and-mouth crisis. Scheduled, as usual, for Easter Monday, the Department of Agriculture in Ireland had recently clamped down on the movement of horses to prevent the spreading of the virus, and as such, the race took place a few weeks later on 6 May.

Commanche Court and Foxchapel King, first and second in the previous year's race, reopposed each other in the 2001 Irish Grand National in what was the richest Jump race ever run in Ireland. After following up his win the season before with victory at the Punchestown Festival, Commanche Court had gone through the current season winless, although the horses he had faced had been of the highest calibre, with the likes of Moscow Flyer, Florida Pearl and Young Spartacus lowering his colours. On his most recent run, Commanche Court had got a piece of birch wedged in his sheath, and the horse had to be pulled-up in discomfort. Ted Walsh also admitted giving weight away (Commanche Court was top weight with 12st) to some of the horses in the field would be extremely difficult. Despite this, Commanche Court started second favourite at 8/1, again ridden by Ruby Walsh.

Favourite was the 2000 runner-up, Foxchapel King. The horse had begun his season with a fine win in a handicap chase at Cheltenham, a victory that suggested the horse was capable of taking one of the really big chases during the season. But when Foxchapel King disappointed in both the Hennessy Cognac Gold Cup at Newbury and the Ericsson Chase at Leopardstown that seemed unlikely. However, Foxchapel King bounced back to form with a good second behind the useful Micko's Dream in the Thyestes Chase at Gowran Park, while trainer Mouse Morris, who had ridden Billycan to win in 1977, and sent out Cahervillahow to finish second in 1991, suggested the Irish National had long been the target for his horse.

With no British-trained runners due to the foot-and-mouth crisis, interesting newcomers to the race included Sheltering, Kings Valley and Shannon Gale. Trained by Edward O'Grady, Sheltering was Ireland's leading hunter-chaser and had won three hunter-chases during the season. By the excellent sire Strong Gale, Sheltering was considered the dark horse of the race and was expected to give his rivals a strong test, provided the horse adjusted to handicap company. Although 11lbs out of the handicap, Kings Valley was well fancied for trainer Noel Meade. While talented, Kings Valley was somewhat inconsistent, having fallen twice and won twice during the season. Shannon Gale, a novice, had finished second, also to Micko's Dream, in the season's Leopardstown Chase, and was considered a sure stayer. Trained by Christy Roche and owned by J.P. McManus, Shannon Gale had long been one of the market leaders for the race, and eventually started 9/1.

With long-time ante-post leader Feathered Leader again in the field, one horse that had caught the eye recently had been Davids Lad, trained by the shrewd Tony Martin. Davids Lad had started the season in nondescript fashion and was being aimed at the Kim Muir Chase at the Cheltenham Festival, a race for which Martin believed he had the horse in peak condition. However, when that meeting was cancelled due to foot-and-mouth, Davids Lad ran at Fairyhouse eleven days before the Irish National. The horse showed his total well-being there, winning as he liked

by twenty lengths, a victory that hinted at better things to come. There were doubts that Davids Lad would get the trip in the Irish National, but the fact the ground was good and that he was ridden by hold-up specialist, Timmy Murphy, increased the likelihood of the horse lasting home.

Sure enough, as the field were sent on their way, Davids Lad could be seen, wearing a distinctive white noseband, held-up at the back of the field, as Shannon Gale led from Sheltering, Lanturn and Peggy's Lad. The only casualty in the early stages was Martin's second runner, the veteran Linden's Lotto, who unseated Adrian Maguire at the second fence.

Lanturn was next to go when falling in the lead at the ninth, badly hampering Shannon Gale in the process, while, sadly, Peggy's Lad broke a hind leg having jumped the seventh last. But, as the race entered its latter stages, many of the leading hopes were very much involved.

Foxchapel King had tracked Commanche Court for most of the way as Sheltering led on, all three holding every chance. However, the picture changed drastically when outsider Rathbawn Prince, trained by Dessie Hughes, hit the front three fences from home, increasing the slow pace considerably and quickly coming clear, leaving most of his rivals for dead.

Davids Lad, meanwhile, had been patiently guided round by Murphy. From the rear of the field, the horse had made headway six fences from home and had

Tony Martin and Davids Lad.

Davids Lad comes to challenge the leader Rathbawn Prince at the final fence.

By the line, Davids Lad has outgunned Rathbawn Prince.

moved into a position just behind the leaders four out. When Rathbawn Prince had made his bid for glory, Davids Lad had been the only horse able to give chase, setting up a thrilling finish. Challenging the leader by the final fence, the battle to the line was tremendous, with the nine-year-old Rathbawn Prince running the race of his life, giving his rival 13lbs. But edging in front on the run-in, it was Davids Lad that stayed on the stronger, and at the line, emerged victorious by a length-and-a-half. Eleven lengths back in third came Sheltering, with Kings Valley plugging on at one-pace in fourth ahead of old adversaries Commanche Court and Foxchapel King. Of the others, Feathered Leader had fallen with two fences to jump when beaten, while Shannon Gale had never sufficiently recovered from being hampered by Lanturn's fall, and trailed home last of the thirteen finishers.

Martin, known for his well-plotted, winning raids on British courses, immediately targeted the 2002 Aintree Grand National for his progressive chaser, one that had risen 43lbs up the handicap during the season, providing the biggest career win for his trainer. It had been Davids Lad's first season over fences, and his dam, Cool Nora, had been Martin's first winner as a trainer. Much praise went to twenty-six-year-old County Kildare native Murphy for the wonderfully calm, waiting ride he gave the winner, cementing his position among the leading riders in the sport. Davids Lad did make it to Aintree the following season, and was in the process of running a huge race when agonisingly falling four fences from home, and although he also ran in the 2004 renewal of that race, it was the 2002 running that would be his finest chance of glory.

2001 IRISH GRAND NATIONAL RESULT

FATE	HORSE	AGE/WEIGHT	JOCKEY
1st	DAVIDS LAD	7.10.0	T.J. MURPHY
2nd	RATHBAWN PRINCE	9.10.13	K.A. KELLY
3rd	SHELTERING	9.10.1	N. WILLIAMSON
4th	KINGS VALLEY	7.10.0	P. CARBERRY
5th	Commanche Court	8.12.0	R. Walsh
6th	Foxchapel King	8.10.13	J.R. Barry
7th	More Than A Stroll	9.10.0	D.J. Casey
8th	Knights Of Kerry	6.9.11	S.P. McCann
9th	Florida Light	9.10.0	T.P. Rudd
10th	Nuzum Road Makers	10.10.0	K.P. Gaule
11th	Private Peace	11.10.2	P.A. Carberry
12th	Ardnataggle	9.9.7	S. Fitzgerald
13th	Shannon Gale	9.10.0	P. Moloney
Fell	Feathered Leader	9.10.1	C. O'Dwyer
Fell	Lanturn	11.10.2	J.L. Cullen
Pulled-Up	Northern Sound	8.10.0	G. Cotter
Pulled-Up	Peggy's Lad	8.9.9	R. Geraghty
Pulled-Up	Slaney Native	8.10.13	B.J. Geraghty
Unseated Rider	Linden's Lotto	12.10.0	A. Maguire

6 May 2001
Going – Good
Sponsor – Powers Gold Label
Winner – £65,725
Race Distance – three miles five furlongs
Time – 7mins 40.5secs
19 Ran
Winner trained by A.J. Martin
Winner owned by Eddie Joe's Racing Syndicate
Davids Lad, bay gelding by Yashgan – Cool Nora.

Betting – 9/2 Foxchapel King, 8/1 Commanche Court, 9/1 Shannon Gale & Sheltering, 10/1 DAVIDS LAD & Feathered Leader, 11/1 Kings Valley, 14/1 Slaney Native, 20/1 Northern Sound, 25/1 Knights Of Kerry, Lanturn, More Than A Stroll, Nuzum Road Makers & Rathbawn Prince, 33/1 Linden's Lotto & Private Peace, 40/1 Peggy's Lad, 66/1 Florida Light, 200/1 Ardnataggle.

2002 – THE BUNNY BOILER

Despite not having won since his victory in the 2000 Heineken Gold Cup at the Punchestown Festival, Commanche Court remained the apple of trainer Ted Walsh's eye, and quite rightly so. The horse was a real class act, having won a Triumph Hurdle and an Irish National. On his latest start, Commanche Court had delivered a career best performance when valiantly chasing home the new chasing sensation, Best Mate, in the Gold Cup at Cheltenham, with the chestnut jumping, travelling and staying admirably, only outdone in the closing stages by his conqueror's superior class. Following that heroic effort, Commanche Court lined-up at Fairyhouse for the 2002 Irish Grand National, his third attempt at the race, and was promptly made the 7/2 favourite on the day, with Ruby Walsh again in the saddle.

The significant factor concerning the participation of Commanche Court was that the weights were kept down. Carrying top weight of 12st, Commanche Court was one of just three horses in the race (Rathbawn Prince and Arctic Copper being the others) that raced from their correct handicap marks. Not surprisingly, the race was labelled one of the poorer renewals of recent times, yet included in the field were a number of intriguing candidates, some of which were considered to be progressive. The one horse perhaps more on an upward curve than most was The Bunny Boiler, a bay chaser with a distinctive white mark on his forehead, trained by Noel Meade. Having idolised Tom Dreaper, it had long been an ambition of Meade's to win the Irish National, and in The Bunny Boiler, he had an eight-year-old that had won twice during the season, at Thurles in December and, most impressively, at Uttoxeter in March when winning the Midlands National. His win at Uttoxeter had proven The Bunny Boiler to be a thorough stayer, for the horse prevailed very easily in testing conditions, and although he was not the most reliable of jumpers, the distance of the Irish National was expected to be one that he would relish, despite ground far better than he had encountered at Uttoxeter. On board The Bunny Boiler was 5lb claimer Ross Geraghty, the older brother of former Irish Champion jockey Barry Geraghty, and whose father, Tucker, was a close friend of Meade's. In addition to the Bunny Boiler, Meade also ran Arctic Copper and Oa Baldixe. Arctic Copper had an element of class about him, though was considered a better horse at shorter distances, while the tall, lean Oa Baldixe was a former Group Three winner on the flat, and smart hurdler that had finished fourth in the four-mile chase at the Cheltenham Festival.

Recent Wincanton winner Trouble Ahead, trained by Venetia Williams, was the sole British representative, while Rathbawn Prince was fancied to improve on his second place of the year before. Also in the field were Timbera, second in the same four-mile chase as Oa Baldixe at Cheltenham, the talented Edward O'Grady-trained seven-year-old Takagi, and the chestnut Cregg House, representing Paddy Mullins, having been a good second in the Cathcart Chase at the Cheltenham Festival.

Despite it being the usual good-spirited Easter Monday occasion, there was a slightly sombre mood attached to the Irish National of 2002, for it was the first big race staged since the sad passing of Queen Elizabeth, The Queen Mother the Saturday before. The Queen Mother was a huge supporter of National Hunt racing,

and all those present at Fairyhouse hoped the race would develop into one that would have pleased her immensely.

The Paul Roche-trained mare, Northern Sound, set off in a clear lead, followed by Takagi, Ellenjay, Timbera, Cregg House, Commanche Court, Good Shuil and Give Over, the lattermost travelling on the wide outside under Tom Rudd. Despite the large size and stiffness of the Fairyhouse fences, there were no casualties until the prominent Ellenjay made a bad mistake and unseated his rider seven fences from home.

Give Over, a horse that had disappointed during the season, had come back to form with some aplomb in the Irish National. Having raced on the outside for much of the way, the horse went up to dispute the lead with Northern Sound six out, and two fences later, held the lead on his own. In behind, Takagi and Timbera were mounting challenges, while The Bunny Boiler had sauntered through from a midfield position to begin a bid for glory. However, Commanche Court, having been guided round the inside by Walsh, was unable to quicken when the lightweights turned on the pressure, and soon weakened, while Rathbawn Prince too could make no impression, ultimately capsizing at the third last.

Mistakes in the closing stages were to ruin the chances of a number of the leading players. Takagi was close up in second place when clouting the third last, while Timbera was in third place but probably held when coming down a fence later. Both of those two had run well, but the race now centred on Give Over and The Bunny Boiler, as the two prepared to battle out the finish.

The Bunny Boiler had jumped well throughout the race and had moved smoothly into contention. The horse had managed to head Give Over by the last

Trainer Noel Meade.

The Bunny Boiler makes a mistake at the last, tracked by Give Over.

Winning jockey Ross Geraghty is congratulated by Paul Carberry (yellow cap) who finished fourth aboard Arctic Copper.

fence, but a horrific mistake there very nearly spoilt the chance of Meade's charge. However, carefully collected by Geraghty, The Bunny Boiler lost little momentum and was soon plugging on up the run-in. Give Over pressed the leader for all he was worth, but The Bunny Boiler was to confirm himself a most progressive stayer, and driven out powerfully, won the day by a length-and-a-half. Give Over lost little in defeat, while Northern Sound shocked many by coming third, a mere four lengths back, at a price of 40/1. Next home came Arctic Copper, Takagi and Oa Baldixe, with the favourite Commanche Court eventually pulled-up before the last.

The victory of The Bunny Boiler was the highlight of a tremendous day at Fairyhouse for Meade, who achieved a four-timer on the card. Meade knew his horse was far from the greatest jumper, but was overjoyed with the way The Bunny Boiler tackled Fairyhouse, despite his late scare. It was also a very special day for Ross Geraghty, who achieved the biggest win of his career, and who was riding his first winner for Meade. The Bunny Boiler completed a season of high promise and was then put away for the following campaign. The horse would twice run in the Grand National at Aintree, unseating his rider at the first in the 2003 race, won by Monty's Pass (ridden by Barry Geraghty), and finishing tenth behind Amberleigh House in 2004.

2002 IRISH GRAND NATIONAL RESULT

FATE	HORSE	AGE/WEIGHT	JOCKEY
1st	THE BUNNY BOILER	8.9.9	R. GERAGHTY
2nd	GIVE OVER	9.10.0	T.P. RUDD
3rd	NORTHERN SOUND	9.10.0	J.R. BARRY
4th	ARCTIC COPPER	8.10.0	P. CARBERRY
5th	Takagi	7.10.0	K. Whelan
6th	Oa Baldixe	8.10.0	D.J. Casey
7th	Delgany Royal	10.9.7	P.T. Wade
8th	More Than A Stroll	10.10.0	C. O'Dwyer
Fell	Rathbawn Prince	10.10.8	B.J. Geraghty
Fell	Timbera	8.10.0	K.A. Kelly
Pulled-Up	Champagne Native	8.10.0	P. Moloney
Pulled-Up	Commanche Court	9.12.0	R. Walsh
Pulled-Up	Good Shuil	7.9.9	D. Crosse
Unseated Rider	Ellenjay	8.9.9	D.J. Howard
Refused	Copernicus	7.10.2	J.L. Cullen
Refused	Cregg House	7.9.11	M.P. Madden
Refused	Trouble Ahead	11.10.0	B.J. Crowley

1 April 2002
Going – Good to Yielding
Sponsor – Powers Gold Label
Winner – £65,693
Race Distance – three miles five furlongs
Time – 8mins 3.1secs
17 Ran
Winner trained by Noel Meade
Winner owned by Usual Suspects Syndicate
The Bunny Boiler, bay gelding by Tremblant – Danny's Charm.

Betting – 7/2 Commanche Court, 13/2 Rathbawn Prince, 7/1 Timbera, 11/1 Cregg House, 12/1 Arctic Copper, Takagi & THE BUNNY BOILER, 14/1 Ellenjay, Oa Baldixe & Trouble Ahead, 16/1 Champagne Native, Copernicus, Good Shuil & More Than A Stroll, 25/1 Give Over, 33/1 Delgany Royal, 40/1 Northern Sound.

2003 - TIMBERA

Again, it was hardly a vintage renewal of the Irish Grand National in 2003, with twenty-one runners going to post, headed by the hero of 2001, Davids Lad. Since Brown Lad had won the race for the third time in 1978, only Desert Orchid and Flashing Steel had carried 12st to victory in the race, yet that was the task facing Davids Lad, a horse that would not have been in the class of those two at level weights. The horse was making his first appearance since being banned for forty-two days at Naas in February. Davids Lad had been banned under the non-trying rule that basically opined that connections had used the racecourse as a training ground for the horse. It was one of the most talked about topics of the entire National Hunt season, and was to be a decision that proved most costly, since the ban ruled Davids Lad out of a second crack at the Grand National at Aintree, a race for which his entire season had been geared and for which the horse had long been amongst the ante-post favourites. Trainer Tony Martin was of the opinion that Davids Lad could gain rich compensation in the Irish National, but it was also his belief that, although Davids Lad was a big horse, giving large amounts of weight away could prove a problem. In addition to Davids Lad, Martin also saddled Ross Moff, a horse that had been troubled by wind problems in his career, and the lightweight Falcon Du Coteau, a horse that had run well recently over the big Aintree fences in the Topham Chase.

As well as the former good bumper horse, Native Jack, Arthur Moore saddled the seven-year-old chestnut Eskimo Jack, and it was to be that horse that started favourite. Eskimo Jack was a promising novice that jumped and travelled well in his races, and had finished third in the prestigious Leopardstown Chase during the season. The horse was ridden by thirty-seven-year-old Conor O'Dwyer, who was still seeking his first Irish National win. While O'Dwyer had ridden in many Irish Nationals before, the 2003 race would be the first time that leading British-based jockeys Tony McCoy and Mick Fitzgerald had competed. Fitzgerald, a Gold Cup and Aintree National winning rider, was on board Ross Moff, but it was the booking of McCoy for the Oliver McKiernan-trained Winning Dream that was seen as a big plus for that horse's chance. Though there was some doubt over the ability of Winning Dream to fully see out the distance of the Irish National, the horse had been most impressive when winning at Navan last time out and had been backed significantly in the days leading up to the race.

Takagi, winner of the Troytown Chase and runner-up in the Thyestes Chase during the season, was the mount of Norman Williamson, while Ruby Walsh opted to ride the novice One Night Out, a course winner for trainer Willie Mullins. It had been expected that the ground for the 2003 Irish National would be good to firm, greatly benefiting the likes of Davids Lad and Winning Dream. This ground, however, would have been most unsuitable for three-time course winner Timbera, considered a soft-ground performer. However, on the day of the race, rain arrived, turning the going to good, and allowing trainer Dessie Hughes to give the all clear for his horse to take his chance. Timbera was considered a good jumper and strong stayer, despite falling in the 2002 race, and the horse began at 11/1 for jockey Jim Culloty, who had already won two Cheltenham Gold Cups on Best Mate and an Aintree National aboard Bindaree.

Torduff Boy and Beausheram were the two horses that disputed the running, with Timbera running freely on the first circuit and taking a prominent position on the inside, while the leading group was tracked by Takagi, Satcoslam and Princess Symphony on the outside, and The Dell and I'Vehadit towards the centre.

Native Jack and Ross Moff took crashing falls at the sixth fence, but there were no more casualties until One Night Out fell seven fences from home and Satcoslam suffered a bad mistake at the same fence and was pulled-up shortly after by Garrett Cotter.

That last open ditch seven fences from home was where Timbera finally settled into a rhythm, having run far too keenly early on. The pace on the first circuit had been slow and Timbera had been particularly headstrong, but now the horse was preparing to mount a serious challenge on the inside. In contrast, the baby of the race, the six-year-old Knock Knock, had travelled smoothly throughout, although an awful mistake at the fourteenth had threatened to ruin his chance. However, the horse had recovered sufficiently, and by two out, Knock Knock had come through to take the lead, with Timbera his closest challenger, while Winning Dream too began a challenge at the second last with Davids Lad, having been held-up by Timmy Murphy, running on strongly from off the pace.

A thrilling finish lay in store, with very little to separate the principals at the final fence. Once on the flat, Knock Knock and Timbera emerged as the key players, and the struggle to the line was enthralling and intense. Carrying significantly more weight, it was the courageous Timbera that found that little bit extra in the dying strides, and though Knock Knock threw everything he had into the finish, the youngster was to be denied by a head at the line. Winning Dream had kept on under pressure to finish a mere two lengths back in third, with Davids Lad running

Timbera (green and white) beats Knock Knock.

Above: *Jim Culloty (centre) is congratulated by Rathbawn Prince's jockey, Kieran Kelly, (red and black).*

Left: *Trainer Dessie Hughes.*

it there. Timbera had been made ante-post favourite for Aintree in 2004, but the bitter twist of fate that so often curses racing saw the horse suffer a setback just days before the race, forcing Hughes to withdraw Timbera. A few weeks later, fit and well, the horse was back at Fairyhouse to defend his title in the 2004 renewal.

2003 IRISH GRAND NATIONAL RESULT

FATE	HORSE	AGE/WEIGHT	JOCKEY
1st	TIMBERA	9.10.12	J. CULLOTY
2nd	KNOCK KNOCK	6.9.13	M.D. GRANT
3rd	WINNING DREAM	9.10.5	A.P. McCOY
4th	DAVIDS LAD	9.12.0	T.J. MURPHY
5th	Torduff Boy	10.10.4	G.T. Hutchinson
6th	Wotsitooya	11.10.0	P. Moloney
7th	Eskimo Jack	7.11.1	C. O'Dwyer
8th	Kirmar	9.10.0	K.P. Gaule
9th	Good Vintage	8.10.0	P. Carberry
10th	Spot Thedifference	10.10.10	D.J. Casey
11th	Takagi	8.11.13	N. Williamson
12th	Princess Symphony	7.9.7	A.J. Donoghue
13th	Beausheram	9.9.11	R. Geraghty
14th	Rathbawn Prince	11.11.5	K.A. Kelly
15th	The Dell	10.10.7	B.J. Geraghty
16th	I'Vehadit	9.10.5	Mr R. Loughran
17th	Falcon Du Coteau	10.10.0	J.R. Barry
Fell	Native Jack	9.10.9	D.J. Howard
Fell	One Night Out	7.10.6	R. Walsh
Fell	Ross Moff	10.10.11	M.A. Fitzgerald
Pulled-Up	Satcoslam	8.10.0	G. Cotter

21 April 2003
Going – Good
Sponsor – Powers Gold Label
Winner – £69,207
Race Distance – three miles five furlongs
Time – 7mins 43.8secs
21 Ran
Winner trained by D.T. Hughes
Winner owned by Mrs J.M. Breen
Timbera, bay or brown gelding by Commanche Run – Morry's Lady.

a gallant race, ending his long-running saga with an admirable fourth place. The favourite Eskimo Jack had been towards the rear early on before arriving to challenge by the third last, but was soon beaten, and the common feeling was that the horse did not stay.

Having tried to hold-up Timbera in the early stages, Culloty had ultimately got his horse in to a beautiful jumping pattern, and the horse emerged victorious from a titanic duel with the novice Knock Knock. Hughes, for whom Timbera provided a first Irish National win, had admitted to fearing the worst when viewing the opening sequence of the race, yet in the end, his horse put a cap on what had been a fine season for the trainer, one in which his Hardy Eustace had won the Champion Hurdle at Cheltenham. Hughes instantly nominated the 2004 Grand National at Aintree as Timbera's long-term target, and the horse very nearly made

Betting – 8/1 Eskimo Jack, 9/1 Ross Moff & Winning Dream, 10/1 Davids Lad, 11/1 TIMBERA, 12/1 I'Vehadit & The Dell, 14/1 Native Jack, One Night Out, Rathbawn Prince, Torduff Boy & Wotsitooya, 20/1 Falcon Du Coteau, Good Vintage, Knock Knock & Takagi, 25/1 Princess Symphony & Satcoslam, 28/1 Spot Thedifference, 33/1 Beausheram & Kirmar.

2004 – GRANIT D'ESTRUVAL

The 2004 Irish Grand National was a highly competitive but not very classy renewal, swelled by a large number of novices. Originally, a record-breaking field number of thirty had been declared to race, but the late defections of Bennie's Pride and Where Now meant twenty-eight went to post, one shy of the record set in Bentom Boy's year of 1984. With the likes of Desert Orchid, Cool Ground, Flashing Steel, Papillon, Bobbyjo and Commanche Court all carrying the mantle of top weight in recent renewals, the fact that the Sue Smith-trained Artic Jack shouldered the burden this time (12st) suggested a below-par edition in terms of quality. Artic Jack was a big, old-fashioned type of chaser that had won the season's Peter Marsh Chase at Haydock, but the horse was an unreliable jumper best suited to dictating proceedings in small fields, and the horse had recently fallen at the first fence in the Grand National at Aintree.

Among the novices in the field were Direct Bearing, Colnel Rayburn, Xenophon and Marcus Du Berlais. Direct Bearing, trained by Dermot Weld, was having only his fifth run over fences in the Irish National and was previously a smart Flat race performer. Owned by Michael Smurfit, Direct Bearing won his chase debut but had been running at distances of around two miles, and while his stamina was unproven, his popularity was high, as punters sent the horse off 9/1 joint-favourite. A giant of a horse with an unusual 'parrot-mouth', Colnel Rayburn was tough and consistent and was considered to be a sure stayer. A grand jumper too, Colnel Rayburn had defied top weight when winning at Navan in March and was well fancied to provide a first Irish National success for up-and-coming trainer Paul Nolan. Xenophon, a horse that appreciated cut in the ground, had won the Coral Cup at the 2003 Cheltenham Festival and was highly rated. However, Tony Martin's charge had found difficulty in adjusting to fences, falling once in his four starts during the season and failing to win. Xenophon did, however, appear to be improving each time he ran, and in a race where novices with a touch of class normally performed with credit, the horse was well supported. Marcus Du Berlais was a grey horse trained by Arthur Moore that was having his first run in a handicap. The horse had been a progressive hurdler the season before, but was another that had yet to find his feet over fences, however, with his trainer always respected in the Irish National, the grey shaped as one of the dark horses of the race.

Timbera had sufficiently recovered from a lung infection that had caused his absence from the recent Aintree National, and took his place in the line-up, while others in the field included Ted Walsh's runner Never Compromise, runner-up in the Cheltenham Foxhunters' and carrying the Commanche Court colours, and the other joint-favourite, Hume Castle, a horse trained by Jessica Harrington and considered to be a good, solid stayer, and one that had run well in the season's Paddy Power Chase at Leopardstown. Also in the field, although somewhat ignored in the betting, was the injury-plagued ten-year-old, Granit D'Estruval. Trained in Britain by Ferdy Murphy, Granit D'Estruval had not won since 2001 but had recently finished fourth behind the progressive Tyneandthyneagain in the four-mile Eider Chase at Newcastle, and held an outside chance in a very open contest.

It was to be a race of much incident, many casualties and a pulsating finale. Many of the field missed the break as they were let go, including Timbera, and the rush to the first caught out Never Compromise, who fell at the opening obstacle. Then at the second fence, Eamon Sheehy's mare, Rose Perk, fell heavily, fatally breaking her shoulder, and in the process badly hampering Killultagh Thunder.

Escaping the early mayhem, What Odds, carrying the same colours as the 2003 Aintree National winner, Monty's Pass, led onwards, followed by Montayral, Run For Paddy, Artic Jack and Lanmire Glen, and tracked most closely by Golden Storm, Native Performance, Good Vintage and Native Jack, the lattermost on the wide outside.

Ross Moff had fallen at the fifth, an incident that had severely interfered with the trailing Direct Bearing, all but bringing down the joint-favourite, and although staying upright, the horse was never a factor thereafter, eventually pulling-up four out. With Colnel Rayburn also a faller when towards the rear at the fourteenth fence, What Odds led on deep into the second circuit.

Having been well in touch at the halfway stage, Granit D'Estruval had moved nicely through the field under British-based jockey Brian Harding, and at the fifth last fence, the horse had come through strongly to take it up from long-time leader What Odds, who subsequently weakened rapidly. Closely grouped in behind the new leader were Marcus Du Berlais, Golden Storm, Native Jack, Montayral and Hume Castle, but with the lattermost fading alarmingly when asked to challenge the leaders, a shock result appeared on the cards as the race entered its closing stages.

Granit D'Estruval, 5lbs out of the handicap, went for home in the straight, and by the final fence, it was left to the novice Marcus Du Berlais to challenge him. Both horses threw everything into the finish having sailed the last, and there was little to separate the two as they surged to the line. Marcus Du Berlais was galloping home resolutely, but at the line, Granit D'Estruval prevailed by half-a-length, becoming just the sixth British-trained winner. The leading group finished in close proximity of one another, with Golden Storm and Native Jack only a couple of lengths behind, followed in by Timbera, who had kept on well in the latter stages to take fifth. Sadly, in touch but beaten at the time, Xenophon took a tired fall two fences from home, and although the horse had jumped well by and large, he broke his back and had to be destroyed.

The result provided a huge boost to a Ferdy Murphy yard that had struggled all season fighting a ringworm problem. Murphy had achieved success in Ireland previously, winning the Kerry National with Mac's Supreme four years before, and the trainer stated that going right-handed made a huge difference to Granit D'Estruval, a horse that had endured problems in the past and had received keyhole surgery on a clipped joint. The win came for wheelchair-confined owner Walter Gott, whose previous best horse had been the good chaser Addington Boy, while Harding, from Castletownroche, County Cork, had previously been associated with the stable of the late Gordon Richards, and had ridden the great One Man to Queen Mother Champion Chase glory. It was a first victory in Ireland for Harding, and the gallant Granit D'Estruval very nearly recorded a memorable double just five days later when taking his chance in the Scottish Grand National at Ayr. Locked in a duel with the popular Grey Abbey, Granit D'Estruval was bitterly unlucky to take a spectacular last fence tumble when holding every chance of victory.

Left: *Trainer Ferdy Murphy and jockey Brian Harding with their trophies.*

Above left: *Granit D'Estruval flies a fence.*

Above right: *Granit D'Estruval beats the grey horse Marcus Du Berlais.*

2004 IRISH GRAND NATIONAL RESULT

FATE	HORSE	AGE/WEIGHT	JOCKEY
1st	GRANIT D'ESTRUVAL	10.10.0	B. HARDING
2nd	MARCUS DU BERLAIS	7.9.11	D.J. HOWARD
3rd	GOLDEN STORM	7.9.9	J.M. ALLEN
4th	NATIVE JACK	10.11.4	C. O'DWYER
5th	Timbera	10.11.2	J. Culloty
6th	Montayral	7.10.12	S. Durack
7th	Garvivonnian	9.10.6	L.A. Hurley
8th	Kadoun	7.11.4	Mr D.W. Cullen
9th	What Odds	8.10.1	R. Geraghty
10th	Thari	7.10.1	P. Carberry
Fell	Colnel Rayburn	8.10.8	J.L. Cullen
Fell	Heart Midoltian	7.10.9	I.J. Power
Fell	Killultagh Thunder	8.9.9	S. Curling
Fell	Munster	7.10.3	M.D. Grant
Fell	Never Compromise	9.9.13	G.T. Hutchinson
Fell	Rose Perk	8.9.7	P.W. Flood
Fell	Ross Moff	11.10.10	R.P. McNally
Fell	Satco Express	8.10.9	J.R. Barry
Fell	Xenophon	8.10.9	D.N. Russell
Pulled-Up	Artic Jack	8.12.0	R. McGrath
Pulled-Up	Back On Top	10.10.11	Mr J.T. McNamara
Pulled-Up	Colonel Bradley	10.10.0	A.P. Crowe
Pulled-Up	Direct Bearing	7.10.8	B.J. Geraghty
Pulled-Up	Hume Castle	8.10.2	R.M. Power
Pulled-Up	Lanmire Glen	7.10.0	T.P. Treacy
Pulled-Up	Native Performance	9.9.10	R.M. Moran
Pulled-Up	Run For Paddy	8.10.1	K. Hadnett
Refused	Good Vintage	9.9.9	D.F. O'Regan

12 April 2004
Going – Yielding
Sponsor – Powers Gold Label
Winner – £79,802
Race Distance – three miles five furlongs
Time – 7mins 45.30secs
28 Ran
Winner trained by Ferdy Murphy
Winner owned by W.J. Gott
Granit D'Estruval, bay gelding by Quart De Vin – Jalousie.

Betting – 9/1 Direct Bearing & Hume Castle, 11/1 Never Compromise & Timbera, 12/1 Native Jack, Satco Express & Xenophon, 14/1 Colnel Rayburn & Montayral, 16/1 Kadoun & Lanmire Glen, 20/1 Artic Jack, Back On Top, Marcus Du Berlais, Ross Moff & What Odds, 25/1 Golden Storm & Thari, 28/1 Colonel Bradley, 33/1 GRANIT D'ESTRUVAL & Munster, 40/1 Garvivonnian, 50/1 Good Vintage, Heart Midoltian, Killultagh Thunder & Native Performance, 66/1 Rose Perk & Run For Paddy.

2005 – NUMBERSIXVALVERDE

With Ireland's richest jumps prize on offer, the 2005 Irish Grand National would develop into one of the most exciting of recent years. Twenty-six horses went to post, headed by top weight Le Coudray, a former smart staying hurdler and consistent chaser. But it was to be the Tucker Geraghty-trained What Odds, ninth the year before, having led for much of the way, that started favourite for the valuable and prestigious race.

What Odds had won the Punchestown Grand National Trial in January and, in the long-term, was seen as a candidate for the Grand National at Aintree, a race that the horse's owners, Dee Racing Syndicate, had won in 2003 with Monty's Pass. The syndicate was headed by Mike Futter, a Blackpool-born bingo club owner, who had reputedly staked £10,000 each-way that What Odds – a good stayer and jumper – would win the Irish National.

Marcus Du Berlais and Golden Storm ran in the race again, the former winning the Leopardstown Chase earlier in the season, while 2002 winner The Bunny Boiler was also back. Of the newcomers, Paul Nolan thought highly of his Thyestes Chase runner-up Kymandjen, while three-times winning trainer Michael O'Brien had specifically trained the talented Kadoun – the mount of Tony McCoy – for the Irish National. The Pat Hughes-trained youngster, Point Barrow, had been well fancied for the four-mile chase at the Cheltenham Festival but had failed to make an impression up the finishing hill, yet retained plenty of supporters, while Ted Walsh's runner, Jack High, had won the season's Troytown Chase at Navan and was opined to be one of the more stamina-rich runners in the field.

Also new to the race was the nine-year-old bay Numbersixvalverde, winner of the Thyestes Chase at Gowran Park. The horse was trained in County Kildare by Martin Brassil and was one that appreciated the soft ground present at Fairyhouse in 2005. Numbersixvalverde was a first runner in the race for Brassil, and despite being hampered when finishing third at Navan the month before, Brassil was confident his horse would get the trip and love the ground. A vital indicator to the possible outcome was noted when the brilliant jockey Ruby Walsh wasted down to a near minimum weight to take the ride on Numbersixvalverde, the horse being officially 1lb out of the handicap.

In contrast to the 2004 race, there were very few casualties in 2005, although the one faller in the race was sadly fatal. The incident occurred at the sixth fence, an open ditch, where Noel Meade's runner Native Sessions crashed and broke his neck. The poor horse was still lying on the ground as the runners raced on the second circuit, so the fence was omitted.

As was his style, Kymandjen led enthusiastically on the first circuit, bounding along under John Cullen from What Odds, Hume Castle, Golden Storm, Howaya Pet, Heroic, Green River and Le Coudray, until Hume Castle joined the leader at the head of affairs at halfway.

On the second circuit, the race developed into a most interesting contest. Beforehand, Tucker Geraghty had indicated he had done much work on trying to get What Odds to settle in his races, yet it was apparent that the horse was again running too freely, and although he was still third at the halfway point, the horse

would not be able to find any extra as the pace increased during the second lap. Le Coudray too had been up with the leaders under his burden of 12st, but when he weakened alarmingly approaching the fifteenth, his jockey J.T. McNamara believed that something was wrong with the horse, and though he was pulled-up a fence later, thankfully, the veteran chaser was fine afterwards.

At the fourth last, many horses remained in the thick of the battle. Kymandjen still held an advantage, but in behind a plethora of challengers were emerging, many improving from off the pace such as Numbersixvalverde, Jack High and Marcus Du Berlais, while the unconsidered Coolnahilla was bang in touch, as the likes of What Odds and Golden Storm began to struggle.

Two out and Jack High had stormed through to take a menacing looking lead, followed by Coolnahilla, Marcus Du Berlais and Numbersixvalverde, and by the last, it was the lattermost that had emerged as the biggest threat to Ted Walsh's hopes of winning a second Irish National. Ironically, Numbersixvalverde was ridden by Walsh's son Ruby and trained by his close friend, Brassil, and in an emotional fight to the line, both Jack High and Numbersixvalverde could have emerged victorious in what was a rousing conclusion. Coming up the inside rails as Jack High hung left towards the stands side, Numbersixvalverde was able to grab the lead early on the run-in, and with the authoritative urgings of Ruby Walsh to cajole him, proved the stronger in a dour struggle, holding Jack High by three-quarters-of-a-length. Again running admirably in the race, Marcus Du Berlais finished just a length-and-a-half back in third, the same distance separating the next three home in Howaya Pet, Coolnahilla and Kymandjen. What Odds had burned out close home and eventually came in eighth, ahead of Point Barrow in tenth and Kadoun thirteenth.

Both Numbersixvalverde and Jack High gave the impression that they could be Aintree Grand National horses of the future, with the latter capping his season

On opposite sides of the track, Numbersixvalverde (green) beats Jack High to win the 2005 race.

Left: *Trainer Martin Brassil.*

Below: *In between the two grey horses, Jack High sets sail for the finish line having jumped the last in front, but it was to be Numbersixvalverde (second left) that emerged victorious.*

2005 IRISH GRAND NATIONAL RESULT

FATE	HORSE	AGE/WEIGHT	JOCKEY
1st	NUMBERSIXVALVERDE	9.10.1	R. WALSH
2nd	JACK HIGH	10.10.0	G. COTTER
3rd	MARCUS DU BERLAIS	8.10.6	D.J. HOWARD
4th	HOWAYA PET	9.10.0	J.R. BARRY
5th	Coolnahilla	9.10.0	D.J. Condon
6th	Kymandjen	8.10.4	J.L. Cullen
7th	Golden Storm	8.9.9	J.M. Allen
8th	What Odds	9.10.0	R. Geraghty
9th	Star Clipper	8.10.0	A.P. Crowe
10th	Point Barrow	7.10.9	J.P. Elliott
11th	Jaquouille	8.10.0	P.A. Carberry
12th	Mullacash	7.10.0	P. Carberry
13th	Kadoun	8.11.3	A.P. McCoy
14th	Darrens Lass	9.10.0	M.D. Grant
15th	The Bunny Boiler	11.10.0	G.T. Hutchinson
16th	Takagi	10.11.2	D.N. Russell
Fell	Native Sessions	10.10.0	N.P. Madden
Pulled-Up	Alexander Banquet	12.11.9	B.J. Geraghty
Pulled-Up	Garvivonnian	10.10.6	Andrew J. McNamara
Pulled-Up	Green River	11.9.9	R.C. Colgan
Pulled-Up	Heroic	9.10.0	D.J. Casey
Pulled-Up	Hume Castle	9.10.1	R.M. Power
Pulled-Up	Le Coudray	11.12.0	Mr J.T. McNamara
Pulled-Up	Lord Alphieross	7.9.11	P.W. Flood
Pulled-Up	Native Jack	11.10.13	B.M.Cash
Ran Out	Pearly Jack	7.9.11	T.G.M.Ryan

28 March 2005
Going – Soft
Sponsor – Powers Gold Label
Winner – £100,354
Race Distance – three miles five furlongs
Time – 8mins 3.6secs
26 Ran
Winner trained by Martin Brassil
Winner owned by O.B.P. Carroll
Numbersixvalverde, bay gelding by Broken Hearted – Queens Tricks.

with victory in the race formerly known as the Whitbread Gold Cup at Sandown. Numbersixvalverde finished his season by running at the Punchestown Festival, but it was his Irish National win at Fairyhouse that provided the golden moment for trainer Brassil, as the horse was able to come through the field and pick off tiring horses, showing determined stamina in victory. Brassil gave much credit to the inspirational ride Ruby Walsh had given Numbersixvalverde. Walsh had already won the season's Welsh Grand National on the Paul Nicholls-trained Silver Birch, and shortly after Numbersixvalverde's triumph, guided the Willie Mullin's-trained Hedgehunter to victory in the big one at Aintree. Walsh very nearly made it an historical clean sweep in the Nationals, for he was only denied by the narrowest of margins aboard Cornish Rebel, again for Nicholls, by Joe's Edge in the Scottish National at Ayr. With Walsh having put up a mere 1lb overweight on Numbersixvalverde at Fairyhouse, it was unanimously agreed that the winners of the 2005 Irish Grand National were truly worthy. Proving his brilliance as a staying chaser, Numbersixvalverde followed his Fairyhouse triumph with victory in the Grand National at Aintree twelve months later. Ridden on that occasion by Niall 'Slippers' Madden, Numbersixvalverde won at Aintree from Hedgehunter, ridden by none other than Ruby Walsh.

Betting – 8/1 What Odds, 9/1 Jaquouille, Marcus Du Berlais & NUMBERSIXVALVERDE, 10/1 Jack High, Kadoun & Point Barrow, 12/1 Kymandjen & Pearly Jack, 16/1 Mullacash, 20/1 Golden Storm & Native Jack, 25/1 Alexander Banquet, Garvivonnian, Hume Castle, Le Coudray & Takagi, 33/1 Coolnahilla, Heroic & Howaya Pet, 50/1 Native Sessions & Star Clipper, 66/1 Green River, Lord Alphieross & The Bunny Boiler, 100/1 Darrens Lass.

2006 – POINT BARROW

Less than a fortnight before the 2006 Irish Grand National (which carried the sponsorship of Powers Whisky), Numbersixvalverde had seriously franked the form of the 2005 edition of the Fairyhouse showpiece by out-gunning the great force that had become Hedgehunter (2005 Aintree National winner and second in the 2006 Cheltenham Gold Cup to Ireland's War Of Attrition) at Aintree, winning the Grand National in glorious style for softly spoken trainer Martin Brassil.

Numbersixvalverde's win at Aintree was strikingly similar to the success that Bobbyjo had enjoyed in both races, and was a further illustration of the dominance that the Irish horses had enjoyed over their British counterparts for a number of seasons. Indeed, at the cherished Cheltenham Festival in March 2006, the three major Championship races – the Gold Cup, Champion Hurdle and Queen Mother Champion Chase – had all been won by Irish-trained horses in War Of Attrition, Brave Inca and Newmill. A golden chapter in Irish racing was being written, and with the Ferdy Murphy-trained outsider Supreme Developer the only British-trained runner in the twenty-six strong Irish National field, another major prize looked virtually assured for the home team.

Experienced campaigners such as What Odds, Coolnahilla, Kymandjen and Harbour Pilot (twice placed in a Cheltenham Gold Cup) featured amongst the runners, but it was with younger horses such as Dun Doire, GVA Ireland and Our Ben, that the betting public sided. Having enjoyed an extraordinary season winning six races in a row including the Thyestes Chase at Gowran Park and the William Hill National Hunt Chase at the Cheltenham Festival, the Tony Martin-trained Dun Doire was rightly made strong favourite for glory. A super jumper and rugged stayer, the sheepskin noseband-wearing bay had failed to make the cut for Aintree, although his success during the season saw his handicap mark improve dramatically by the time Fairyhouse arrived. Dun Doire had come from so far back in the field to win at Cheltenham it almost defied belief, yet that was the horse's style, and the longer the race distance, the better the horse performed, though it remained to be seen how well Dun Doire – partnered by Mick Fitzgerald – would cope with his weight rise. The eight-year-old GVA Ireland was another with stamina to burn, the horse's breakthrough success coming on heavy ground in the Midlands Grand National at Uttoxeter earlier in the season. The progressive GVA Ireland was the mount of Barry Geraghty and was trained by Francis Flood, while the big chestnut Our Ben – a leading novice stayer – was top weight and well backed, despite disappointing in the Royal and Sun Alliance Chase at Cheltenham when boasting a big reputation. Our Ben was trained by Willie Mullins and ridden by Ruby Walsh.

Tony McCoy's mount Far From Trouble – unlucky in his race at the Cheltenham Festival – and Kerry National runner-up Monterey Bay from the yard of Pat Hughes, were also fancied, as was Dessie Hughes' young contender Oulart, a maiden over fences but a previous winner of the Pertemps Hurdle at the Cheltenham Festival. Not among the leading fancies this time was Pat Hughes' second runner, Point Barrow. Having failed to make an impact on the 2005 Irish National, Point Barrow had returned only modest form during the current season, although a recent run

over hurdles at Navan had hinted at better to come. Even so, the odds of 20/1 appeared to realistically indicate Point Barrow's chance. The horse was ridden by Philip Carberry, younger brother of Paul.

On good ground, the runners were sent away without any delay, as Well Presented and Coljon set the early pace to GVA Ireland, Harbour Pilot and What Odds. Tracking the leaders on the first circuit was a tightly bunched group consisting of Oulart, Doodle Addle, Black Apalachi, What A Native and Manjoe. As usual, Dun Doire was positioned well out the back early on, where he was grouped with other hotly fancied horses such as Monterey Bay and Our Ben.

The Charlie Swan-trained six-year-old One More Minute was the first casualty when falling at the fourteenth, but by six out, many of the leading fancies had run their races. GVA Ireland, having been prominent early, had already faded tamely on unsuitable ground and was pulled-up before Far From Trouble – having made eyecatching progress – tipped up at the fence, and as he crashed out, the disappointing pair of Monterey Bay and Our Ben also called it a day. The favourite Dun Doire was still in the race but was nowhere near the leading group as the race entered its final stages that even his customary late charge seemed impossible to imagine.

With the likes of Well Presented, Doodle Addle and Manjoe – each running admirable races – weakening rapidly, it was Point Barrow that had made the

Point Barrow holds off Oulart to win the 2006 race.

smoothest progress through the field, eventually grabbing the lead from Doodle Addle at the fourth last and was quickly kicked clear by Carberry. Behind him, Oulart and the Michael Hourigan-trained A New Story gave chase.

Over the closing fences, Point Barrow jumped with precision and a newfound determination that had seemed lacking in a number of his previous races. In the home straight, victory looked assured, yet the combative Oulart – ridden by Roger Loughran – refused to give in. From the final fence, Point Barrow was made to battle as Oulart came with one final effort to snatch victory. But ultimately it was Point Barrow that proved the stronger, holding on for a length victory. Eight lengths away in third came A New Story with the mare American Jennie fourth. One-paced over the final fences, Dun Doire failed to shine on this occasion, yet had enjoyed a memorable season and remained one very much for the future.

The same feeling now applied to both Oulart and the winner, Point Barrow. The latter had been a fine novice the season before yet had seen his reputation slip somewhat following a number of disappointing showings. However, the positive ride that Philip Carberry gave him enabled the horse to win the big race he had promised to one day deliver, and gave Pat Hughes yet another success in the Irish Grand National following Insure's win in 1986.

Philip Carberry punches the air in delight.

2006 IRISH GRAND NATIONAL RESULT

FATE	HORSE	AGE/WEIGHT	JOCKEY
1st	POINT BARROW	8.10.8	P.A. CARBERRY
2nd	OULART	7.9.12	R. LOUGHRAN
3rd	A NEW STORY	8.10.6	ANDREW J. McNAMARA
4th	AMERICAN JENNIE	8.10.7	D.N. RUSSELL
5th	Solar System	9.10.11	T.J. Taaffe
6th	Coolnahilla	10.10.4	J.R. Barry
7th	Dun Doire	7.11.6	M.A. Fitzgerald
8th	Well Presented	8.10.13	R.M. Power
9th	Doodle Addle	10.10.3	A.P. Crowe
10th	Black Apalachi	7.10.8	N.P. Madden
11th	Supreme Developer	9.10.5	Keith Mercer
12th	Coljon	8.10.8	R.M. Moran
13th	Montayral	9.10.5	Mr R.O. Harding
14th	Star Clipper	9.10.11	Miss N. Carberry
Fell	Far From Trouble	7.10.10	A.P. McCoy
Fell	One More Minute	6.10.0	M. Darcy
Pulled-Up	Our Ben	7.11.12	R. Walsh
Pulled-Up	Harbour Pilot	11.11.6	D.F. O'Regan
Pulled-Up	Kymandjen	9.11.1	J.L. Cullen
Pulled-Up	GVA Ireland	8.11.0	B.J. Geraghty
Pulled-Up	Romaha	10.10.13	T.G. M.Ryan
Pulled-Up	Colonel Monroe	9.10.8	P.W. Flood
Pulled-Up	What A Native	10.10.8	D.J. Casey
Pulled-Up	Manjoe	8.10.6	T.P. Treacy
Pulled-Up	What Odds	10.10.1	R. Geraghty
Pulled-Up	Monterey Bay	10.10.0	T.J. Murphy

17 April 2006
Going – Good
Sponsor – Powers Whisky
Winner – £97,586
Race Distance – 3 miles 5 furlongs
Time – 7 mins 41.7 secs
26 Ran
Winner trained by P. Hughes
Winner owned by Mrs P. Clune Hughes
Point Barrow, bay gelding by Arctic Lord – Credit Transfer.

Betting – 9/2 Dun Doire, 7/1 Far From Trouble, 9/1 Monterey Bay, 10/1 GVA Ireland, Oulart & Our Ben, 14/1 Black Apalachi, 16/1 American Jennie & A New Story, 20/1 Coolnahilla & POINT BARROW, 25/1 Coljon, Kymandjen & Well Presented, 33/1 Manjoe, Romaha, Star Clipper, Supreme Developer & What A Native, 40/1 Harbour Pilot & One More Minute, 50/1 Solar System, 66/1 Colonel Monroe, Doodle Addle, Montayral & What Odds.

IRISH GRAND NATIONAL ROLL OF HONOUR

YEAR	HORSE	JOCKEY	ODDS
1870	Sir Robert Peel	J. Boylan	9/2
1871	The Doe	J. Boylan	Evens Fav.
1872	Scots Grey	Mr G. Moore	5/2 Fav.
1873	The Torrent	M. Toole	100/6
1874	Sailor	W. Ryan	8/1
1875	Scots Grey	Mr G. Moore	6/1
1876	Grand National	Mr T. Beasley	100/30
1877	Thiggin Thue	Mr T. Beasley	4/1
1878	Juggler	Mr J. Beasley	3/1 Fav.
1879	Jupiter Nonans	Capt. S.F. Lee-Barber	7/1
1880	Controller	Mr H. Beasley	6/4 Fav.
1881	Antoinette	S. Fleming	4/1
1882	Chantilly	D. Canavan	5/2 Fav.
1883	The Gift	T. Kelly	5/1
1884	The Gift	T. Kelly	5/2
1885	Billet Doux	Mr W. Murland	5/1
1886	Castle Lucas	Mr Atkinson	100/30
1887	Eglantine	Mr R. Brabazon	4/1
1888	Maroon	Mr W. McAuliffe	4/1
1889	Citadel	Mr H. Beasley	3/1
1890	Greek Girl	Mr H. Gore	5/2 Fav.
1891	Firewater	Capt. J. Burn-Murdoch	10/1
1892	Springfield Maid	Mr L. Hope	6/1
1893	Thurles	L. Ryan	6/4 Fav.
1894	The Admiral	Mr F.W. Mitchell	8/1
1895	Yellow Girl II	Mr J. Ennis	8/1
1896	Royston Crow	Mr L. Parsons	6/1
1897	Breemount's Pride	R. Hopper	Evens Fav.
1898	Porridge	T. Collier	9/2 Fav.
1899	Princess Hilda	Mr J. Clarke	100/15
1900	Mavis Of Meath	J. Kelly	5/2 Jt-Fav.
1901	Tipperary Boy	T. Moran	4/6 Fav.
1902	Patlander	J. Cheshire	Evens Fav.
1903	Kirko	J. Scully	4/1
1904	Ascetic's Silver	T. Dowdall	3/1 Jt-Fav.
1905	Red Lad	C. Kelly	6/4 Fav.
1906	Brown Bess	J. Bresname	10/1
1907	Sweet Cecil	Mr T. Price	Evens Fav.
1908	Lord Rivers	Mr R.H. Walker	10/1
1909	Little Hack II	Mr R.H. Walker	10/1
1910	Oniche	Mr F. Malone	100/8
1911	Repeater II	Mr J.A. Trench	100/8
1912	Small Polly	Mr R.H. Walker	10/1
1913	Little Hack II	Mr R.H. Walker	10/1
1914	Civil War	Capt. P. O'Brien-Butler	6/1
1915	Punch	Mr R.H. Walker	7/2 Fav.
1916	All Sorts	J. Lynn	5/1
1917	Pay Only	Mr W.F. Stanley	6/4 Fav.
1918	Ballyboggan	C. Hawkins	Evens Fav.
1919	NO RACE	N/A	N/A
1920	Halston	D. Colbert	4/1
1921	Bohermore	D. Colbert	7/1
1922	Halston	J. Moloney	100/8
1923	Be Careful	J. Moloney	100/8
1924	Kilbarry	W. Horan	10/1
1925	Dog Fox	Jos Doyle	8/1
1926	Amberwave	Mr J.E. O'Brien	8/1
1927	Jerpoint	P. Powell	2/1 Jt-Fav.
1928	Don Sancho	T.B. Cullinan	8/1
1929	Alike	Mr F.W. Wise	3/1
1930	Fanmond	K. Lenehan	7/1
1931	Impudent Barney	Mr F.E. McKeever	6/1
1932	Copper Court	T. Cullen	2/1 Fav.
1933	Red Park	D. Kirwan	4/1
1934	Poolgowran	R. Everett	8/1
1935	Rathfriland	T. Regan	8/1
1936	Alice Maythorn	M.C. Prendergast	10/1
1937	Pontet	F.E. McKeever	3/1 Jt-Fav.
1938	Clare County	T. Hyde	4/1 Jt-Fav.
1939	Shaun Peel	J. Wade	20/1
1940	Jack Chaucer	J. Lenehan	5/2 Fav.
1941	NO RACE	N/A	N/A
1942	Prince Regent	T. Hyde	5/2 Fav.
1943	Golden Jack	D.L. Moore	5/2
1944	Knight's Crest	M. Molony	100/8
1945	Heirdom	J.P. Maguire	100/7
1946	Golden View II	M. Molony	7/1
1947	Revelry	D.L. Moore	6/1
1948	Hamstar	E.J. Kennedy	6/1
1949	Shagreen	E. Newman	5/1
1950	Dominick's Bar	M. Molony	8/1
1951	Icy Calm	P.J. Doyle	100/6
1952	Alberoni	L. Stephens	6/1
1953	Overshadow	A. Power	20/1
1954	Royal Approach	P. Taaffe	Evens Fav.
1955	Umm	P. Taaffe	100/7
1956	Air Prince	T. O'Brien	20/1

1957	Kilballyown	G.W. Robinson	10/1
1958	Gold Legend	J. Lehane	100/8
1959	Zonda	P. Taaffe	5/1
1960	Olympia	T. Taaffe	6/1
1961	Fortria	P. Taaffe	17/2
1962	Kerforo	L. McCloughlin	9/1
1963	Last Link	P. Woods	7/1
1964	Arkle	P. Taaffe	1/2 Fav.
1965	Splash	P. Woods	6/4
1966	Flyingbolt	P. Taaffe	8/11 Fav.
1967	Vulpine	M. Curran	7/1
1968	Herring Gull	J. Crowley	5/2 Fav.
1969	Sweet Dreams	R. Coonan	10/1
1970	Garoupe	C. Finnegan	10/1
1971	King's Sprite	A.L.T. Moore	7/1
1972	Dim Wit	M. Curran	15/2
1973	Tartan Ace	J. Cullen	10/1
1974	Colebridge	E. Wright	11/5 Fav.
1975	Brown Lad	T. Carberry	6/4 Fav.
1976	Brown Lad	T. Carberry	7/2 Fav.
1977	Billycan	M.F. Morris	8/1
1978	Brown Lad	G. Dowd	5/1
1979	Tied Cottage	Mr A.S. Robinson	13/2 Fav.
1980	Daletta	J.P. Harty	11/1
1981	Luska	T.V. Finn	11/1

1982	King Spruce	G. Newman	20/1
1983	Bit Of A Skite	T.J. Ryan	7/1
1984	Bentom Boy	Mrs Ann Ferris	33/1
1985	Rhyme 'N' Reason	G. Bradley	6/1 Fav.
1986	Insure	M. Flynn	16/1
1987	Brittany Boy	T.J. Taaffe	14/1
1988	Perris Valley	B. Sheridan	12/1
1989	Maid Of Money	A. Powell	10/1
1990	Desert Orchid	R. Dunwoody	Evens Fav.
1991	Omerta	Mr A. Maguire	6/1 Fav.
1992	Vanton	J.F. Titley	13/2
1993	Ebony Jane	C.F. Swan	6/1
1994	Son Of War	F. Woods	12/1
1995	Flashing Steel	J. Osborne	9/1
1996	Feathered Gale	F. Woods	8/1
1997	Mudahim	J.F. Titley	13/2
1998	Bobbyjo	P. Carberry	8/1
1999	Glebe Lad	T.P. Rudd	8/1 Jt-Fav.
2000	Commanche Court	R. Walsh	14/1
2001	Davids Lad	T.J. Murphy	10/1
2002	The Bunny Boiler	R. Geraghty	12/1
2003	Timbera	J. Culloty	11/1
2004	Granit D'Estruval	B. Harding	33/1
2005	Numbersixvalverde	R. Walsh	9/1
2006	Point Barrow	P.A. Carberry	20/1

If you are interested in purchasing other books published by Stadia, or in case you have difficulty finding any
Stadia books in your local bookshop, you can also place orders directly through the Tempus Publishing website

www.tempus-publishing.com